Afro-Paradise

Afro-Paradise

Blackness, Violence, and Performance in Brazil

CHRISTEN A. SMITH

University of Illinois Press

URBANA, CHICAGO, AND SPRINGFIELD

Portions of Chapter 3 are reprinted from 2013. "Strange Fruit: Brazil, Necropolitics, and the Transnational Resonance of Torture and Death." *Souls* 15(3): 177–98.

Portions of Chapter 5 are reprinted from 2015. "Between Soapboxes and Shadows: Activism, Theory, and the Politics of Life and Death in Salvador, Bahia, Brazil." In *Bridging Scholarship and Activism: Reflections from the Frontlines of Collaborative Research*, edited by Bernd Reiter and Ulrich Oslender, 135–50. East Lansing: Michigan State University Press.

A performance video that accompanies the text can be viewed at http://www.press.uillinois.edu/books/smith/afroparadise/.

Publication of this book was supported by funding from The University of Texas at Austin Office of the President and the Department of Anthropology.

1 2 3 4 5 C P 5 4 3 2 1
♾ This book is printed on acid-free paper.

Library of Congress Cataloging-in-Publication Data
Names: Smith, Christen A., 1977-
Title: Blackness, violence, and performance in Brazil /
    Christen A. Smith.
Description: Urbana ; Chicago ; Springfield : University of Illinois
    Press, 2015.
Includes bibliographical references and index.
Identifiers: LCCN 2015027982
ISBN 9780252039935 (cloth : alk. paper)
ISBN 9780252081446 (pbk. : alk. paper)
ISBN 9780252098093 (ebook)
Subjects: LCSH: Blacks—Brazil—Salvador. Blacks—Race identity—
    Brazil—Salvador. Blacks—Crimes against—Brazil—Salvador.
    Salvador (Brazil)—Race relations.
Classification: LCC F2651.S139 N475 2015
DDC 305.896/08142—dc23
LC record available at http://lccn.loc.gov/2015027982

K'a ja loni agô maa sa ilê ke be lo ja

Contents

Acknowledgments

Afro-Paradise is the culmination of a long, arduous journey that began in 2001 when I first traveled to Salvador and was introduced to the layered and mysterious city that I would come to love. Despite its often heavy topic—violence—it is love that drives this book: love for friends, love for family, and love for the culture and society of Brazil, even with all of its complexities. Along that path there have been innumerous ups and downs, twists and turns—too many to name here. The trials, tribulations, and triumphs that I have faced produced this book. And so did the many wonderful people that supported me along the way. Without these people, this project would not have been possible—it would probably still be sitting in a leather-bound notebook somewhere as a set of forgotten scattered ideas.

Afro-Paradise has been inspired, most directly, by the theater troupe *Choque Cultural* (Culture Shock), whose guidance, wisdom, and insight is the book's spiritual and theoretical thread. I would like to thank Giovane Sobrevivente, Rafael, Vânia, Rogério, Uilton, and the other members of *Choque Cultural* that I have gotten to know (if only briefly) over the years for their willingness to give me a window into their lives, hopes, dreams, and ups and downs since November 2003. They have been patient with me from the very beginning, donating their time continuously in order to support this research project. They have let me tag along on performances and attend festivals and events, and have introduced me to communities, artists, and ideas. During this time we have become friends as well as colleagues. This book is, in every way, for you and all of the uncompromising work that you do. *Obrigada pela inspiração, o carinho e a amizade.*

When I began doing fieldwork in 2001, little did I know that the first interview that I conducted would spark a lasting friendship that would radically reshape the way I see the world. Hamilton Borges dos Santos has been, not only a friend through the years, but also a brilliant and inspiring mentor. He moved me to begin collaborating with the Reaja ou Será Morto/Reaja ou Será Morta! (React or Die!) and Quilombo X (community action campaign). He also introduced me to Andreia Beatriz dos Santos who became not only a role model but also a sister. React or Die! and Quilombo X's unwavering charge for justice on behalf of victims of state violence can only be summarized as revolutionary. Thank you for your inspiration Jamile, Aline, Luis Paulo, Jamerson, Tony, Carol, and Lemos Brito Corpo 2. Your tireless fight will be remembered long after you are gone. *A luta do povo é nossa luta. Não há palavras suficientes para agradecer.*

The early feedback I received on my ideas, particularly the feedback that I received on the analysis of the theater, was absolutely invaluable. As an anthropologist, I had to wade deep into interdisciplinary waters in order to gain the analytical skills to critically engage with the theater from a qualitative and theoretical perspective. I could not have done this without the early mentorship and guidance of Harry Elam, who took the time to teach me about everyone from Antonin Artaud to Luiz Valdez. Peggy Phelan's early critiques of my reading of *Stop to Think* and the video of the play were also truly vital, as were Anita Gonzalez's insights into Afro–Latin American performance and the mentorship of Joni "Omi" Jones.

This is, at its core, an anthropological project, although it is decidedly interdisciplinary. As such it has been developed in conversation with many anthropology colleagues and mentors over the years. One of the first to encourage me to pursue this work and develop it was Paulla Ebron, to whom I am eternally grateful for her support and guidance. Johannes Fabian's wisdom, patience, and guidance were also invaluable, providing support and critical feedback on the early stages of this project. Renato Rosaldo also helped to shape the project's conceptual frame. Christa Amouroux, Aisha Beliso-DeJesus, and Michael Ralph each provided comments on aspects of my work in its early stages that became absolutely essential to its development as well.

At the University of Texas (UT), my colleagues in the Department of Anthropology have been immensely supportive, giving me critical feedback (often multiple times) as it grew and took shape. Special thanks to my African diaspora and activist anthropology colleagues (former and current) Jafari Allen, Maria Franklin, Edmund Gordon, Charles Hale, Jemima Pierre, Shannon Speed, and João Vargas for encouraging me to deepen my engagement with activist anthropology and hone my critiques of white supremacy and antiblackness. I would also like to thank Sofian Merabet, Denné Reed, and

Craig Campbell for their priceless help in the last stages of the project, from reading drafts to editing video and photographs, and helping me navigate cumbersome mapping software. The Department of Anthropology has also generously supported this project by providing subvention funds and general support.

One space on my campus became my home away from home while writing. The Lozano Long Latin American Studies Institute (LLILAS) has consistently and generously supported this book as it developed. The Benson Library was my hiding place while I researched each chapter. Thank you Tiffany K. (T-Kay) Sangwand for helping me to find and acquire the texts I needed. And thank you to all of the staff for assisting me along the way. In 2014 I was the first faculty member to have a book workshop at LLILAS. I thank Paloma Diaz, Charles Hale, and Juliet Hooker for initiating this opportunity and for all of their hard work and support through the years. And I would particularly like to thank Jossianna Arroyo-Martinez and Deborah Thomas for participating in the workshop, reading the complete draft of the manuscript, and giving critical feedback. Your comments were immensely helpful and I truly appreciate your time. My colleagues at LLILAS's Brazil Center also provided key feedback on early chapters of the book, especially the 2011–12 LLILAS Brazil Faculty Seminar. And Deborah Paredez and Frank Guridy have also been very helpful and supportive over the years.

Beyond theater, anthropology, Latin American studies, Brazilian studies also anchors this study. Many Brazilianists have given me important insight during the development of the book, both one on one and at conferences. Lúcia Sa provided invaluable guidance at the beginning of this project. John Burdick and Kia Lilly Caldwell gave important formal and informal feedback. While in the field, I made lasting connections with a cadre of amazing colleagues who also became friends. The sage counsel of Keisha-Khan Perry was indispensible and her anthropological work in Salvador inspired this book in many ways. Okezi Otavo and Tianna Paschel have been wonderful colleagues who gave feedback on the book in its development. And Erica Williams is a longtime friend who, not only helped me while I was in the field, but also contributed a photograph to this book and aided me in processing my research once I returned.

Afro-Paradise is at its core a book about the African diaspora experience. In the middle of writing, the African and African Diaspora Studies Department (AADS) was inaugurated at UT. My colleagues in AADS helped develop this diaspora focus by providing their thoughts, insights, and technical aid as I grappled with the global relevance of what is happening in Brazil. I want to thank the department as a whole for its tireless support, and especially thank

Omoniyii Afolabi, Daina Berry, Tshepo Chery, Lyndon Gill, Kali Gross, Frank Guridy, Stephanie Lang, Deborah Paradez, Anna-Lisa Plant, Matt Richardson, Cherise Smith, and Omise'eke Tinsley for their moral support, time, and critical feedback on various aspects of *Afro-Paradise* as it developed.

Many people have repeatedly read drafts of this manuscript over the years, taking the time to sit down and chat, edit, and formally and informally respond to my work, particularly Jossianna Arroyo-Martinez and Charles Hale. Thank you for being willing to read and reread! Juliet Hooker and Lorraine Leu gave excellent comments on chapter drafts as well.

My students at UT have also been important conceptual interlocutors—particularly my "Politics of Race and Violence in Brazil" students (undergraduate and graduate) and my "Performance, Race, Violence, and the Body" graduate students. I should also acknowledge the many anthropology graduate students who have contributed to this project in one way or another. Instead of naming some and forgetting others, let me just say thank you.

This project has been generously supported by multiple grants. I thank the Ford Foundation and the National Academies for the 2005–6 Ford Foundation Diversity Dissertation Fellowship and 2009–10 Postdoctoral Fellowship. I thank the Woodrow Wilson National Fellowship Foundation for the 2004–5 Dissertation Writing Grant, research support in 2003 and 2004, and the 2010–11 Career Enhancement Fellowship. I received a 2009 summer research assignment from the graduate school at UT Austin to help complete this project. And finally I thank the Stanford Humanities Center and Professor and Mrs. Theodore H. Geballe for the 2005–6 Geballe Dissertation Prize Fellowship.

I wrote early drafts of this book while I was in residence at the Africana Research Center at Johns Hopkins University. Thank you to the center and former directors Ben Vinson III and Franklin Knight for providing the space for me to work, engaging with my scholarship, and making key suggestions for writing.

Visual analysis plays an important role in this book. This was possible because of the generosity of the photographers who allowed me to reprint their work. Thank you M&G Therin-Weise, *A Tarde* newspaper (particularly Edyna Santos), and the Library of Congress. And I would be remiss if I did not include a special word of thanks to Luiz Morier, who contributed two of his prize-winning photographs. Also, the investigative journalism of Lena Azevedo has not only been motivational but has also inspired my mapping of death squads in Bahia. And I would be remiss without thanking Grupo Opni for allowing me to use their artwork for the book's cover

Certain people have gone out of their way to help me take care of the little things behind the scenes to make this book come together. Thank you Luciana

Cruz Brito for your lasting friendship and for your hard work transcribing the play *Pure Puru Pensar* and several interviews. Thank you Luís Carlos Alencar for your help with permissions and for continuously reminding me that this work is worth doing. Thank you Vinicius Xavier for always being ready and willing to resolve difficult logistical questions. Thank you Edinho Alves for your advice and support in this vein as well. Thank you Dotun Ayobade for painstakingly helping me render the dedication to this book in written form—a religious phrase from candomblé that has been transcribed from the archaic Yoruba language used by Ketu practitioners of the religion.

Books do not come together without unfailing editorial assistance; thank you Laura Helper-Ferris for your meticulous eye. And thank you to the editorial staff at the University of Illinois Press, chiefly Dawn Durante, Anne Rogers, and Amanda Wicks, for your patience, your guidance, and your investment in this project.

My friends in the United States and Brazil have been dedicated these years as I've traveled back and forth between two continents. At times they have even picked up and pitched in to help with the physical labor of the book process. At times they have just been there to support. Chiyuma Elliott, Phillip Goff, and Jacqueline Jenkins not only read and edited early drafts of chapters, but have also been unswervingly supportive through the emotional process of writing a book. Thank you Janmile Cerqueira, Janine Garnes, Nicolle Grayson, Jacqueline Jenkins, the McEwen Family, Simone Manigo-Truell, and Melissa Stuckey for just being there.

Family—biological and otherwise—has been my life's breath throughout this process. Countless people have helped me in Brazil over the years—too many to name here—but some have gone out of their way to give me a space of home. I thank my adopted family in Brazil: Maurício Luande, Selma, Dona Teresa, Walmir Damasceno, Iara Damasceno, Patricia Alves, Juarez Xavier, the Soares family, the Rezende family, Ivison Pessoa, Fabiane, Renata, and Toddy. And I especially thank my biological family for their support of me and this book from the beginning. They have sacrificed time, money, and spiritual and emotional energy to make sure this project was realized. Words cannot express my gratitude. My deepest thanks to G. Elaine Smith, Wallace C. Smith, George F. Smith, Annie Wiggins, Bertha Smith, and George Williams. In addition, two of my family members who stood by me throughout this process passed away before they could hold this book in their hands: I dedicate it to them as well—William H. Hand and Zelma Smith.

It is often the ones who are closest to us that sacrifice the most so that we can realize our dreams. They are the ones who give up their days off and pick up the slack when we are holed up typing away. Books are never individual projects; they are collective ones that are the summation of the love of family and community. Thank you Clayton Rogerio Souza, Olukayô, and Hojidiamazy for being there and being you.

To end is also to begin. This book is for the dead and the living. Before it begins, I ask permission to speak of the dead in these pages—in honor and in memory of their lives. Agô.

Afro-Paradise

Introduction

Grainy home videos show a young boy kicking high and bending low in a fast-paced rhythm that glitters with genius. To even the untrained eye he is clearly very good. He does not miss a beat as one of his competitors slips out of the circle and another taps in, kicking, bending, and swirling with choreographed motion. Ten-year-old Joel da Conceição Castro has loved capoeira his whole life. Capoeira is a martial art that was developed by enslaved Africans in Brazil that has survived as a cultural practice (Capoeira 2002). It is a hallmark of the black cultural heritage of Salvador, Bahia—Joel's hometown. His teachers stand by, proudly watching and excitedly and lovingly coaching him. They are training him to be the next great capoeira master in a long community tradition.

Months later, little Joel sits in front of another camera to record a commercial for Bahiatursa, the state of Bahia's tourist agency. Sitting in a bright white T-shirt, head high with a big smile on his face, he talks about his beloved capoeira and one of his favorite people, his dad, Joel "Mestre Ninha" Castro, a capoeira master. His face beams when he talks about his love for the martial art/dance. He laughs and looks up into the sky as if he knows that his inspiration and passion come straight from heaven. He melts our hearts with his round cheeks and brown eyes. The short recording shoots back and forth between high-definition shots of little Joel's smiling face and stock shots of happy, jovial black and white people. The scenes are interposed with images of the sun-kissed beaches of Bahia and recognizable tourist sites of the city. One of many like it produced by Bahiatursa, the video happily announces that Joel is the new face of Bahia as it lists all of the reasons to make the city of Salvador your next vacation spot.[1] It is the perfect publicity piece for a city renowned for its black culture and black people. "I want to be a capoeira master when I grow up just like my dad." *This is the new Bahia.* . . .

In the early morning hours of November 22, 2010, just as little Joel laid down on his mattress to get ready for bed with his dad and his siblings, Salvador military police (PM) invaded his neighborhood of Nordeste de Amaralina. They came in shooting, as the PMs often do during raids on the *periferia* (the periphery)—the literal and figurative marginal zones isolated on the outskirts of urban metropolises (Amnesty International 2005; Holston 2009).[2] These communities are where the majority of black working-class people live in Brazil's major cities.[3] A "stray" bullet pierces the house and strikes Joel in the face while he is lying on his mattress. Distraught, Mestre Ninha begins to desperately call out to his oldest son, Jeanderson, for help, assuming that his young son Joel is already dead. Jeanderson tries to console his father, convincing him to go out into the streets amid the firestorm to seek assistance. Jeanderson picks up his little brother in his arms and he and his father desperately head outside. They go from house to house, but neighbors, fearing for their lives, do not open their doors because of the flying bullets. Mestre Ninha and Jeanderson then turn to the invading police officers for help. The response is vicious. An officer points his gun at Mestre Ninha and says, "Either you turn back now or I'm going to do to you what I did to your son."[4] Seeing what is going on, community members begin to rally, insisting that the PMs help the boy. "Go get help from the people who shot him," the officers quip. "The bullet came from over there," they say, gesturing. "Not here."[5] The implication is that "drug traffickers," not the police, are responsible for the shooting, a statement that contradicts the previous officer's threat. But the community does not buy this story. Angry and exasperated, Mestre Ninha begins to argue with the officers. The crowd of neighbors swells and demands that the police help the boy. A neighbor who recognizes Mestre Ninha and Joel comes out and offers his assistance. He drives the three to General Hospital (Hospital Geral do Estado—HGE). Little Joel is pronounced dead later that day.

"Our womb misses the child that it has borne. . . . My womb, my entrails, my spirit misses Joel," Míriam da Conceição, Joel's mother, says as she looks at the camera. Her eyes are red and filled with tears. Míriam's pain resonates with that of the countless other black mothers who have lost their children to gendered, racialized state violence—not only in Brazil but across the Americas. The documentary *Menino Joel* (2013), directed by Italian Bahian Max Gaggino, chronicles Joel's story, featuring the testimony of his family and his community as well as the counternarrative of the state police forces that deny killing him. When the film was scheduled to premiere in Nordeste de Amaralina in August 2013, the military police refused to let the filmmakers show it, stating that the project compromises police work (Correio24horas 2013). In response, the director made the full documentary available on Vimeo, creating one of the only public archives of Joel's life and death.[6] To watch the documentary is to bear witness to Joel's tragic story, and also to the crisis of state violence in Bahia.

The tale of Joel da Conceição Castro encapsulates a cruel irony. There is a paradoxical relationship between Bahia's identity as an exotic, black, jovial playland where anyone, especially tourists, can enjoy black culture and black people, and the state's use of terror against the very black bodies that ostensibly produce this exotic space—Afro-*paradise*.[7] This gendered, sexualized, and racialized imaginary has made the region a sizzling tourist industry on the one hand, and fueled the violent repression of black bodies on the other. These two seemingly conflicting actions are not in opposition to one another. Rather, Bahia as a space of black fantasy and Bahia as a space of death for black people are two sides of the same coin. Afro-paradise is a choreographed, theatrical performance between the state's celebration of black culture and the state's routine killing of the black body. This book is an attempt to unpack this reality. When we recognize that blackness in Bahia is defined by pain and violence as much as it is defined by folklore and culture, we acknowledge that black people exist, have a history, have a present, are sentient beings, and have the right to lay claim to rights. The rhetoric of Bahia's racial melting pot, racial democracy, and Afro-paradise go hand in hand; this relationship is key to deconstructing the complexities of racial politics in Brazil. The atmosphere of violence in Bahia is not in contradiction to the city's identity as a "paradise." To the contrary, one cannot exist without the other.

Rio de Janeiro is famous both for its beaches and beautiful people and for its legendary crime, guns, and militarized favelas (as immortalized in Hollywood films such as *Fast and Furious 5* [Lin 2011]). Yet the capital city of Salvador, home to the oldest colonial neighborhood in the Western hemisphere and renowned for its African cultural heritage and alluring black people, is rarely considered a place of violence.[8] A quick look at Wikipedia is telling, not because of the site's esteemed factuality, but because of its structure as a global, collectively authored encyclopedia. As a public site with entries that can be modified or contributed by anyone around the world, Wikipedia reflects transnational popular perceptions. Here, we find Salvador described as "Brazil's *capital of happiness*" (Wikipedia 2013).[9] Indeed, for years Bahiatursa has used the slogan "Bahia: Terra da Felicidade (Bahia: Land of Happiness)" as its catchphrase.

Recent national studies, however, reveal that Bahia is one of the most violent places to live in Brazil, particularly for black youth (Waiselfisz 2012, 2013). Likewise, according to the results of the Seventh Brazilian Yearbook of Public Security by the Fórum Brasileiro de Segurança Pública (FBSP 2013), Bahia had the highest index of police-related homicide in the nation.[10] In 2011, the civil police killed 60 people and the military police killed 224 people in Bahia, totaling 284 (FBSP 2013, 24, 25). In 2012, the civil police killed 60 people and the military police killed 284, totaling 344 (ibid.).[11] These numbers sharply contrast to the number of officers killed in the line of duty. In 2011, six military police officers and four civil police officers were killed in the line of duty in Bahia (FBSP 2013, 26). In 2012, no civil police officers and three military police officers died (ibid.). Moreover, the demographic information that we have on police killings is in no way straightforward.

Beginning in January 2013, the FBSP began compiling statistics on law-enforcement killings during the previous twelve years. They sent questionnaires to military and civil police headquarters and the secretary of public security in each state. The response that they received was telling. Of the eighty-one questionnaires that they distributed, only twenty public safety secretaries and sixteen civil police offices responded with their data, and no military police offices responded (FBSP 2013, 120). Faced with this overwhelming resistance, FBSP employed Brazil's *Lei de Acesso* (Law of Access) to require states to comply.[12] Once they finally compiled the data received, they found that nineteen of the twenty-six states and the federal district had mediocre or low-quality records on police killings. Bahia was one of the states with low-quality records. In other words, even when states do keep records of police-caused deaths, they are paltry and difficult to analyze—an indication that the problem might be much bigger than it appears (Lemgruber et al. 2003).

Despite gaps in the records, we do have some information on police use of deadly force by state. For every 100,000 inhabitants, the Bahian military police officially killed two people in 2012 (FBSP 2013, 24). In São Paulo, the largest city in Brazil and the seventh-largest in the world (measured by population), civil and military police officers officially killed 1.3 people per 100,000 (ibid.). Bahian secretary of public security Mauricio Barbosa says that Bahia's numbers are abnormally high because the state is more transparent in its reporting (*O Globo* 2012). There is indeed a chronic problem with the lack of reliable data on police killing and aggression across Brazil as previously mentioned. However, the statistics still return us to the fact that the Bahian police routinely kill civilians at an alarming rate. The city of Salvador, home to approximately three million people, is about the size of Los

Angeles. In 2011, the Los Angeles police, notorious for their police brutality, reported killing fifty-four people (Rubin and Ardalani 2012). According to *official* counts, Brazilian police kill approximately six people per day, totaling 11,197 over the past five years (CBS News 2014; FBSP 2013). This compares to approximately 11,090 people officially killed by the police in the United States during the past *thirty years* (ibid.). The classification of these killings is also deeply disconcerting. When Brazilian law enforcement catalogues police killings, they tend to do so according to three categories: *resistência seguida de morte* (resistance followed by death), *autos de resistência seguidos de morte* (acts of resistance followed by death), and *morte em confronto* (death in confrontation). In other words, they recast police homicides as victim suicides (FBSP 2013, 120). Direct violent action at the hands of the state is an egregious aspect of the culture of public safety in Brazil and distinguishes it from other nations also known for violent racial profiling (Chevigny 1995; Chevigny et al. 1987). And Salvador is a key point on this map.[13]

The realities of state violence require that we rethink Bahia's iconic image as an exotic black space. Why has state terror against black people become so acute, and what does it tell us about the relationship between the commodification of black culture and the killing of black people not just in Bahia but also elsewhere? Afro-paradise is a paradox that hides the economies of black suffering that sustain it. In order to disclose these hidden economies, we must peel back layers of secrecy. An important step in this process is understanding that Afro-paradise is a performance that is staged and scripted, choreographed and performed over and over again against the backdrop of the black body in pain.

The New Racial Democracy: Afro-Nationalism

As the politics of race continue to shift in Brazil and the nation increasingly discusses and addresses the question of race openly, particularly at the national level, race is no longer the taboo subject it once was. Brazil, a republic that once declared itself free of racism, is now faced with the reality that racism does exist. And this realization has been at the forefront of national politics at least since the advent of the affirmative-action era (Telles 2004). In response, the country symbolically performs rituals of racial tolerance—always itself a complex term—by publicly and dramatically including black people in the national fabric in order to forge a new identity. Government initiatives like the establishment of the Secretariat for the Political Promotion of Racial Equality (SEPPIR) by the Lula government in 2003 and the institution of the Statute of Racial Equality (Estatuto de Igualdade Racial) by the Dilma government in 2010 have radically changed the racial landscape of the nation.[14] These gestures have paralleled sweeping economic changes that have altered the realities of class in the nation. The implementation of widely successful social welfare programs such as Bolsa Família (which has reduced Brazil's poverty rate by half, helping eleven million people out of poverty) has forever changed Brazil's internal economic realities (Soares, Ribas, and Osório 2010).[15] And these programs have greatly benefited people of African descent—the majority of those living in poverty. At least since the 1990s, with the gradual implementation of racial quotas in the university system and beyond, black visibility and economic access have increased exponentially. Laws such as 10.639, the mandate that requires teaching African and Afro-Brazilian culture in schools (passed in 1996), and milestones such as actress Tais Araujo's debut as the first black female protagonist in the history of Brazilian television (also 1996) have seemingly placed blackness, black people, and issues of race at the forefront of national discourse.

Afro-nationalism has taken the place of racial democracy. Black Brazilians have become symbolically incorporated into the national culture and identity—but at a price.[16] The appropriation of blackness to the national identity has served to assert the nation's status as an emerging world power. But increased visibility equals neither full inclusion nor an epistemological acknowledgment of psychic presence (Phelan 1993). Black inclusion into the national fabric follows a logic of permissibility that allows only those black bodies and spaces marked as acceptable to participate in the national project, and leaves the black masses at the margins. Indeed, as Jean Muteba Rahier observes, throughout the Latin American region, the shift in multicultural politics has led to the emergence of the *negro permitido* (permissible black), "a populist manipulation of blackness for political gain" (Rahier 2014, 146; Hale 2004).[17] Yet while the federal government implements radical social reform, Brazil's states continue to engage in a routine politics of gendered, racialized terror toward the majority-black working class that manifests in the systematic killing of black people by the police throughout the country. Hegemonic discourses of public safety tie blackness to criminality and morally exclude black bodies from citizenship in ways that offset many of the advances that have been made.

Indeed, as Benedict Anderson (1991) has argued, often the nation as a project depends on the death and/or erasure of the Other in order to succeed. In the case of Brazil, everything indicates that the national project is built on the deaths of black people. Although society continues to hold on religiously to the ideology of racial democracy and to discursively celebrate the vitality of blackness, the state engages in a racialized necropolitics that, in tension with biopolitical practices, marks the black body as violable and expendable yet necessary to the maintenance of the nation's saleable world image. In other words, there is a tension-cum-symbiosis between the nation's celebration of blackness and the routine killing of black people. This tension is not functional. Instead, it is complex, uneven, and constantly strained. It is an entangled relationship and suggests that killing the black body is a performance that the nation-state engages to declare itself a heteropatriarchal society that is true to the global politics of white ascendancy to world leadership.[18] Thus, despite the material, lived reality of blackness, the black body is a ghost that sits in the shadows of the nation's popular imagination. Amid this process of Afro-nationalism, however, there is another countermovement of political subversion that seeks to upturn this political reality: protests from the black community.

On the evening of May 12, 2005, the grassroots, collective, black-action campaign, React or Die!/React or Be Killed!, staged a vigil in front of the Office of the Secretary of Public Security of the State of Bahia (Secretaria de Segurança Pública do Estado da Bahia) at historic Praça da Piedade in downtown Salvador. Protestors laid a coffin in the middle of the road in front of the building's entrance. They stopped traffic and demanded the city's attention, provoking the tension and frustration of bus passengers, drivers, and motorists. The gatherers, *soteropolitanos* (native residents of Salvador), chanted slogans, recited poetry, made speeches, and gave testimonies about black experiences with state violence in the periphery. At one point, demonstrators even physically invaded the public safety office, refusing to leave and camping out in the lobby all night. Their demands were clear: stop the genocide against black people. They charged that the state of Bahia is not only complicit in the routine, violent death of black youth but also responsible for it, perpetrating lethal police raids, killing young people in the streets with impunity (then claiming, postmortem, that the youth were resisting arrest), orchestrating clandestine death squads, and encouraging gang violence and violence between drug traffickers. The marchers also claimed that the state government, through both direct action (lethality) and indirect action (negligence), was guilty of hunting down and seeking to eliminate its own denizens.

A long history of community experience corroborated the cries of the demonstrators at the vigil that day in 2005, and some of it was still fresh. Just weeks before the event, six young people from the peripheral neighborhood of Paripe—Itázio (age nineteen), Renan (age twenty-two), Tamires (age fourteen), Filipe (age nineteen), Alessandro (age fifteen), and Daniela (age twenty-two)—had been found beaten and shot, then burned. One of the victims, Daniela, had been burned while still alive. Although police investigators blamed their deaths on drug-related violence, families and community organizers asserted that a police death squad (*grupo de extermínio*) executed the youth. Unfortunately, the story of Itázio, Renan, Tamires, Filipe, Alessandro, and Daniela is not unique. Almost daily, newspapers report cases of mass torture and murder in the working-class, majority-black neighborhoods of the periphery. Death squads are an egregious hallmark of police brutality in Brazil.[19] In 2005 the United Nations reported that the number of death-squad murders in Bahia had increased 212 percent over the previous ten years (Ramos 2005). Since then these numbers have grown steadily (Waiselfisz 2013). Black people between the ages of eighteen and twenty-nine represent a disproportionate number of those killed (Waiselfisz 2012). In fact, black youth are thirty times more likely to be the victims of death-squad murders than their white counterparts regardless of socioeconomic status (Reis 2008).[20] In other words, despite the fact that class is an important factor, being black is a unique social determinant that has a particular relationship with state terror. Blackness as a social condition shapes Brazilian's interactions with the state and the nation, and more and more black residents are organizing to denounce this reality.

The May 2005 protest at the Office of the Secretary of Public Security would turn out to be a historic event in which the React or Die!/React or Be Killed! campaign emerged as a national movement. In the years that followed, that project would expand into one of the most influential national black political campaigns of the past twenty years.

The impetus behind React or Die! is the desire to survive. Cofounder Hamilton Borges dos Santos recalls:

> The campaign *Reaja ou Será Morto* arose in the streets of Salvador in 2005 in the same month the youth from the community of Paripe were assassinated. . . . In a meeting with more than eighteen organizations of the Black Movement, we came to two conclusions: The first one was that we no longer would invite the Human Rights Movement, because that movement didn't fit with us. . . . The second was that we would "politicize our death." We were inspired by the Palestinian people, who, when they lose a loved one they give prominence to the coffin and go to the street in a protest march. We would turn the funerals in our community into a political space, a space for amplifying our pain. Let's politicize our death! (personal interview 2012)

Almost ten years later, in August 2013, the campaign held the first March Against the Genocide of Black People in Salvador, which drew approximately five thousand protestors, many of whom were the family members of young people who had been killed. One of the family members who spoke was Mestre Ninha, Joel Castro's father. On August 22, 2014, approximately 51,000 people in major cities across Brazil participated in the II (Inter)National March Against the Genocide of Black People, also organized by React or Die! Ironically, as black residents marched in the streets of Brazil, #BlackLivesMatter protestors were filling the streets of Ferguson, Missouri, to protest the killing of Michael Brown—a black teenager who was shot by a white police officer on August 9, 2014. Much like the protests in Ferguson, the marches in Brazil were born out of frustration and pain. The protests in Brazil were political, funeral marches. In Salvador, the coordinators, led by the women of the campaign, dressed in black and maintained a somber tone. The demonstration began with the reading of a long list of black people who had been killed by the police not just in Brazil but also around the world—including Michael Brown and Aiyana Stanley-Jones[21]—a reminder that antiblack genocide is transnational. The friends and family of the dead carried posters with their loved ones' photos and signs that asked the world when the killing would stop. One young man, who towered above the crowd in stature, simply walked along the streets with the march and cried. He carried a sign that said, "When will they stop killing us?" A mass movement against antiblack state violence has emerged in Brazil and it is, not coincidentally, in sync with the growing global movement against antiblack state violence.

In 2013, President Dilma Rousseff declared violence against black youth living in the periphery one of the priorities in the federal government's Youth Statute—an important first step toward acknowledging this violence, albeit only a rhetorical one (SEPPIR 2013). However, although it is tempting to read the vigil as a catalyst, we must situate this moment, and the React or Die!/React or Be Killed! Campaign, as part of a genealogy of grassroots, collective black struggle against antiblack genocide in Brazil. Black Brazilians have been organizing and speaking out against state violence and its genocidal effects for generations—in fact, since slavery. The React or Die! campaign's accusations of genocide resonate with similar claims that have been made by black radical organizers (*militantes*)[22] over time, including the tireless and often-unremarked actions of black mothers seeking justice for their disappeared, tortured, and/or murdered children since the military dictatorship (1964–85). In the 1970s, black Brazilian scholar and activist Abdias do Nascimento (1979) argued that Brazilian racial democracy was "the social lynching of the Black in Brazil." Beginning with its founding in 1978, the Movimento Negro Unificado (MNU) articulated state violence as one of the primary threats affecting black people (Movimento Negro Unificado

1988). Today, grassroots organizations such as the community action campaign Quilombo X (Salvador), the black youth organization Núcleo Akofena (Salvador), and dozens of other collectives around the country continue to both theorize about and fight against the antiblackness of state terror. As a result, antiblack genocide has become a topic of political debate that is not only shaping the national discourse on human rights and police violence but also shifting the conversation around race and violence in Brazil.

Scenarios of Racial Contact

To begin a discussion of this new moment in Brazil's history, we must first contextualize it and present the analytical parameters and challenges to the conversation. One of the primary problems in opening debate about the realities of state violence against black Brazilians has been the controversy over racial classification. Traditionally, racial classification and racial stratification have been contentious issues in Brazil (e.g., Telles 2004). The myth of Brazilian racial democracy is the idea that a plethora of racial classifications exist in rainbow-like harmony, a mixed-race nation with no discrete racial identities (e.g., Twine 1998). Consequently, scholars have historically argued that racism does not exist here in any serious way because it is impossible to distinguish discrete racial identities that would produce such a tension (e.g., Degler 1971; Frazier 1942; Pierson 1947). This dispute about who should be classified as black or white and who should not continues to affect social science research (e.g., Bailey and Telles 2006; Loveman, Muniz, and Bailey 2012; Telles 2004). However, for more than fifty years, many social analysts have insisted that Brazil is a nation divided by race, documenting how the multicolored populace is divided along a black/white classed line (Hasenbalg 1984; Hasenbalg and Silva 1988). Yet many Brazilians still hold on religiously to the myth of racial democracy and adamantly defend the idea that Brazil is a racially harmonious nation with little racial conflict. Take, for example, the 1995 Datafolha survey (Turra, Venturi, and Datafolha 1995), which found that although the majority of Brazilians acknowledge that racism exists, they also believe that racism is relatively mild in Brazil. The same mentality continues today as the debate over affirmative action rages on (Fry 2007; Fry and Maggie 2004). Still, racially charged realities like that of state violence against majority-black communities increasingly serve as a counterpoint to these views. Embodied practices of state violence, like the police raid that killed little Joel, reveal that racism is rooted in the very structure of the Brazilian state and that blackness is very material and real. The lived black experience of state violence is one site where blackness becomes palpable, which leads us to rethink our methodological approach to understanding racial politics in the region.

In 2007, BBC Brazil launched a special series, *Raízes Afro-Brasileiras* (Afro-Brazilian Roots), investigating the genetic racial breakdown of nine prominent Afro-Brazilian celebrities (Glycerio and Salek 2007).[23] In partnership with geneticist Sérgio Pena, a professor of biochemistry at the Federal University of Minas Gerais (UFMG), the report found, not surprisingly, that each of the celebrities had some genetic mixture of African, European, and Amerindian heritage. The responses to these findings were varied, but several participants in the study noted that there was a disjuncture between the scientific conclusions of their "genetic" racial background and their racial positioning within Brazilian society. One participant and well-known black activist, Father David Santos of EDUCAFRO (São Paulo), had strong observations to make: "I've never seen a police beating in a bus, for example, where they asked what percent African the person was before discriminating against them" (Glycerio 2007). Father David's observation echoes the feelings of many of Brazil's black political organizers: that despite the fact that race is sometimes understood to be nebulous in Brazil, there are tangible effects of racial discrimination that define racial subjectivities and make them legible. These moments are often violent. The following quote from Djaci David de Oliveira's exposition of homicide and race relations in Brazil, *A Cor do Medo* (1998), expounds on this nearly ten years prior to the 2007 study:

> The Brazilian intellectual is no longer able to identify who the black people are in Brazil, but the police, the bosses, the media (especially the television media), in addition to other social groups and institutions, know how to identify black people the moment they physically and symbolically assault them, in the moment they deny them jobs they are qualified for. (Oliveira et al. 1998, 47)

In other words, when the police and employers discriminate, who is black in Brazil is never a question.[24] Denying that race is coherent, and by extension that blackness exists, stands in contraposition to the hyperrealities of blackness in the nation.

Violence against the black body is a rehearsed, embodied, haunted script. Moments of violent encounter between the police and black residents are *scenarios of racial contact* that make visible the ghosts of racial tension that haunt the nation. Scenarios of racial contact are the moments of violent encounter when racialized bodies meet in performance zones defined by discourse, power, and action (Smith 2008). The phrase gathers elements from Mary Louise Pratt's (1992) definition of the *contact zone*[25] and joins it with Diana Taylor's (2003) definition of the *scenario,* "a sketch or outline of the plot of a play, giving particulars of the scenes, situations, etc." (2003, 28). Scenarios are not only applicable to the theater but also to "real" life away from the stage.[26] The scenario is that which "makes visible, yet again, what is already there: the ghosts, the images, the stereotypes" (ibid.). Scenarios of racial contact are analytical frames for understanding how violent interactions produce and embody racial meaning in Brazil at the site of the body through time and space.[27] In this sense, they entail *restored behavior*—a reiteration of something that has already occurred, twice-behaved behavior (Schechner 1985).[28] These are necessarily diasporic processes, lending a transnational perspective to our discussion of Afro-paradise. In other words, scenarios of racial contact, through transtemporal violence, link one moment and time in the black Atlantic experience to another. In the case of Bahia, state terror defines *Afro-paradise* as the juncture of these moments. These scenarios are not only unique to Brazil but also to collective, political experiences of blackness that push us to move beyond discourses of Brazilian exceptionalism to recognize transnational patterns of global antiblack violence (Vargas 2008). We need only cite the crisis of antiblack police killings in the United States, and the current U.S. rise in visibility of the #BlackLivesMatter movement, to find concrete examples of this resonance.

For generations, anthropologists have observed the pervasive code of silence that haunts the question of race in Brazil (Caldeira 1988; Sheriff 2001; Vargas 2004). Even as Brazil witnesses a new epoch of openly addressing racial issues, silence continues to cocoon candid conversations about race. The embodied practices of scenarios of racial contact, however, tell a very different story about the politics of blackness, violence, and the body in the nation. Gestures, looks, glances, movements, and unspoken codes—the *repertoire*—present a body of knowledge that is critical for deciphering the current political moment but often goes ignored (Taylor 2003).[29] Even when no overt transcripts of race accompany state terror, the *actions* of this violence adhere to a racialized logic of antiblackness that is readable.

Race and racism become explicit in Brazil during the performance and performativity of violence at moments of racialized encounter. Whether it is the physically violent moment when the police decide to use force against black bodies, the structurally violent moment when employers decide to discriminate in hiring based on appearance, or even the symbolically violent moment when children's entertainment stars associate black women with ugliness and foul odors; words, gestures, actions, movements, looks, and attitudes produce racial meaning dialogically. Racial formation in Brazil, in addition to being constituted by historical context, social reality, and epistemology, is also constituted by the nonarbitrary ways that race is inscribed onto the body. The embodiment of race and racism has everything to do with its repetition and the perpetuation of embodied actions over time, and it is this corpus of knowledge—this unspoken epistemology—that allows us to deepen our understanding of its politics. Performance in this sense is not an elective act, but a social imperative that is at times conscious and at other times semiconscious or unconscious.

In Brazilian studies there has been a long history of scholarly work on black culture in Bahia (e.g., Dunn 1992; Perry 2005; Pierson 1947; Sansone 2001; Walker 1973). Recently, much of this scholarship has focused on the question of culture and ethnicity from a critical perspective, employing the work of theorists Paul Gilroy and Stuart Hall to assert that blackness is an elusive and slippery concept within the Bahian context (e.g., Pinho 2010; Sansone 2003). These scholars argue that the idea of discrete racial identities pushes up against the realities of racial fluidity in Bahian society. In essence, for them, blackness is a strong Bahian cultural concept that is part of the *regional* (and by extension *national*) identity, but not an ethnicity anchored to black bodies or a lived black experience. Other scholars make similar assertions about blackness in Brazil nationally (e.g., Bailey 2009). From this perspective, blackness and black people are mutually exclusive, and claims to the contrary are a dangerous form of essentialism. The effect of this approach is twofold: It dismisses the possibility of *blackness as presence* and instead reinscribes the notion of *blackness as absence* (Wilderson 2008), dissociating black culture from black people and dehistoricizing blackness as a political space. Engaging with the performance and performative aspects of race/gender/sexuality allows us, however, to recorporealize blackness. We can then recognize antiblack violence and acknowledge blackness as a materiality tied to black people and their experiences.

Race is not an essence. It is a social reality that has material effects on material people (e.g., Omi and Winant 1986).[30] And although blackness is not a monolith, it is lived and marks bodies and creates transnational patterns in experience across time and space. Blackness in this way is an incontestable "fact" born out of history, social experience, and violent encounter. Frantz Fanon (1967) defines the "fact of blackness" as the incontrovertible moment when one's blackness becomes salient during moments of racial encounter.[31] In using the terms *black* and *blackness* to refer to people of African descent in Brazil, to their history, and to their contemporary lived experiences, I am not ascribing to a flattened-out, one-dimensional interpretation of *black* that does not reflect the complexities of racial formation and subjectivity in Brazil. To the contrary, my use of the term mirrors the way that the terms *negro* and *negritude* are used to define blackness and black people in contemporary

Brazil, both by the state and by people of African descent themselves (Perry 2013; Reiter and Mitchell 2010; Santos 2006). This use of the term *black* reflects a diasporic theorization of blackness that frames racial formation as global (Winant 2001). It is therefore a political category in addition to a social one and it is defined by encounter.

Whether Brazilians targeted by the police identify themselves as black, and whether the police who target black people explicitly do so because of some racial bias, these moments produce and reflect racial antagonisms that are defined by metonymical race and epistemologies of blackness and whiteness. Metonymical race is the "socio-symbolic calculus" by which racial identification gets collapsed with class and social status in the Caribbean and Latin America (Wynter 1994, 54). Thus, race is not a naturalized essence that emerges solely from the body. Rather, it is a social marker that is influenced by popular interpretation (phenotype coupled with class, geographic location, education, and so on) and social positioning. An implicit racial hierarchy is at play within society that is tied to bodies but not essentially anchored by them. For example, not only do police officers and death-squad agents identify black people when they enact violence on the black body, but they also *produce* blackness through these acts. This is an important political distinction because the dialogic nature of racial formation requires us to move away from an analysis that overdetermines race as an elective identity marker toward a discussion of structural antagonisms—historical, social blocs that define what position people hold in society based on racial hierarchies.[32] Racial discourses and epistemologies often solidify race, anchoring it to the body in ways that inextricably link gender, sexuality, and class as well. We cannot separate this process from violence. Although race is performative, it is not somehow fluid, contingent, and wearable.[33] Racial performativity is keenly political (Munoz 2006).[34] Reading race as performative can therefore allow us to get a better understanding of how race works in our contemporary world, especially given the increasing lean toward dismissing race as a social consequence because of its absence of biological realness. Reading the performativity of race allows us to think about its effects—what it does—and avoid many of the "conceptual impasses" of racial discourse (Munoz 2006, 679). Scripted performances of violence that operate according to logics of white supremacy—like the actions of death squads and police aggression—define blackness in tension with its *fungibility*—the summation of its accumulation and giveness—attempting to fix and control it (Hartman 1997; Wilderson 2008).[35] As Allen Feldman (1991) observes, "Within the ecology of violent practice one cannot . . . assume that subject positions are fixed in advance" (20). We must move away from symptomatic notions of violence toward understanding violence as a process that "transforms material and experiential contexts and becomes the condition of its own reproduction" (ibid.). State terror is not only demonstrative of the racial politics of violence as performance, but also a disciplining act that demarcates the boundaries of the social order, putting black people in their "proper place" by disciplining the body publicly and repeatedly (de Certeau 1984; Gonzalez 1983).

Embodied practices of violence, like police violence, are spectacles of racialization that produce and articulate the moral and social boundaries of the nation. Violence against the black body is a boundary-making performance that is produced out of and into the ineffable. Without saying anything, people interact with one another in ways that define race and create racial antagonisms. And in the aftermath of these moments, the mechanisms of race and racism remain unspeakable. The theater, as we will see in this book, is one of the few places that permit us to see these spectacles in all of their complexity.

We must situate our analyses of performativity outside of the realm of positivism in order to consider performativity as a politics of effect rather than chance. How do social scripts of race define racial identity? Analyzing the performative aspects of race in Brazil provides a methodological approach to race that allows us to conceive of white supremacy and antiblackness as the underlying tension that maintains the myth of racial democracy. Violence erupts from this tension precisely because racial democracy requires the invisibilization and silencing of racial tensions in order to exist—*Afro-paradise*.

Genocidal Assemblages

At the heart of the emergence of React or Die! is the controversial claim that the Brazilian nation-state is guilty of genocide against black people. In 2005, shortly after the launch of the campaign, the *militantes* that coordinated the campaign—a collective of black organizations—produced the React or Die! manifesto, reprinted here in the English translation.

*   *   *

REACT OR DIE!
A campaign for a unity beyond the conjuncture. . . .
"Every police car has a bit of slave ship in it . . ."
                    —*O Rappa (Brazilian Rock Band)*

For more than five hundred years, we, Black women and men, have confronted and reacted to the violence of racial hatred. The

*State of Brazil—at its core slavist, racist and exclusionary, has,
throughout the centuries, tried to annihilate and assassinate our
people, extorting our lives in the name of the interests of its White
elite. Throughout the centuries, we have responded, creating strategies of negotiation and confrontation. We resist, and beyond anything else, we react!*

*Black children and adolescents have been the victims of sexual
violence when forced to trade school for work, while the adults sit
on the margins, unemployed or searching for a drudgery job.*

*It is on the backs of Black women that the weight of oppression
bears down most heavily in a lethal combination of sexism and
racism. It is the Black mother who cries over the death of the murdered child; and there is no specific age reserved for the violence of
racism and sexism in Salvador.*

*Gays, lesbians, bisexuals, trans-gendered, and transsexuals, vic-
tims of all sorts of sexual hatred, find themselves condemned by
an oppressive social logic that bases itself on sexual orientation in
order to eliminate human beings: homophobia kills.*

*This manifesto, yes, is for peace: Not the peace of cemeteries,
where the voices of women and young Black people are silenced.
Not the peace of hypocrisy that tolerates the overcrowding of prisons—true gravediggers, warehouses for young Black women and
men subjected to all sorts of poor treatment. The peace we want
is a peace without fear, without privilege, accompanied by justice,
and dignified living conditions, for all the people of this country.*

To us, all lives carry the same worth!

*Not only bullets worry us, but the lack of emergency health care
that causes us to die or be mutilated by diseases that could have
been avoided had they been treated adequately; the lack of education that condemns us to a unqualified participation in conversations that pertain to our interests; lack of access to cultural
goods and services; the crime of religious hatred openly practiced
by neo-Pentecostal churches against African-descendant religions.
All of this results in the perfect chemical reaction for a storm of*

*ungoverned rage emanating from our black community, a rage that
pleases the White elite in Brazil—Blacks killing Blacks.*

*We invite all to react, to fight, to organize: a black rage organized
by ancestral values of collective self-defense.*

*We will not treat any one exact case; we will combat the course
of the extermination of the Black people in Bahia and across the
nation.*

*We demand that the governing bodies and politicians act where
criminal activities and omissions are being committed.*

React or die!

A campaign for Life, against racism, sexism and homophobia.

*   *   *

The claim that the Brazilian state is guilty of genocide goes against the
dominant rhetoric of Afro-nationalism, particularly in the state of Bahia.
But the React or Die! manifesto is one voice in a long history of radical black
political action denouncing the deadly antiblack violence that black people
experience around the world as genocide. These political claims have been
articulated in response to the conditions of violent repression that black
people often suffer globally as a legacy of slavery, colonialism, and persistent
neglect and marginalization within the nation-state. Inspired by the work of
Abdias do Nascimento (1979) and William Patterson (1951 [2007]), anthropologist João Costa Vargas argues that there is a need to use the framework
of genocide in order to contemplate the "deadly, often state- and society-
sanctioned, yet seldom overt contemporary campaigns against peoples of
African descent" throughout the African diaspora (2005, 270, 267).[36] Vargas
uses the phrase "genocidal continuum" (2005, 274) to define this related
experience and maps Brazil onto this genocidal continuum. React or Die!
presents a different, unique definition of genocide.

The React or Die! manifesto rethinks the definition of genocide from the
perspective of contemporary Brazil. Its concept of genocide echoes Abdias do
Nascimento's (1979) definition but also differs from it in its gendered, sexualized reading and its direct references of physical, state violence.[37] Genocide,
according to React or Die!, is what we might call an *assemblage*. Deleuze and
Guattari define *assemblages* as "lines of articulation or segmentarity, strata

and territories; but also lines of flight, movements of deterritorialization and destratification. Comparative rates of flow on these lines produce phenomena of relative slowness and viscosity, or, on the contrary, of acceleration and rupture. All this, lines and measurable speeds, constitutes an assemblage" (1987, 3–4). Disrupting heteronormative, patriarchal assumptions about race, gender, class, and nation, React or Die! addresses the multilayered and multivalent dynamism of genocide against black people by identifying it as inextricable from sexism and homophobia. Genocide includes "all sorts of sexual hatred" and the "lethal combination of sexism and racism." Genocide emerges from the problematics of the myth of racial democracy but is also a fundamental element of the nation-state structure itself. It is also necessarily diasporic (ancestral). Thus, the React or Die! manifesto echoes many of Nascimento's ideas about antiblack genocide but also recasts it as a deterritorialized concept that incorporates various, related forms of oppression. Genocide for React or Die! is not only multivalent, multilayered, raced, gendered, sexualized, and classed but also resonant across time and space.

One historical hindrance to applying the term *genocide* to the case of Brazil and black people in the African diaspora has been the overdetermination of genocide as a historically specific term rooted in the experience of the Nazi holocaust (Hinton 2002; Vargas 2005). However, by thinking of genocide as an assemblage rather than a historically determined, location-specific occurrence, we not only take into account its gendered/racialized/sexualized/classed contours, but also how it is tied to other similar iterations of violence across space and time. Antiblack genocide morphs the bodies of the victims of police violence and death-squad murders across Brazil into other violated bodies transnationally.[38] The bodies of Afghani children whose communities are raided by the U.S. military are also those of the children that the Bahian military police kill when they raid communities like Nordeste de Amaralina. Although antiblack genocide is locally specific and grounded in the black condition in Brazil and elsewhere in the African diaspora, it is at the same time unbounded, transnational, and comingled with other times and other spaces outside of the immediate material boundaries of the nation. It is collective and at the same time individually felt and experienced. Returning to the manifesto, unemployment, unequal access to schooling, sexual exploitation, misogyny, heterosexism, uneven access to health care, and religious intolerance constitute the genocidal assemblage of terror that black people face from society. This violence—a legacy of slavery—has led to physical and social death (Patterson 1982). And yet, the very authoring of the manifesto itself emerges from a deliberate and direct black political action reminding us that black Brazilians, despite having been rendered ghosts by state terror and white supremacy—political and social invisibles—remain active, fighting political subjects who not only articulate the contours of their suffering but do so in an organized manner defined by the "black rage organized by ancestral values of collective self-defense" as well. Social death is tempered by its taught relationship with the politics of black subversion: this is war.

At the heart of the manifesto is also a basic observation that is subtle and simple yet profoundly important. Antiblack genocide is a performance and it is also performative—it enacts the very problems that define it. Even when no overt discourses of race and racism accompany the practice of state violence, the repertoire of this violence engenders the question of race. Embodied practices are what make genocide knowable and readable as antiblack racism, and these practices are necessarily entwined in history. *"Every police car has a bit of slave ship in it."*

Necropolitics and Bare Life

Violence is a pervasive, classed aspect of the habitus of life in the nation; state, structural, and symbolic violence haunt the lives of Brazilians in the everyday. However, for the most part, the question of race has been glossed over in anthropological theorizations of this violence. Anthropologists have constructed violence in Brazil, particularly the experience of premature death (either by disease or by the state) as a classed phenomenon that disproportionately affects the poor because of their precarious social position (e.g., Zaluar 1994; 2004; 2010; Zaluar and Alvito 1998). To be sure, violence is a defining aspect of Brazilian citizenship and democracy writ large (Caldeira 2000). Yet most analyses have ignored the ways that this violence is also part of a racialized imaginary. State negligence and abandonment produce bare life, which situates the poor and the destitute on the edges of Brazil's moral economy (Biehl 2001). This negligence and abandonment are not apolitical or unraced, however. They are keenly plugged into the nation-state's legacies of racial democracy and slavery.[39]

The React or Die! discourse of genocide implies that reading violence in Brazil as apolitical or nonracial is inadequate for theorizing the totality of this experience. For example, João Biehl (2005) argues that the moral economy of Brazilian society abandons the poorest and the sickest to die.[40] Biehl's argument resonates with Nancy Scheper-Hughes's (1992) early work on death and dying in Brazil, which also frames the realities of death as the aftereffect of state abandonment—letting die. However, the experience of Afro-paradise exists in tension with this interpretation. Not only does the state—in this case manifest through the police—routinely kill, but also, if we follow React or Die!'s interpretation, these deaths are political deaths. A racial analysis of death and dying in Brazil shifts our anthropological approach to understanding violence in the nation. If death is also racialized and deliberately executed by the state, then it has an *inherently political* meaning that should not be ignored.

Afro-paradise is both biopolitical and necropolitical.[41] While the nation seeks to proliferate the life of some black people—Afro-nationalism—it operates according to a politics of death toward others, and this death is not apolitical. Biehl is correct when he observes that "the ones incapable of living up to the new requirements of market competitiveness and profitability are socially included through their dying in abandonment" (2001, 139). However, the state's intent to kill—evidenced by the lethal actions of the police and death squads—also demonstrate that those who cannot be incorporated into the nation are purposefully killed to be removed out of the way. Afro-paradise sits somewhere between the passive neglect of letting die and the intentional, political acts of state killing.

Brazil's approach to the black body is to invisibilize it; as Denise Ferreira da Silva argues, "the arms of the state—the police and the military—deploy total violence as a regulating tactic" that produces a *horizon of death* (2009, 212). This horizon of death renders the deaths of young black people a forgotten issue and in effect, like the physical burning of their corpses, makes their bodies ghosts—shadows disintegrated into the unrecognizable, "consigned to the outermost fringe of reality" (Mbembe 2001, 173).[42] In the case of black Brazilians, there is no process that strips off the "legal and moral protection (the 'ban') that produces the bare life" (2009, 233). Black people, not just in Brazil but globally, are already located as nonhuman and non-citizen (Wilderson 2010; Wynter 1994). Consequently, there is no possibility of stripping off legal and moral protection—by definition, to be black means that you exist already without these coverings (2009, 233).

State violence against black bodies does not depoliticize black people as subjects.[43] Rather, it is because black people were never considered human to begin with that the state feels empowered to commit genocidal acts.[44]

Necropolitics is a more apt description of the contemporary politics of Afro-paradise. Achille Mbembe defines *necropolitics* as "contemporary forms of subjugation of life to the power of death" (Mbembe 2003, 39). For him, necropolitics, rooted in the legacies of racism, colonialism, and slavery, "under the guise of war, of resistance, or of the fight against terror, makes the murder of the enemy its primary and absolute objective" (Mbembe 2003, 12). This requires that we rethink Foucault's notion of biopolitics in order to consider the central role that death plays in the states' engagement with the bodies of its subjects. The epidemic of police violence in Brazil, its economy of death, and its hegemonic racial logic all suggest that the genocidal assemblages that affect black people emerge out of the nation-state's necropolitical strategies toward black residents (Smith 2013b). These strategies are discriminatory and raced according to structural antagonisms between whiteness and blackness—necropolitics is not the state's policy toward everyone. Yet, it is the duality of biopolitics and necropolitics that constitutes the paradox of Afro-paradise. The state's two-pronged approach to blackness—micromanaging black life in order to harness its symbolic power while at the same time ensuring black death—means that we must think of Afro-paradise as a choreographed duet between the imperative of death and the management of life that cannot be uncoupled.

Diasporic Connections

In order to fully understand Afro-paradise and its political consequences, we must take a transnational approach. Bahia is part of what Joseph Roach (1996) has called the "circum-Atlantic," a concept of the black Atlantic that "insists on the centrality of the diasporic and genocidal histories of Africa and the Americas, North and South, in the creation of the culture of modernity" (Roach 1996, 4; Gilroy 1993).[45] Performance, memory, forgetting, and intercultural exchange define the circum-Atlantic. Thus, any cultural (and I would extend that to include social and political as well) analysis of this region must center performance as a methodology.

For black performance scholar Anita Gonzalez, "performance . . . involves enactment, re-creation, or storytelling . . . it is also a metaphoric, or symbolic, iteration of life" (DeFrantz and Gonzalez 2014, 6). Black performance "expands, synthesizes, comments, and responds to imaginations about black identity. . . . If black identity is constructed and articulated by those outside of the 'race' then performances of blackness are created in response to these imagined identities as well as to cultural retentions and African histories" (ibid.). In this way, it is also global, transnational, and diasporic. Black performance is both "artifact and artistry" (ibid., 5). Performances of blackness are dialogic engagements with black life that speak back to lived experiences of black people.

As Roach observes, "circum-Atlantic societies, confronted with revolutionary circumstances for which few precedents existed [like slavery and genocide], have invented themselves by performing their pasts in the presence of others" (1996, 5). Within the context of Bahia, these performances have emerged in both oppressive performances of violence (like state terror) and subversive performances of antiviolence (like theater). State violence is a theatrical, temporally layered performance just as the theater is, but for different ends. Although these two spaces present different perspectives on performance (one theatrical, the other social), they both bring us back to the fundamental importance of the genre as an analytical tool. What we cannot always see but feel and know viscerally constitutes the complex totality of actions, behaviors, narratives, and embodied practices that define Bahia's Afro-paradise. This includes transnational resonances in politics and experience with other spaces from the United States to Afghanistan as I discuss later. That which makes visible, yet again, what is already there and is performed in the presence of others is a reformulation of the past. These moments—from police raids to their parodied, politically charged reenactment—are restored behavior that not only reference what has been but also what is and what will come across the circum-Atlantic. Decoding Afro-paradise means deconstructing the diasporic racial narratives that are emplotted in this space/time and the spiritual and phenomenological violence that permeates the air (Mbembe 2001).[46] This process returns us to Bahia.

Imagining Afro-Paradise

Just after dawn on the morning after React or Die!'s vigil in 2005, I sat in the Praça da Piedade waiting to meet with black street theater troupe Culture Shock. The troupe had participated in the vigil as one of the several black political organizations that had come together to inaugurate React or Die! At the vigil they recited poetry and joined the crowd when it invaded the public safety office. I had been working with the troupe for almost two years, and was going to accompany them to a teach-in on racial discrimination in the workplace also sponsored by local black movement organizers. The event was part of the tradition of holding educational events and protests on the anniversary of the legal abolition of slavery in Brazil—May 13, 1888 (Rios 2012). The vigil had also been strategically planned to coincide with this date. Instead of reading this anniversary as a day of commemoration, militantes read this date as a day of demonstration, emphasizing the fact that conditions of slavery continue to relegate black people to second-class status (Fontaine 1985). I soon met up with Sobrevivente and William and we walked over to the nearby Brazilian Bar Association (OAB) building where the teach-in would be held. Still exhilarated from the vigil, the actors presented an energized presentation of their signature play, *Stop to Think* (*Pare Para Pensar*) to a room of approximately one hundred people.

Culture Shock's *Stop to Think* introduced me to the realities of Afro-paradise. It was first through the theater that I began to understand the complex

connections between performance, race, violence, and the black body in
Brazil and the material consequences that this web has on the lives of black
soteropolitanos. In fifteen short minutes, Culture Shock uses theatrical elements like allegory, metaphor, parody, and incomplete mimesis to re-present
black residents' lived experiences with violence in the periphery back to the
people who live with this reality daily. They refract it just enough so that the
scenarios of racial contact that conduct the state's use of lethal aggression
become readable. Up on stage, the social discrimination that is normally
shrouded in secrecy and invisibilized by the rhetoric of racial democracy
comes to light. We come to know Afro-paradise through performance.

When the play ended that day, the actors, tired and sweaty, retired to a
basement room in the building where they performed to catch their breath.
Seizing the opportunity to talk with them again about the significance of
their work, I pulled out my video camera as I had many times before.[47] The
momentum of the vigil was still carrying us all forward. We began by talking
about Culture Shock's founding and purpose, and specifically its use of the
theater as a space of political intervention. One of the actors said, "What I am
doing . . . for my part . . . is a revolution . . . a verbal revolution . . . completely
without firearms . . . our group [Culture Shock] is ready to tear down the big
house." He added,

> The name "Cultural Shock" came about to go against the "shock" forces, because
> here in Salvador there exists a "shock" force called the Shock Police. This is the
> only time we see the State in our community. We see it through the police. The
> State is present in our peripheral community bringing violence . . . we resolved
> to create this name, Culture Shock, to go against [that Shock Police presence],
> to even say we don't want a violent police; we want . . . a cultural police, a shock
> of culture, a shock of information. Because we see in research that we never see
> any police invading any upper-middle-class home. But in the periphery, every
> day, every hour, even at this moment, a house is being invaded and black youth
> are being murdered by a police force commanded by a white man. (interview
> with Sobrevivente, May 13, 2005)

On the way to the bus stop after our interview, his words kept echoing in my
mind, sparking questions: What does it mean to launch a revolution completely without firearms? What does it mean to tear down the "big house?"
What does it mean to do all of this on the stage and using performance?

The emergence of the React or Die!/React or Be Killed! campaign as a
national platform and the theater work of Culture Shock draw our attention to a historical phenomenon: how embodied practices of antiblack violence generate structural antagonisms that in turn consolidate the nation
(Goldberg 2002; Wilderson 2010).[48] Such violence is the accretion of state

power in its rawest form (Bayley 2010; James 2007). This book unpacks the paradox of Afro-paradise by demystifying its layered, historical, embodied meaning using performance as a methodological and theoretical tool. With these performer/activists, I argue that we can only begin to comprehend Afro-paradise by reading the meaning that emerges from the interstices of what is said and what is not said in the everyday. Racialized moments of violent encounter with the state (like the death of Joel Castro and the deaths at Paripe) produce the nation as a racial project (Omi and Winant 1994).[49] These scenarios have been performed over and over again—albeit always in different iterations—since the colonial period.

Inspired by Culture Shock's theater work and the grassroots movement of React or Die!, this book imagines Afro-paradise as a performance. My use of the term *performance* emerges from black performance theory. Saidiya Hartman's (1997) theorization of subjection, performance, and the black subject inspires my reading of the fundamental relationship between violence, performance, the black body, and the modern American nation-state. Fred Moten's (2003) reflections on black performance as a necessary rupture that reinforces the ontology of blackness; its relationship to the gendered, sexualized racialized experience of black suffering; aesthetics; and the generative ineffability of black pain also influence this work. Performance is at once the site of black social death and the site of its redress. It is that which reproduces pain and that which ruptures it.

My engagement with performance is also an outgrowth of anthropological approaches that frame everyday life as a kind of performance, as well as performance theory frameworks that use performance as a framework for reading and understanding social phenomena (Schechner 1985; 1988). Performance is not only the bounded and staged practices that we engage with in the theater, but also the ways that we perform our daily actions (Bauman and Briggs 1990; Goffman 1959). Erving Goffman (1959) suggests that our daily actions are in actuality a social performance defined by the presence of others whose existence and proximity impacts the contour and nature of social actions. Goffman's definition implies that as humans, we are always acting. Thus, everything we do, everything we say, is either onstage (as when waiters and waitresses are serving restaurant customers) or backstage (as when coworkers gossip by the watercooler in the back during lunch break). The concept of audience, stage, and actor are fluid in this configuration as one begins to realize that each member of society simultaneously acts as audience and player.[50] The idea of the individual becomes wholly wrapped up in his or her role as a member of society; because the individual and the collective society are so closely intertwined, one's audience is always in one's midst. There are several "plays" going on at one time, and the audience is quite possibly performing in one "play" while watching yet another. In Salvador, layers of witnessing produce Afro-paradise. The police perform for the nation-state and the people. The people perform for and watch the police as well. The world watches it all. And when Culture Shock enters the stage, its parodied representations dramatically interpret this reality.

Focusing on the city of Salvador, *Afro-Paradise* uses performance as a methodological frame for deconstructing gendered antiblack violence. Following the work of performance theorist D. Soyini Madison (2010), the book employs performance analytics as a method of social analysis in order to travel back and forth between onstage and offstage (2010, 1–2). It makes five claims: (1) that the maintenance of racial democracy as a national ideology in Brazil (exemplified by the myth of Bahia's Afro-paradise) depends on the spectacular and mundane repetition of state violence against the black body; (2) that these repetitions of violence are entangled in time and space, implicating the past, the present, and the future; (3) that therefore state violence against the black body is not only a performance but also palimpsestic—embodied, disciplining, and marked by erasure, reinscription, and repetition; (4) that the trauma of the black experience with state violence is a kind of gendered terror that not only harms the bodies of the immediate victims but also inflicts pain on the families and communities of the victims, defining the political stakes of these moments and, in part, blackness itself; and, finally, (5) that the close relationship between Afro-paradise and performance has also led the black community to turn to performance in order to demystify and undo its violence.

By focusing on the ways in which racialized bodies enact (and subvert) racial oppression, this book casts a wider analytic lens on how race functions in a global moment of retreat from explicit racial bigotry. Through an engagement with Culture Shock's play *Stop to Think,* I explore the extent to which performance, the very modality of racial violence, can also be a possible path toward effecting social change. Although Culture Shock defines itself as a verbal revolution without firearms, I suggest that the troupe's theatrical interventions do more than produce a verbal discourse. In its staged, physical critiques, it reveals aspects of racism in Brazilian society that are embodied and not necessarily spoken. Culture Shock's performances demonstrate the critical role that performance plays in defining racial formation in Brazil and how performance as a theoretical lens might be a methodology that lays bare the mechanisms of racism in the hopes of undermining—if not dismantling—it.

Structurally, this book documents an ethnographic conversation between Culture Shock's play *Stop to Think* and the grassroots work of React or Die! Together, their stories not only help us to get a better understanding the current political moment in Brazil, but also critically interrogate the dangerous, dialectical politics of performance, race, violence, and the body that increasingly define the relationship between the state and the black body globally. This ethnography spans 2001 to 2013. This period is an era in global politics between the 9/11 attacks in 2001 and the protests in Brazil in 2013. It also covers the time that I began traveling to Brazil to conduct research for the writing of this book. In 2001 I met several of the militantes who would later found React or Die! From 2003 to 2005, I conducted field research in Salvador with Culture Shock. The focus of my research was *Stop to Think*, Culture Shock's work in peripheral communities across Salvador, and the harsh realities of antiblack violence in the city. I followed the troupe across the peripheral neighborhoods of Salvador, from the Subúrbio Ferroviário to Sussuarana, for two years, lugging my video camera everywhere. I recorded their shows and processed the recordings for the group (see the appendix), taught English classes in their community-outreach programs in San Martins and Sussuarana, and offered general technical support during their performances. What I learned those two years about the periphery carried me deeper toward a political commitment to address the urgent questions of violence facing black people across Brazil. In 2005, Culture Shock joined the coordinated struggle to denounce antiblack state genocide and to confront it in new ways. That same year, I also began to work closely with the antigenocide campaign React or Die! as it first formed in Salvador. Since then, I have continued to collaborate with React or Die! and the grassroots community-action network Quilombo X, an offshoot of React or Die! Culture Shock and React or Die! are two separate but related organizations. They are connected through their political networks but do not overlap much beyond their brief collaboration at the vigil in 2005. My work with the two organizations was sequential and represents two independent phases of my research. The vigil is in many ways the crossroads between these two moments. At the end of 2005 I stopped my full-time research on Culture Shock. That same year I began to volunteer with React or Die! My research with the campaign emerged gradually from this political work.

This is an activist research project. According to Charles Hale, activist research is set apart from cultural critique; although cultural critique includes research that has political conviction, challenges existing power structures, acknowledges authority, and deconstructs oppressive ideas (including those of traditional anthropology), it introduces very little change in the material relations of anthropological knowledge production because it is not aligned with an organized political movement (2006, 98). Hale's thoughts follow a tradition of politically engaged anthropology that has sought to decolonize the field (Harrison 1991). This process of decolonization, according to Edmund Gordon (1991), *requires* aligning oneself with the struggles of the oppressed and *actively* working in solidarity with oppressed communities to further the political pursuit of liberation. This is particularly applicable for African diaspora anthropology, which Faye Harrison maintains requires that we address "persistent black dehumanization and struggles for rehumanization" of black people globally (2012, 9). There is precedent for this work in Brazil, particularly Bahia. Keisha-Khan Perry (2013) works alongside the black women in the neighborhood of Gamboa de Baixo to contest that peripheral community's forced removal from its ancestral territory in downtown Salvador. Gamboa de Baixo is an excellent example of a "peripheral" neighborhood that ironically exists in the center of the city. Her approach to black feminist anthropology is an inspiration for this work. In this project, I seek to continue in the legacy of activist anthropologists who align themselves with black political struggles not only to advance their struggles (which in the case of Culture Shock and React or Die! is the struggle to end antiblack state terror and its repercussions), but also to decolonize anthropology as a field, continuing to challenge the discipline's traditional possessive investment in patriarchy, colonization, and white supremacy (Lipsitz 2006).

The organization of this book is an important aspect of its analysis. It is, in many ways, a play within a play. It is organized around the conceptual framework of *Stop to Think*: our map of Afro-paradise. In between each chapter there is an interlude that presents an ethnographic transcript of *Stop to Think*. The first interlude introduces the performance ethnographically; the subsequent three interludes present transcripts of the three principal vignettes of the play (but not the play in its entirety), including the setting and audience dynamics. The interludes and chapters fit together into a dialectical montage—a style of editing and placing images, written text and ideas in juxtaposition with one another in order to create a narrative collage. This approach, inspired by dialectical materialism, plays back into the general focus of this book on the productive qualities of dialogism (Bakhtin 1981). The play adds conceptual and illustrative depth to the "real-life" situations and conversations that I present in the chapters. The play is a window into how working-class black people feel about and reflect on the violence they experience. This structure has precedent in anthropological writing. Diane Nelson's (2009) ethnography of duplicity in Guatemala, following Lévi-Strauss, uses dialectical montage in order to "interpret alternately one with the help of the other" (2009, xxi). For Nelson, this model allows us to leave things messy, letting our gaps in knowledge push us to reflect more deeply on the implications of the information presented. This methodology once again returns us to performance. Not only are the interludes a method for engaging the reader in dialectical montage, but they are also a direct reference to the play itself. The refrain of *Stop to Think* is its alliterative title, "pare para pensar," which repeatedly and deliberately induces the breaks in the performance that compel the audience to pause and reflect. Paralleling this format, the interludes are an opportunity for the readers of this book to pause and reflect—stop to think. Beyond reflection, the totality of the book is designed to position its readers as virtual witnesses, like theater attendees, to Bahia's milieu of race and violence. To reiterate, violence is in no way the only sociocultural context that defines Bahia. Bahia is a place with a rich black cultural history and a dynamic and vibrant yet complex social reality. Yet most scholarship on Bahia has focused on its folkloric, cultural elements (particularly regarding blackness)—often to the detriment of grappling with real-life issues that make being black and living in Bahia complex.[51] Witnessing the lesser-known politics of Bahia—its fraught connection to racialized state violence—thus draws our attention to aspects of it that are less familiar but nonetheless equally important for understanding the space. There are many things going on at one time—too many to explain all of them in detail. It is up to the reader to look around the stage for clues that will help elaborate her or his interpretation of the plot and the broader play.

The transcriptions that I present in the interludes are of the performance of *Stop to Think* in the neighborhood of Fazenda Grande do Retiro in November 2003. The performance occurred outside, in front of residents who live in a neighborhood that is often plagued with the same violence that the play presents. Thus, this particular performance was emblematic of the work that Culture Shock does and presented a unique insight into the ways that the play's intended audience—black people living in the periphery—react to the performance. It also illuminates the troupe's engagement with improvisation as a theatrical tool. These transcripts are my interpretations and narrations based on the video footage that I took of the performance, not formal stage instructions. The dialogue is, however, directly quoted from the play. The video footage of the three vignettes that I discuss is available via this book's website with the University of Illinois Press.[52] I encourage readers to use it as a reference to supplement the text because it captures aspects of the performance that I inevitably miss and also relays the energy and affect of the performance in important ways.

The first interlude introduces the November performance at Fazenda Grande do Retiro by describing the space and the beginning of the play. The next interlude presents the first vignette, "The Berlin Wall," a critique of the spatialization of racial apartheid in Bahia. The third interlude presents the second vignette, "Terrorism," an examination of police racial profiling as a form of terrorism that maps black Bahian bodies onto transnational "terrorist assemblages" (Puar 2007). The fourth interlude presents the last vignette, "The Police Raid," addressing police operations in peripheral neighborhoods and the politics of white supremacy that structure police action. The chapters that follow the interludes return the conversation to the "real" by discussing either the sociopolitical, historical context of Salvador or cases that the React or Die! campaign has taken up in the past ten years and the conditions that define the city. Chapter 1 exposes the ironic relationship between Bahia's Afro-paradise and the black body in pain through a discussion of carnival and the Pelourinho (the historic city center). Chapter 2 discusses the politics of citizenship, blackness, and exclusion in Bahia, taking up the question of Afro-nationalism. The third chapter discusses death squads, particularly their relationship to transnational politics of state terror. What does it mean to classify Bahia as a war zone? Chapter 4 looks at the repetition and performance of antiblack violence over time and the relationship between space, time, the body, and the visual. Here I analyze photographs of state violence as archives of black pain and suffering on the one hand, and historical documents that reveal hidden truths on the other. Finally, chapter 5 discusses the gendered impact of state violence on the black family.

It is risky to reproduce scenes of violence and torture of the black body. Such scenes can convey impact to our readers, but they can also reify the very abasement of the black body that the original torture was meant to inflict (Hartman 1997, 7). Throughout this book, I find myself frequently caught within this tension, drawn at times to recount the details of torture and death because of its complete unfamiliarity to a non-Brazilian audience; at other times drawn into silence in recognition of the inherent political complexities of retelling and the other violences that act produces. I do not wish to promulgate terror or create a museum of suffering, although I realize that this may be inevitable (Feldman 2004).

This book tells stories about specific people, families, and neighborhoods, but it cannot be reduced to a single, linear narrative about any one location or one small group of people. Consequently, it is not a classical ethnography of the minute details of a location. It is also not an ethnography that documents the political efficacy of the theater. Although I recognize the relationship between the material and the realm of performance, I cannot prove that the performances I discuss here have led to any measurable political change. Indeed, most theater scholars who do work on social-protest theater note the difficulty of this task (e.g., Elam 1997; Kershaw 1992). I do, however, recognize the political import that performance has for understanding political moments.

This is an ethnography that intends to provoke the reader to recognize the intricacy and complexity of a place like Bahia. It is disingenuous to pretend to do a comprehensive ethnography of Salvador. Instead, by presenting images, stories, and the play, together, this narrative presents a critique of the image of Bahia as an Afro-paradise and the ironic relationship that the space of Bahia has to the black body in pain.

Culture Shock

I knew that I had arrived when the public bus I was riding slowed to a crawl because of the people parading in the streets. Some were dressed as clowns and some as giant-sized puppets. Many people just walked along with the parade, following the beat of a small band of teenage boys drumming. When I got off the bus to catch up with the members of Culture Shock, I soon found one of them laughing and joking around, holding the daughter of another actor. They were wearing their faded black-and-white insignia T-shirts with their motto emblazoned on the back: "*Nós somos a voz da favela que faz parte dela*" (We are the voice of the favela that comes from the favela). It was dusk, not quite dark yet, and everyone was enjoying the night summer air and the lighthearted atmosphere of the parade. People were laughing and joking as they walked through the streets. I walked along with the parade through Fazenda Grande do Retiro past storefronts, houses, and tiny squares. This part of the city exemplifies the demography and topography of Salvador's periphery—the low-income, mostly black literal and figurative margins of the metropolis (Espinheira 2004). At the time of the performance, the neighborhood had one of the higher indices of violence in Salvador (Paim et al. 1999). As we walked, we joked around, sang, and chanted slogans. By the time we circled the central hub of the neighborhood, we arrived back at the bus stop. The streetlights were on now and the paradegoers gathered around the concrete plaza to wait for the show to start. It was the kick-off event for the Tenth Meeting of the Cynics of Scenic Arts (*X Encontro de Cínicos de Artes Cênicas*), a theater festival that brought together amateur dramatists from across the state. The concrete plaza that would serve as the initial stage was the depot at the end of the bus line. It sits tucked away in the middle of the commercial district of the neighborhood, just next to the community school where the next two days of the theater festival would be held.

The sandy-colored concrete of the plaza's awnings and benches are a sharp, sterile contrast to the loud, buzzing energy of the children, teenagers, adults, and elderly people who are chatting and playing while waiting for the opening performances to begin outside. About half of the crowd consists of children still hyper and smiling from the parade. The gatherers are a mix of brown faces. The monotonic concrete is the perfect stage—a contrast that emphasizes the theater's role as a symbolic interruption of everyday routine. As people come to watch under the streetlamps, they form a circle in the middle of the plaza, creating an embodied stage for which the audience members are the human markers. A group of about a dozen young boys, all around ten or twelve years old, climb on top of one of the concrete awnings covering a bench to get a better view—a makeshift balcony.

When the acting begins, more people gather from the community, drawn by curiosity, word of mouth, or a bit of both. There seem to be as many people from the neighborhood observing as there are dramatists and actors. Everyone appears comfortable and it is hard to tell who is a theater participant and who is not. Some who stop to look veer from their paths to the grocery store or the lottery to see what is going on. Many of them stick around, and others stay for a bit and then pick up and move on. Throughout the evening, people come and go as they please. Although the presentations are a clear disruption of the normal space of the bus stop, it is not an uneasy one.[1] As the actors perform, the crowd laughs and jokes loudly, creating a constant hum of voices over which the actors project their lines.

Several theater groups present that opening night of the Cínicos festival. The first play is by a group from the Bahian countryside. This is a more traditional moralistic play about poverty and caring for others. The second play is *Stop to Think* by Culture Shock.

In 2003, seven years before the death of Joel da Conceição Castro, black street-theater troupe Culture Shock performed its signature play *Pare Para Pensar* (*Stop to Think*) across the city of Salvador. When I met them, there were five principal actors—four men and one woman—and three to five actors that participated off and on. Everyone was under thirty-five. The play explores the overlapping injustices of classism and gendered racism that disproportionately affect black working-class residents in Salvador's peripheries, focusing principally on racial violence. It is a sharp and edgy form of theater that interrogates local, national, and global power structures and challenges those who live in Bahia to "stop to think" about how being "black" in Brazil means something more than just carrying certain phenotypical traits or the unifying force of historical experience. *Stop to Think* discusses everything from "sell-out" soccer players to the absence of black faces on national children's television programs. However, the primary focus of the collection of short vignettes is the state terror that defines the lived experience of working-class soteropolitanos and its social and political significance.

On May 1, 1994, Giovane Sobrevivente and Jorge Arte founded Culture Shock in the peripheral neighborhood of San Martins on the lip of the Subúrbio Ferroviário region of Salvador. Motivated by the constant "shock and siege" of police raids, racial profiling, poverty, and inequality in the region, the two wanted to create a community-based organization that would provide a positive form of recreation for neighborhood youth, while allowing them to speak out against the injustices they experience every day. They attributed these injustices to racism, and their goal was to use the theater to bring attention to what they perceived to be this structural link. Inspired by the politics of long-standing black Brazilian political organizations such as the Movimento Negro Unificado (MNU) and the Afro-carnival group Ilê Aiyê, the founders positioned themselves as an antiracist, problack organization (Covin 2006; Dunn 1992). The result was a sharp and edgy form of theater that interrogates everything from Brazil's infamous racial cordiality to the transnational and translocal interconnections between the United States' wars on Iraq and Afghanistan to police invasions of the peripheral neighborhoods of Bahia. However, their performances are much more than just a reflection on the dehumanizing effects of racism. Culture Shock also reveals how antiblackness and state violence are part of the very fabric of black life in Bahia, and define the space of the city itself. The theater in this case decodes the layers of secrecy and silence that define Bahia as an Afro-paradise.

Stop to Think's interventions are as much content as they are structure. The fifteen-minute play is a series of allegorical vignettes that metaphorically and literally denounce the racism, white supremacy, and antiblackness that frame the politics of race, class, gender, and sexuality in Brazil. It is not only a play, but also an ethnographic narrative itself, one that in some ways brings ethnography into conversation with magic realism by refusing to privilege tropes of truth telling over parody, satire, poetry, and dance as media for remembering, telling, and producing community.

For Culture Shock, community is the periphery. The periphery region that they called home during my time working with them was the Subúrbio Ferroviário (Railway Suburbs), and the peripheral region north of the city, particularly the neighborhood of Sussuarana. These zones played a key role in their identity formation. The Railway Suburbs are situated on the western half of the city and expanding along the coast of the Baia de Todos os Santos (Bay of All Saints). It extends from the neighborhood of Calçada just north of Cidade Baixa (the lower city) to the neighborhood of Paripe situated at the far north of the city and it is home to an estimated 500,000 people (Espinheira 2004). The name literally refers to the train that runs from Calçada to Paripe. After some of Culture Shock's performances in the region, we would catch the train back toward downtown instead of taking the bus. Along the trip, we would watch the house lights come on in the neighborhoods in the hills that line the track. The lights would beautifully illuminate the sky at dusk like stars, and the cool breeze from the ocean would set in.

Historically, the suburbs were fishing communities. Yet demographic changes over the past thirty years have increased the population considerably, attracting "squatters" and low-income residents looking to settle somewhere more affordable in the metropolitan region of Salvador. The influx of low-income residents, the majority of whom are of African descent, has caused mainstream society to stigmatize the region. Sociologists describe the Subúrbio Ferroviário as one of the most violent areas of the city

(Espinheira 2004). Government officials describe the suburbs as a set of "disorderly settlements . . . without any planning, with precarious and inhumane living conditions" that were set up by an influx of "impoverished residents" who rushed to the region to squat (Viana 2004, 9; my translation). The news media's description of the region is similar (Fonsêca 2003). However, this perspective is acutely dismissive of the state's role in failing to provide an infrastructure for impoverished people that would not require relocation to the outskirts in order to find affordable housing. It is as if this population intentionally chose to establish settlements "without any planning, with precarious inhumane living conditions, needy for equipment and efficient educational, health, recreation and security services" (ibid., 3; my translation). It is this negative stereotyping that Culture Shock and the other theater groups of the region work to deconstruct.

Stop to Think is a creative collage of poetic vignettes, accented by dramatized allegory. There is little dialogue, no clear plot, and no chronological story progression. Without linearity, the play tells a series of short figurative tales. Each of these tales allegorizes an aspect of racism and violence in Brazil. The stories might be called scenes, but are neither formally titled nor thematically or sequentially ordered. Rather, they are more like vignettes. Together they spin a lyric tale about the experience of racial violence in the periphery and its broader political significance. There is a written informal script, but improvisation drives the performance. It is not only a way to help the flow of the play; it is also a way to engage the audience. Not tied to the script, the actors are able to adjust the performance to the spectators, allowing the actors to interact with onlookers directly. The actors emphasize fluidity rather than adherence to the text, so if words are missed or scenes are forgotten, they are simply passed over or changed.

Culture Shock produces a theater that refracts rather than reflects the politics of racism to reveal how it truly works in society. As Elin Diamond (1996) suggests, theater cannot rid itself of the impetus to mimic or the search for the real. The theater is infinitely caught up in the politics of representation. However, the mimicry in which the theater engages is always incomplete, always not quite how things "really are." It is the almost and not quite nature of Culture Shock's performance, its outlandishness, and its refusal to appeal to the real in order to interrogate social processes that makes the play so successful. The interludes that preface each chapter in this book demonstrate how this works within the play.

Culture Shock has a performance style akin to agitprop.[2] The group's treatment of the stage is Brechtian,[3] continuously violating the boundaries between audience and performance in order to dislodge spectators from their dissociated placement outside of the performance and draw them into the political space of the performance as partial participants. Their work is also clearly influenced by Augusto Boal (1979).[4] The actors engage assertively with the audience—yelling, pushing, and sometimes grabbing audience members out of the crowd in order to take a combative approach to discussing issues. These forceful tactics are meant to startle and jolt. Alongside this aggressiveness, the performance also incorporates a substantial portion of comedy that tempers the shoving and shouting with joking, laughter, and lighthearted fun. The actors use this contrasting combination to further jar spectators and force them out of their comfortable positions of not knowing or not caring about racism. They also use these tactics to help the audience understand just how subtle and overt violent racism is.

Stop to Think has a hip-hop style (Rocha, Domenich, and Casseano 2001). Culture Shock employs a poetic, theatrical lyricism that is best characterized as a monologic dialogue narrated by allegorical gestures. The play mimics the structure of rap in some ways. As Imani Perry argues, "Rap music is a mixed medium. As an art form it combines poetry, prose, song, music, and theater" (2004, 38). Like rap itself, *Stop to Think* combines poetry, prose, song, music, and theater onstage to produce vignettes that have a lyrical quality. Movement and action are overlain by poetic discourse. For example, because the play is without significant dialogue, the actors recite the script in rounds; that is, monologues are interwoven but not in direct conversation with one another. The play subsequently flows together into a rhythmic web of recitations. The vignettes transition quickly and are fluid. The flow of these transitions gives the play the vivacity it needs to sustain the audience's attention. As one person terminates one part of their monologue, the next actor immediately picks up the text. Interactive and descriptive movements by the actors complete this discursive flow.[5] A distinct aspect of the play is its emphasis on the choreography of words and actions.

The style and structure of the flow of the play is not the only aspect that gives it a hip-hop feel. The play's engagement in reflections on everyday black life also remind us of hip-hop. "Part of the theater of hip hop becomes life and a representation of how life is conducted" (Perry 2004, 39). Part of *Stop to Think*'s theatrical hip-hop style is its constant reference to the real—the lived experience of the violence in the periphery. By reenacting things like police violence (police raids, racial profiling) on stage in conversation with a discussion of the mundane, banal, and everyday manifestations of racism in the lives of black residents, *Stop to Think* uses the real as a referent for reaching its audience. This reference to the real is different from what scholars like Michael Eric Dyson (1996; 2007) identify in the hip-hop culture of U.S. "gangster rap," however. Rather than producing an imaginary community based on the fantastical production of tales of prowess and grandeur, Culture Shock uses parody to take the edge off the "real" experience of state terror and the structural and symbolic violence of racism in order to audaciously push black residents out of the silence that surrounds the question of race and forces people to confront the realities of the terror of racism and their lived experience with this terror. This action encourages the audience to associate their personal experiences with similar violence with racism and to consider the commonalities between their experiences and those of others around the world. Culture Shock challenges the community to stop and think about how being black is not solely about historical legacy or cultural heritage, but also about the experience of blackness in the everyday.

The ephemerality of *Stop to Think* is its vivacity. Ephemerality gives the performance its energy and makes it almost impossible to analyze on the page. Thus, like all theater, *Stop to Think* is fleeting, ever-changing, and constantly being remade. Nevertheless, as Peggy Phelan (1993) argues, we try to capture this moment by writing about it and recording it. In my case, I used my video camera to record their shows during my time working with them. Mark Schuller and Deborah Thomas note that "[t]oday anthropologists are using film and other forms of visual representation as methodological interventions and as dissemination strategies, often collaborating with research partners, in order to create broader dialogues about the issues they face, and developing a contextual frame through which ethnographic work can be more obviously positioned as a kind of relation of complicity" (2013, 153). Although it is a stretch to call the video work that I did with Culture Shock filmmaking, the process of recording, sharing, and editing their performances on video not only facilitated my relationship with them, but also helped us to create a public archive of the work in collaboration with one another. This process of archiving has been important not only for my analysis of the work but also for the maintenance of my relationship with the troupe.[6] These video recordings are the methodological backdrop for the book and the source of the transcripts of the play that serve as interludes and textual "glue" between the chapters. This not only facilitated my relationship with the troupe but also gave me a unique perspective on the play itself. Often, I was so busy recording the shows and enjoying them myself that it was only when I actually sat down to review the footage, edit it, and produce it for the troupe that I began to really gain perspective on the work (in the videos I often hear myself laughing and interacting with the play just like the audience—a sign of my engagement with the work and also my complete lack of videography skills). For this reason, as mentioned in the introduction, I encourage readers to watch the video of the performance while reading the text. Again, the metaphor of the play within the play emerges—Goffman's audiences watching audiences watch audiences.

The following narration introduces the play. Each subsequent vignette in the book picks up on this narration where the previous one left off.

*   *

Silence! I said Silence!

One actor enters the auditorium where the performance is being held and interrupts the speaker onstage. The interjection "Silence" initiates the "shock" element of the performance. Immediately after an actor quiets the crowd, the opening scene begins. Another actor enters the stage shouting, "Knock down, knock down, knock down the structures,[7] the instances of power, I say yes to yes and no to no."

Their voices strain as they scream and shout the first few lines of the play. The yells are aggressive but not angry. It is as if they are struggling to be heard against the silence of the world in the face of the realities of the black Brazilian condition. "Knocking down the structures" refers to the structures of power and hierarchy in society—the structures of the big house/mansion (casa grande)*, a reference to the plantation houses that became the iconic reference for white supremacy during slavery. Several actors come in and echo the first actor's words and repeat this chant. Each speaks with one fist raised, pounding the air as if on top of a political soapbox. Just after this, another actor, offstage, begins to play a catchy beat on a snare drum. The founder of the troupe, the MC, comes in the scene crouched low, head bowed, bobbing to music that he makes with the rhythm of his head, beatboxing, and clapping from the crowd. He's wearing goggles, a hat, and a sweater, distinguishing himself as the show's MC. The other actors wear black T-shirts with Culture Shock's logo: "Nós somos a voz da favela que faz parte dela" (We are the voice of the favela that comes from the favela). Sobrevivente's entrance lightens the mood. He begins to rap while dancing:*

MC: *The theater group Culture Shock presents a very special play . . . that talks of children who live in the favela and speaks of a government that robs our lands. And no one . . .*

ACTORS: *Does anything!*

MC: *No one . . .*

ACTORS: *Says anything!*

MC: *[The government] Arrests the worker, arrests the unemployed, and enacts terrorism [on] a people who are uninformed. And no one . . .*

ACTORS: *Does anything!*

MC: *No one . . .*

ACTORS: *Says anything!*

[THE MC BEGINS TO JUGGLE]

MC: *No one does anything, no one says anything, but all of this would be different if I were [a little rich boy] raised on Ninho milk. Private school, and after that university. . . . But no, no, no, this is not my reality.*

The MC's rap is accented by moments of call and response. Although the rhyming aspects of the verse do not translate into English, they are clearly present in Portuguese. The clapping of the audience, drum playing, and rapping stops when the MC begins to juggle. Paradoxically, juggling, a sport usually associated with clowns, signals a transition to a more serious tone. The audience begins to realize that just as juggling is a delicate balance, so is the situation of working-class black people living on the economic and social margins of Brazil. As the juggling ends, the introduction to the play does as well. The tone is now serious again. Two actors enter the stage and the first one shouts the first line of the next vignette. The two then recite their parts in a kind of musical round, rhythmically bouncing prose off one another but never entering into intense or elaborate dialogue.[8] All of this is done while they walk in circles at the front of the auditorium, using movements to gesture or emphasize parts of the discourse. The audience is weighted by a silence that was not present when the lively beat of the MC's rap made it seem like music was playing in the background. The play begins . . .

1 Afro-Paradise

Where the Whip Tears the Flesh

It was an insult to many. During carnival in Bahia in 2006, Carlinhos Brown, the polemical founder of the wildly popular Bahian carnival group Timbalada, made a shocking political statement at the wrong time, in the wrong place, and in front of the wrong people. Each year during Salvador's biggest revenue-producing event, thousands of people descend onto the city from all over the world. In a short week, Salvador transforms into a gigantic party square with twenty-foot-high truck speakers blasting music—*trio* elétricos. People dance and have a good time laced with beer, drugs, sex, and, ironically, police violence. That particular year, the carnival parade had crawled to a halt on Barra Avenida (Barra Avenue) along the beachfront parade route near downtown Salvador. All of the bands with their large crowds of screaming fans were forced to stop because several altercations had erupted in the *pipoca* (popcorn)—the thick crowd of thousands of general-audience participants that stand at the sidelines of the parade where they are jostled, pushed, and constantly threatened by multiple forms of physical and symbolic violence, including aggressive force from the police. Participants and performers had to wait for the military police to clear the fights in order for the parade to resume. Frustrated with the crowds, and conveniently positioned in front of the skybox of then Brazilian minister of culture and pop-music icon Gilberto Gil, Brown turned to face the minister and his guests. He boldly asked the living legend when he was going to put an end to this "apartheid escroto"—"damned apartheid" (a mild translation, to put it lightly). Brown was referring to the intensely racialized, classed segregation of Bahian carnival and Bahia itself.

Gilberto Gil was immediately taken aback. Brown's statement sparked controversy in the media, inciting scathing critiques and a mini war between

Gil and Brown, two iconic black cultural figures. Gil was deeply offended by the implication that Bahian carnival was anything other than a consonant representation of Brazil's racial democracy. Indeed, given Brazil's passionate ideological investment in racial democracy as the nation's identity, Brown's insinuation that Bahian carnival was racist was antipatriotic. The controversy between Gil and Brown became so intense that a few days later Brown made a very public (and in my eyes, sarcastic), dramatic apology to Gil on his knees in order to try to quell the storm. However, the damage had been done. Brown had drawn attention to a very big white elephant in the living room of Bahian culture—racialized-classed segregation sanctioned by state violence—during an international event intended to proclaim Brazil's racial democracy. The celebration that many have historically interpreted as a space of liberation in fact reifies social norms, exemplified by the continued practice of racialized violence against black bodies.

In general, carnival is a very violent time. In 2006, 4,151 people sought treatment for wounds suffered from violent aggression during carnival (FASEC 2007).[1] Of the total victims, 67 percent were men and 37 percent women; 71 percent were black and 28 percent were white (2007, 19–20). More complexly, 71 percent were paraders and only 16 percent were from the pipoca. Yet 45 percent of the perpetrators were identified as people from the pipoca, with an astounding 48 percent of the perpetrators listed as unknown (ibid.). In other words, although the vast majority of those who seek medical care from wounds present themselves as paraders, when asked who assaulted them, most state that they were assaulted by the general crowd—a strong indication of a perceived class divide between the two. When seeking public-health services, people are more likely to present themselves as paying patrons who have been assaulted by "nonpaying" participants. This class divide is even more multifarious when we factor in the ways that race and state aggression complicate this picture.

When I first heard about Carlinhos Brown's denunciation, I remembered my personal experiences with violence during carnival. Each day of the festival, groups of five or more military police officers walk in a straight line through the crowds, fully armed in riot gear, hitting and arresting anyone who engages in any fight or looks like they might do so. The police literally do not veer from their paths. If you do not move out of their way, they hit you. As a black woman who has lived in Bahia off and on for several years, in many moments I am read and treated as Bahian, partly because of my blackness and partly because of my familiarity with the city.[2] Carnival is one such moment, but luckily, I have suffered only a few sharp pushes and rough nudges with nightsticks. Many Bahians are not so lucky.[3]

Although there are many fights and many assaults in the general crowd during carnival, the pipoca is the disproportional target of harsh police practices. Yet the pipoca is in no way the exclusive enclave of criminality during the event. The military police use a double standard to identify whom they arrest or rough up for disturbing the peace and criminal activity and whom they leave alone. Race, class, gender, and sexuality script this standard. Young black Bahians of all genders get their arms twisted for throwing a punch, not moving out of the way of the police, or looking potentially aggressive, while white tourists (Brazilian and foreign) are allowed to snort cocaine openly inside the VIP sections of the carnival groups and commit sexual assault—particularly interracial assault by white men against black women (FASEC 2007; Lewis 1999). The police play a critical role in maintaining the boundaries of racial moral social order during and beyond carnival, and these performative enactments operate according to a logic of white supremacy, classism, and imperialism rather than native Brazilian status.

Much has been written about carnival as the inversion of reality. Mikhail Bakhtin (1984) argues that carnival unsettles social hierarchies and inverts power structures through laughter and parody. Brazilian anthropologists say that this inherently subversive nature of carnival is what makes Brazil Brazilian (e.g., Matta 1979; Queiroz 1992). Carnival's ability to disrupt social hierarchies and norms gives birth to the "rogue" (*malandro*), the quintessential Brazilian who, Roberto da Matta famously argues, "introduce[s] the possibility of revitalization into the closed world of everyday routinized reality" (Matta 1991, 131–32). Brazil is Brazil because, like carnival, it possesses an enchanting *malandragem*—a rogue persona. And yet, the enchantment of carnival is only one aspect of its reality.

The myth of Bahia's Afro-paradise—which produces an image that portrays Bahia as a theme-park global playland where (national and international) tourists come to savor exotic blackness—is a reality embedded in the world's popular imagination, and also entrenched in the space of the city of Salvador itself. Bahian carnival is emblematic of this space and its relationship to Afro-paradise. In the popular imagination, Bahian carnival encapsulates black cultural expression (e.g., Agier 2000; Risério 1981). Yet the maintenance of carnival as a playful, theatrical celebration of black culture and pleasure zone *depends upon* the violent, spectacular repression of the boundaries between (white) elite enjoyment and the black space that surrounds it. Bahian carnival is an introduction to the tensions between the lived experience of violence and the projected image of Salvador as the "happiest city in Brazil." Afro-paradise is a spatial project, and carnival is the apex of its performance. As Robin Sheriff observes, carnival "bears a metonymic relation to the Brazilian nation in ways other than those typically invoked" (1999, 4). "The glittering surfaces of *carnaval,* like the polite discourses of *democracia racial*—both of which are performed not only for Brazilians but also for a transnational audience—conceal complex forms of contestation that engage both the political and the moral economy of race in Brazil" (ibid., 23). Yet, in the case of Bahia, carnival does not conceal Afro-paradise. It encapsulates and epitomizes it. The violence of carnival reveals the ironic, material relationship between Afro-paradise and the black body in pain.

Carnival emerges at the intersection of the material and the theatrical. It is literally the space that evidences the performativity of state violence. I use the term *performativity* in accordance with J. L. Austin's (1962) definition of the speech act, and the word *performatic* to refer to "the adjectival form of the nondiscursive realm of performance" (Taylor 2003, 6). Beyond the music, fun, and dance, at the juncture of carnival, the performance of violent repression against black bodies performatively and performatically enacts the racialized, violent discourse of Afro-paradise. This in turn delineates the space of the city, as it has done for generations. The exceptional theatricality of carnival, traditionally interpreted as an interruption of the norm, actually extends the everyday, mundane, and routine. The very public, dramatic performance of violence against the black body during carnival also circumscribes the relationship between the black body and the state for the rest of the year.

Two genealogies help us to analyze this relationship between carnival and Afro-paradise: racial violence in the national legacy of the use of the black body as an ironic transfer point, a fulcrum for constructing the Brazilian nation, specifically at the site of the *pelourinho*—the place where enslaved Africans were publically whipped in Brazilian colonial society; and black Brazilians' use of performance (theater and dramatic play) to disrupt and refract this process of violence. For generations, the theater has been a key political space for radical black Brazilians to denounce the myth of racial democracy and declare this myth genocidal (Mendes 1993; Nascimento 1961). Their use of the theater highlights both the performative nature of violence in a racial democracy and the essential role that performance plays in its undoing. The state's performance of spectacular violence against the black body consolidates authority and has done so since the colonial period. As Allen Feldman observes, "A performance can exceed the social conditions of its production and thus exceed any particular ideological closure associated with its site of emergence" (1991, 15). The spectacular performance of public discipline and torture in Bahia exceeds the ideological closure of Afro-paradise. Thus, like a marionette, Afro-paradise is tied to violence, entangled in layers of memory and forgetting that take us all the way back to slavery. This chapter considers these two interlocking genealogies through a look at race, space, and violence in Bahian carnival, the historical relationship between Afro-paradise and the black body in pain, and the relationship between these two contexts and contemporary black political performance in Salvador.

Carnival

The traditional image that we have of carnival, exemplified by Rio de Janeiro and Trinidad and Tobago, is very different from its Bahian version. There is no Sambódromo (the samba-carnival stadium created solely for this event in Rio de Janeiro), and you do not need tickets to watch the parades. There are no elaborately ornate costumes with jeweled headdresses and bikinis as worn by the samba schools of Rio or by the parade participants of Trinidad. The musical focus of Bahian carnival is not samba, but *afoxé*: a kind of music that mixes reggae with samba and traditional Afro-Brazilian religious (*candomblé*) rhythms (Perrone and Dunn 2001). Bahian carnival is very much a big, sweaty party without the traditional glitz and glamour of the pre–Ash Wednesday tradition. Imagine New Year's Eve at Times Square all day and all night for a week.

While most public attention is on Rio, the majority of Brazilians, particularly those from the south, head to Bahia to enjoy the biggest street party in the world. Moneyed national and international tourists pay large sums (prices can range upward of $1,000) for a few days' privilege to parade with the famous carnival groups of their favorite artists like *Chiclete com Banana*, *Bloco Coruja* (Ivete Sangalo), and *Banda Eva*. This elite side of carnival concentrates along the popular parade route in the beach neighborhoods of Barra and Ondina. Hefty fees buy patrons an official group T-shirt (*abada*) or costume (*fantasia*) and the exclusive privilege of walking in the carnival parade within a roped-off VIP section. Those tourists who do not feel like walking the circuit pay for one of many chic skyboxes that typically provide food, alcohol, and private entertainment.

The contrast between those who are able to enjoy this organized, controlled fun of carnival and those who are not is starkly raced, gendered, and classed. My first experience with Bahian carnival in 2004 opened my eyes to the visible and invisible spatializing practices that reflect and reproduce Bahian apartheid. That February I saw how Bahian Afro-paradise (in this case exemplified by carnival) necessarily relies on racialized violence that is not just spectacular and physical, like police violence, but that is also mundane, subtle, and structural. I was both excited and apprehensive about experiencing my first carnival. I had heard stories from both extremes. Some friends told me the event was nonstop fun and excitement; others cautiously advised me to get out of town while I could. These friends offered to take me along as they booked their tickets on the last ferries leaving the city. I would soon learn why. I was living in Dois de Julho, a historic downtown neighborhood, right in the middle of one of the two main carnival circuits. I had heard that the neighborhood would change drastically during the six-day street party from a relatively peaceful neighborhood alcove to a trash dump/temporary workers camp, literally and figuratively. But I really had no idea what to expect.

By the Tuesday before carnival, people had set up makeshift tents and living spaces made of cardboard next to state porta-potties in the open square at the entrance to my street. At least fifty people had provisionally moved into the neighborhood. Many were equipped with Styrofoam chests that could be filled with ice for selling cold beer and liquor. Others had small outdoor grills and cheap pieces of meat for *churrasco do gato* ("cat barbeque," which is actually grilled beef with sides of tomato, onion, and sometimes manioc flour). Whole families had set up shop in the streets, with many women accompanied by young children and even babies. My new neighbors had come to the city to earn what money they could during the festivities and remedy some of the extreme poverty of being unemployed or underemployed in Bahia, the state with one of the highest unemployment rates in the country. But many of these vendors would barely break even. For this reason, families take a multifront approach to their business strategy. Because they cannot travel to and from home each day (a round-trip bus fare was about two U.S. dollars then) and still turn a profit, they take the bus in from the peripheral communities of the city and camp out downtown. The adults sell beer and *churrasco* while the kids collect the empty aluminum cans that carnivalgoers toss onto the ground after they finish their drinks. It is not unusual to see a seven-year-old child, barefoot at two o'clock in the morning, dodge in and out of the throngs of parading people to snatch a can someone has tossed. Those who know Bahia are familiar with the economy and fall into the rhythm of exchange. I am no longer startled or taken aback to see these children and I, like many of the other people out and about enjoying the moment, try to make sure I consider them when I'm ready to discard my beer can. I either hand my can directly to a young child or crush it on the ground so the kids can easily find it. Unable to pay the exorbitant fees to participate in most carnival groups, young, mostly black Bahians typically enjoy carnival as workers or part of the marginalized pipoca. In the general audience, they stand feet away from the parading bands, squished into the precariously dense, mosh-pit-like crowd of the pipoca, where people are pushing and shoving just to be able to stand, let alone see or enjoy the bands. *Soteropolitanos* who enjoy carnival from the margins and the Bahian "tourists" from the interior regions of the state are the other faces of carnival's Afro-paradise, and most moneyed visitors would not see them or even know they were there.

Indeed, most of the camping workers in my neighborhood looked completely different from the elite white tourists arriving in the city every day from places like São Paulo, Rio de Janeiro, and Rio Grande do Sul. And although thousands of mostly white elite Brazilians, Europeans, and North Americans make the pilgrimage to Bahia to party, the largely black underemployed populace of Salvador is relegated to second-class status in its own city. Two sets of human guards maintain this moral, racial, classed social order: *cordeiros* and the police.

The cordão is a widely recognizable symbol of the spatialized racial apartheid of Bahian carnival, and also a material marker of the racial boundary. It is a long thick rope the length of a football field that one to two hundred workers called cordeiros carry to mark—literally—the boundary between those who have paid for the privilege to walk close to the many carnival bands and those who are in the general audience. The human chain of cordeiros ensures that black, poor residents will not "contaminate" mostly white elite spaces during carnival festivities.[4] The cordeiros maintain a twenty-foot barrier around the bands' trucks. Your official bloco T-shirt/costume is your permit to cross it. Once the cordeiros let you through and you emerge from the tense, stuffy atmosphere of the prodding and pushing of the general crowd into these privileged sections, the space inside the rope is a relief. Often (but not always) you can walk and breathe here. The air is cooler, and during the hottest part of the summer, this matters tremendously. Some blocos even offer perks like cleaner bathrooms or free alcohol and water.

Carnival groups hire Bahians desperate for income to carry the rope and make sure nonpayers do not get close to the huge trio elétricos. They pay them about twenty reais (about eight dollars) plus a snack for twelve to fifteen hours of work—a tiny fraction of the often $1,000-plus fees *each* bloco participant pays to parade[5]—and cordeiros often do not receive their payment until several months after carnival has come and gone.

The cord's weight is something that people who have never experienced Bahia's carnival cannot imagine. It takes twenty-five to fifty cordeiros to carry a rope for an average-sized carnival group. When the tension between the pipoca and the bloco is minimal, as it is in the middle of the night on off days of carnival, the rope is a loose hanging barrier that is not only easily traversable, but also easily carried. When the blocos are less formal, like many of the neighborhood-based Afro-blocos I have seen or participated in, cordeiros routinely break the rules and let people in the crowds run through the bloco or temporarily come inside the cord for a respite from the tight sideline walk. But when the tension between the pipoca and the bloco is at its height, the cord stretches taut and heavy, making it almost impossible to push and pull without extreme effort. Cordeiros have to wear heavy working gloves to avoid getting rope burn on their hands, and pull with all of their might to walk along with the trio elétricos. When the biggest carnival groups parade down the streets, you can see cordeiros of all ages and genders (but overwhelmingly black) leaning and straining to maintain the social order of carnival. When the tension between the two worlds is high, the crowds routinely push, pull, and almost knock down cordeiros. In short, this dividing line comes at high cost. Apartheid depends on the participation of the very residents it seeks to segregate in order to function. Cordeiros, however, are not morally invested gatekeepers. More often than not, they are tired, worn-down, hard-working people of African descent who struggle politically (occasionally letting friends, family, and acquaintances break the rules and run through) and physically to secure the dividing line. The police are a different story. The police represent a very different human wall that divides this space. They are the cordeiros who segregate the city not just during carnival but all year round as well.

When the city sets out to "clean up" the streets in preparation for the influx of national and international tourists during carnival, it engages in spectacular practices of policing that demarcate gender/race/class/sexuality lines throughout the city. In discussing the politics of urban renewal and the removal of black communities from the downtown prime real-estate areas of Salvador, Keisha-Khan Perry observes, "The act of policing is central to constructing, maintaining, and disposing of black marginalized landscapes and the people who occupy them" (2013, xvi). The state's efforts to "clean up" the city extend far beyond the months and weeks that lead up to the event—preparation for carnival is all year round. This process is literal and symbolic, and reflects the state's disavowal of its majority-black, poor, urban residents.

During my first experience with carnival in 2004, I became intimately familiar with the city's multivalent cleanup efforts. A few days before the event, I saw something that horrified me. I was coming home about midnight when industrial trucks spraying a mysterious white mist crept up behind me on the street. My gut knew this was pesticide and I was right. The city's cleanup project includes killing potential dengue-carrying mosquitos along with boarding up public parks and building the huge risers and stands that will hold skyboxes for the media. These literal cleanups are paralleled by more symbolic ones. In "fine-tooth-comb" operations, the police invade peripheral communities, roughing up "suspects" who are either known criminals or fit the profile of "potential criminals." Even though the literal translation of the term *periferia* is *outskirts,* many of the peripheral neighborhoods that the police target are the poor black neighborhoods—such as Nordeste de Amaralina, Joel's neighborhood—that are located close to downtown near elite enclaves. Internal peripheries are often the hardest hit by cleanup efforts because of their proximity to tourist spaces.

In order to "maintain order" during carnival, the state mobilizes the military police (PM) to conduct these fine-tooth-comb operations before the party begins, to patrol the streets during the festival, and to "clean up" the streets after the festival is over. In many ways, the preparation and cleanup for carnival never stops. When we read these practices closely, we begin to see that the police in essence function as a border patrol, and their job is to protect those who are metonymically white and privileged from those who are metonymically black and working class. The police perform this job regardless of their own individual racial classification. In other words, racism does not emerge solely when white police officers assault black civilians. The structure of policing operates according to a logic of white supremacy such that black police officers are often the ones enacting this racism, a phenomenon I discuss in more detail subsequent chapters.[6] This is compounded by the fact that the majority of military police officers are black in Bahia (Hoffman-French 2013; Sansone 2002).

Through the theatrical and very public disciplining of the general population by the state—represented by the military police—Bahian carnival reaffirms social hierarchies. The performance of racial violence during this annual event is the ritual reinscription of race/gender/sexuality hierarchies, reaffirmation of class boundaries, and declaration that these boundaries will be patrolled violently. Aggressive and at times lethal police actions during carnival are extensions of the repressive practices of terror that the police enact daily on black bodies and black spaces throughout the city. Thus, Brown's use of the term *apartheid* was a sharp political statement denouncing Bahia's allegedly harmonious symbolic moment of national pride—carnival—as racist, intensely ironic, and representative of the space of the city itself.

The racialized violence of carnival cannot and should not be characterized as an anomaly. Despite the widespread notion that carnival celebrations are either an inversion or suspension of social norms (Bakhtin 1984), what happens during Bahian carnival, particularly with respect to segregation and violence, is what Giorgio Agamben (2005) might call a state of exception, a politically fictitious state of siege predicated on an alleged state of emergency.

The state uses discourses of crisis, crime, and imminent danger to justify and maintain racial segregation in the city during carnival. However, this state of emergency *is always in place.* The state justifies the use of excessive force because of the influx of people into the city. Yet the police act like this, particularly in relationship to black people, all year round.

By arguing that carnival is not an exception but the rule, I suggest that the Bahian police manage the black population in repressive ways continuously. Police and others in Bahia are always violently marking black bodies as spaces situated outside of the moral racial social order, with baton blows, kicks, choke holds, hard pushes, and other forms of aggressive public humiliation and abuse. Bahian carnival amplifies existing social hierarchies, drawing attention to the macro- and microprocesses of racial formation and citizenship that make race a critical factor in the daily lives of Bahians.[7]

Bahian carnival is an introduction to the tensions between the lived experience of violence and the projected image of Afro-paradise. Yet Afro-paradise is not only a mythos; it is also a spatial project that literally and symbolically delineates the social geography of Bahia. This project traces its roots all the way back to slavery.

Ghosts of Pelourinho

In February 2010, I traveled to Salvador for another brief visit during carnival. I arrived on a Sunday as the entire nation had its eyes fixed on Bahia. I disembarked a plane from São Paulo full of tourists anxious to make their way out of the driving rain into the sun and fun of mythical Bahia. (That year it rained for thirty days straight in São Paulo.) Nonetheless, I could hear grumbling passengers begin to complain about the heat and the humidity that greeted us. The complaining continued (under breath) as we waited minutes that seemed like hours to collect our baggage and move toward the big glass automatic doors that mark the official entry point to the city. In many ways, southern Brazilian tourists' relationship with Bahia can best be defined as disavowal—a desire that mixes attraction and loathing.[8] On the one hand, Brazilian tourists are drawn to the city's tropical mystery; on the other hand, these same tourists look down on Bahia as a backward, uncivilized place typified by its lack of efficiency—such as, for example, bags that emerge too slowly from an airport conveyor belt. National and global fascination constructs Bahia as an exotic, black cultural mecca (e.g., Pinho 2010; Romo 2010; Williams 2013). Yet stereotypes, exemplified by conversations about the heat and the humidity, script Bahia as an out-of-the-way "heart of darkness."

Walking quickly, head down, struggling to push my heavy cart full of luggage, I saw something that caught me off guard. Along with the family members and friends lined up by the rail waiting for loved ones to emerge from the glass doors, there was a young black woman with dark skin and red lipstick wearing a big white sparkling lace head wrap and a white dress with colorful cloth accents greeting the travelers. Before I knew it, with a large grin she thrust two "Lembrança do Bonfim" ribbons in front of me and handed me a tourist guide to the city." "*Seja bem vinda*" (Welcome), she said. The city was putting its best foot forward for its mega tourist event by hiring women who dress up like candomblé priestesses, *baianas,* to greet guests and hand out souvenirs. Baianas sell bean and palm-oil fritters called *acarajé* throughout the city, and are traditionally women of African descent who are priestesses of candomblé. Over the years, these women have become symbolic representations of Afro-Bahian culture (Fonseca 2008). However, the baiana who greeted me at the airport was most likely not a candomblé priestess who sells acarajé. Instead, she was an "actress" hired to embody the baiana in order to represent the city's Afro-cultural heritage, an extension of the city's routine commodification of blackness for tourism.

Black women dressed like baianas greet tourists at the airport during carnival and in the historic city center in the months outside of carnival. Figure 1.1 shows a large inflatable baiana surrounded by red heart-shaped balloons in the Largo do Pelourinho. She is also the virtual face of Salvador on UNESCO's website. The image of the baiana represents the welcoming,

Figure 1.1. UNESCO World Heritage Site promotional picture for Salvador's historic city center. © M&G Therin-Weise, http://www.gm-photography.eu.

black, happy ethos of the city. This gendered, sexualized, and raced imaginary has made the region a sizzling tourist industry. Happy black bodies are not only pleasant but also available (Williams 2013).[10] Happy Bahia means happy, open black bodies, and these black bodies are constantly portrayed as the sensual, exotic, fit, muscular, beautiful, and often sweaty likeness of the city.

Although black bodies seem to be everywhere in Bahia, pastiche smiling black faces, like the inflatable baiana doll sitting in the middle of Pelourinho, dissociate black bodies from their social context and their recent past. The faces have no family and no history beyond their scripted association with the representations they are contracted to portray (in this case baianas). They are devoid of all politics. They don't have communities. And, most important, they are always smiling. Few observers even suspect the violent histories that haunt this image. Black Bahian bodies sell, but at what cost?

One of the first places that tourists visit when they arrive in Salvador is Pelourinho, the oldest neighborhood in the Western Hemisphere (UNESCO World Heritage Centre 1992–2013) and the historic center of the city. Pelourinho is both the literal and symbolic heart of Salvador as an Afro-Brazilian city, and is distinguished by its aesthetic and colonial history, which it traces back to the mid-1500s. Its bright pastel colonial pink, blue, and yellow buildings, and its narrow, labyrinththine, crisscross, steep cobblestone streets converge in open squares. It is also the third route in Bahian carnival—the space where all of the children's activities are located.[11] In 1985, UNESCO named Pelourinho a world heritage site (Collins 2011). It is home to dozens of the city's oldest churches, such as the Church of St. Francis (*Igreja do São Francisco*) and the Church of the Rosary of the Blacks (*Igreja do Rosário dos Pretos*). The Pelourinho is where the oldest houses in the city are also located, many of which have been continuously occupied since the 1500s. Writers, painters, and musicians, from Michael Jackson to Brazilian novelist Jorge Amado, have immortalized this neighborhood for decades, creating the mythic image that gives Salvador its unique charm, privileged place in Brazil's cultural heritage, and association with the "sensuality" and richness of black Brazilian culture.

Timeless novels like Amado's *Gabriela: Cravo e Canela* are set in the Pelourinho and continue to shape the nation's popular understanding of what Bahia looks, feels, and smells like, including the nation's ideas of blackness, race, and Bahian culture. *Gabriela,* for example, has become an important popular reference for the sensuality of the mulata in Brazilian popular culture (Caldwell 2007; Williams 2013). The story is so popular and is steeped in such strong cultural references that it was made into a feature film in 1983 and reappeared on the national scene again as a television miniseries on TV

Globo in 2012.[12] In 1996 Michael Jackson recorded the music video for his song "They Don't Really Care about Us" in Pelourinho.

UNESCO's World Heritage website recalls the colonial history of Pelourinho and the motivations behind choosing it as a world heritage site. UNESCO gave the neighborhood this honor in part because of its legacy as the first capital of Brazil (1549–1763), and its importance as the site of the first slave market in the New World (UNESCO World Heritage Centre 1992–2013). Indeed, there was a slave market in the heart of the district, although most tourists are unaware of this aspect of the neighborhood's violent, racial past and present. Behind the backdrop of its colonial allure, the name *Pelourinho* itself hides a brutal history that situates the black body in pain at the literal and figurative heart of Salvador's Afro-paradise, and Brazil as a nation.

When I first traveled to Salvador in 2001, like most visitors, I took a tour of downtown Salvador. I was traveling in a group, and an independent tour guide approached me and two of my fellow travelers one late afternoon in the Pelourinho and asked us if we wanted to take a private tour. Adventurous, we paid the fee, and he began to walk us through the historic city center. We started in the Largo do Pelourinho, and our private tour began with a story that none of us expected. He explained to us that the neighborhood Pelourinho was named after the place (the pelourinho) where they once whipped enslaved Africans in the very square where we stood. Mortified, we stared at him and wondered whether his English was correct.[13] How could it be that we had been walking up and down the cobblestone streets of this neighborhood for a week, had gone on several tours with our tour group, and no one had ever told us this before? We knew the large hill and open square as the site of concerts and other festive gatherings. During the day there was a *baiana de acarajé* who sat in the square selling snacks. Tourists strolled in and out of the square, taking pictures and watching the city from the view of the hill. Freelance stylists would gesture at visitors, offering to braid extensions into their hair (like Caribbean vacation spots, hair braiding became a way for mostly white foreigners to experience exotic Afro-culture). At night, during events, vendors set up makeshift bars and served fruity cocktails while bands played in front of Jorge Amado's house at the top of the square. Why was there no plaque?[14] Why no sign marking this space, announcing the history of this tourist attraction? As with many places throughout the African diaspora, slavery played an important role in producing the social space in the colonial period, and it continues to delimit the nation-state.[15] The politics of memory in Salvador often erases the memory of slavery and its brutal hauntings (Araujo 2012). Enjoyment of the city is literally mediated by this space, which is embodied by its past. As Perry asserts, "The racial logic of modernization and urban renewal informed by European models of development nurtures a nostalgic desire for the colonial past on the part of white Brazilians" (Perry 2013, xv). The ghosts of the Pelourinho mark the confluence of the commodification of black bodies and the torture of black bodies.

The memory and erasure of the relationship between Pelourinho's past and the brutal history of slavery is emblematic of the complex politics of race, space, and memory in Salvador. Few tourists even know that the cobblestones that line the streets of the neighborhood are known locally as "negro heads." Or, more poignantly, few understand the layers of meaning behind the name of the neighborhood itself.

Comprehending Afro-paradise requires us to read the intricate history of this trope and its specific relationship to Salvador and the birth of Brazil as a nation. The structure is a haunting that shapes the space of the city and the soul of the nation, and is a metaphor for the racial state. The word *pelourinho* is the diminutive form (*inho*) of the word *pelouro* in Portuguese, which, according to Brazilian historian Waldemar Mattos, literally means stone or wood pillar (Mattos 1978). The neighborhood Pelourinho gets its name from the centrally located pillar used to tether, whip, and torture "criminals" from the earliest days of colonial settlement in the late 1500s through September 7, 1835, when the state removed the pelourinho and suspended its use (Mattos 1978, 117). In other words, the pelourinho emerged almost simultaneously with the city itself, and although we do not know much about early Bahian society's interpretation of this structure, we do know that by the nineteenth century, the pelourinho was almost exclusively associated with, as popular Bahian historian Cid Texeira puts it, "*castigo para os negros escravos*," or the punishment of black slaves (qtd. in Félix 1995, 28). The criminal body writ large was transformed by the social imagination into the rebellious, black, enslaved body. The memory of the pelourinho, and its invisibilization in contemporary discourses of Bahia, returns us to the black body in pain. As React or Die! member José Raimundo dos Santos Silva notes, "The historical political-economic exclusion of blacks in Bahia, and its consequent and continuous social degradation, make the 'land of blackness' a nightmare for black people themselves" (Silva 2007). Over approximately three hundred years, the meaning of the pelourinho shifted with the politics of the city, but its haunting presence remains.

Although the pelourinho is no longer standing in Salvador today, it most likely looked like one that sits in Alcântra, Maranhão, today, one of the few remaining pelourinhos in Brazil.[16] Very little has been written about the history of the pelourinho, its use in Salvador, and its social meaning. In fact, it is a memory that the state and the global tourist industry gloss over in their construction of Bahian identity. But I learned in 2001 that most Bahians are very aware of this history. Understanding the pelourinho and the ghostly hold it still has on the city provides a key to deconstructing Afro-paradise and the layered politics of race, space, and violence in Salvador. This story begins with Dom João III's decision to establish the city of Salvador as the headquarters of the Portuguese colony in the middle of the sixteenth century, and its subsequent founding on March 29, 1549, as a "fortress-city" considered the "Head of Brazil"—the "administrative and military headquarters of the Colony" (Silva and Pinheiro 1977, 70). It was also the administrative and economic seat of its hemispheric political supremacy. The Portuguese erected the pelourinho in the late 1500s to link the colony and the metropole explicitly and to establish law and order; Portuguese law dictated that Portuguese cities should have a pelourinho prominently located near the marketplace for the punishment of lawbreakers (Félix 1995, 28). The pelourinho's location in the center of Salvador was a symbol of the city's status as a fortress of war. Its placement was also a performative act that established the crown's authority.

An obviously phallic structure, the pelourinho signifies the masculine and patriarchal nature of colonialism and its politics. It represented colonialism as a project of "phallic domination," and, as the spectacle of colonial authority, it was "the focus of ways of constructing masculinity and power" (Mbembe 2001, 13). In other words, the pelourinho is not only a symbolic representation of the assertion of Portuguese colonial authority in Brazil, but also the spectacle of the phallus as colonial power when viewed through the lens of the race/gender/sexuality economy of colonial rule.

During the three-hundred or so years the pelourinho was in use, Bahian governments moved it repeatedly to different locations in Salvador, and each time its placement shifted slightly in cultural meaning.[17] It came to represent Portuguese social rule, white supremacy, slavocracy, militarism, and Brazil's identity as a crossroads of multiracial encounter. One early location was Terreiro de Jesus, a public square that gained a reputation for being the raucous meeting place for enslaved and freed Africans in the city. Here, Africans and their descendants would dance and play the drums loudly (Reis 2003). The pillar's final resting place was what is now known as the Largo do Pelourinho, the location of the slave market. Each location of the pelourinho carried its own political meaning: center of authority, locale of subversive behavior, economic hub. Even though the torture device moved throughout the city, the government always located it in a prominent plaza in town as a warning symbol to potential "miscreants." The iconic referent to Portuguese authority, the pelourinho was also the literal and symbolic representation of the culture of terror that was the backdrop of slavery in colonial Brazil. One reason the iconic structure moved frequently was that residents complained about the screams of the people who were whipped and otherwise tortured at the site (Mattos 1978, 117). In 1727, for example, local Jesuit clergy petitioned Dom João V to move the pillar from the Praça do Palácio to the Terreiro de Jesus plaza because the "cries of the whipped slaves were disturbing the masses and religious society meetings" (Silva and Pinheiro 1977, 81–82). The pelourinho, like the screams of those who were tortured by it, permeated the social milieu.

The structure produced a noise that could be moved but never altered or muted and, as such, remains a recurring reminder of the sadistic cruelty of Brazil's slavocratic origins, and the fundamental role that slavery and its brutality played in perpetuating colonialism. The black body in pain was the spectacular site for the consolidation of the new nation.

The prominence of the pelourinho in the "Head of the Portuguese colony" meant the protuberant and pervasive presence of the black body in pain as the mise-en-scène of Salvador. One of the important firsthand images that we have of the use of a pelourinho as punishment is a graphic sketch of a public whipping in Brazil done by French traveler Jean-Baptiste Debret in 1826.

Figure 1.2. *Espèce de châtiment qui s'exécute dans les diverses grandes places des villes* by Jean-Baptiste Debret, Rio de Janeiro, 1826 (Bandeira and Lago 2007). An alternate title also used for this painting is *L'exécution de la Punition du Fouet.*

Debret traveled throughout Brazil during the nineteenth century, painting dozens of scenes of everyday life in Brazil, most notably scenes of slavery (Bandeira and Lago 2007). The painting in figure 1.2 portrays an enslaved black man in what appears to be a uniform (a soldier? A police officer?), his jacket draped on top of the pelourinho, whipping another black man whose pants are dropped below his knees and whose buttocks are bleeding profusely, blood dripping onto the cobblestone square beneath him and onto his light-colored pants. We know that the punisher is himself enslaved because of the chains on his waist and ankle. This double status as subjugated and enforcer of slavery recalls the cordeiros and the police officers that also often come from the very communities that they are tasked with patrolling.[18] Off in the distance is a crowd of onlookers made up of men, women, and children of different shades. Their faces are indistinguishable from afar. Closer in, to the left side of the painting, stand four black men tethered together by arms and necks with two white policemen/soldiers standing behind them. The four are waiting to be punished. In his travel writing, Debret describes the repeated scene of whipping at pelourinhos located across the city of Rio de Janeiro. He writes, "Thus, almost every day, between nine and ten o'clock in the morning, you can see a line of blacks queued to be punished, tied two and two by the arms, escorted by the police to the designated location for execution. There are pelourinhos erected in plazas all over the city" (qtd. in Bandeira and Lago 2007, 187). Pelourinhos were iconic fixtures across Brazil.

In his book *Black Milk*, Marcus Wood engages with Debret's depictions of slavery as multivalent artistic pieces that present subtle moments for pause and reflection. He writes, "[I]t is [Debret's] ability to go into this grey zone, to bring out the intimate violence, and the slow-burning apprehensions, locked into the day-to-day existence of slaves, which are unique" (2013, 37). This gray zone, according to Wood, is "the [horror] that lay within the very normalcy of slave existence" (ibid.). This gray zone might be found in the lingering anticipation that frames the image—the four men waiting to be whipped, the crowd standing off away in the distance, quietly held at bay by one lonely police guard, and the torture devices laying on the ground to the left of the frame. It is in the iron shackles that hang on the punisher's waist and ankle, physically and metaphorically tethering him to his post.

Debret's painting represents, among other things, the sexualized nature of the pelourinho as a spectacle of torture. This signification has been captured eloquently and unnervingly by Jorge Amado. In *Bahia de Todos os Santos* (1945), Amado portrays Pelourinho's past and its name in the lyrical, allegorical voice of a novelist. He describes the Ladeira do Pelourinho (the hill and square in the middle of the neighborhood where the pillar stood from 1807 to 1835) as he imagines it must have been in the sixteenth century. Amado depicts it sensually through the allegory of the black male tortured body consumed by the white female mistresses looking out on the scene from their private windows. He writes, "The great stones that line the hill must guard terrible secrets, of the pain that came out of the tortured slaves' breast. From the windows of the enormous mansions, the beautiful little mistresses watch the torture of the *negros*, with some emotion and acute feeling not devoid of pleasure" (Amado 1945, 97; my translation). I leave the word *negros* untranslated to emphasize the two possible linguistic interpretations of the term, either referring to black people generally or black men specifically. The implication, regardless of its reference to heterosexual desire or homosexual desire, remains the same. The display of the tortured black body was not only a spectacular demonstration of Portuguese colonial authority and message of deterrence directed at "criminals" (read in this moment as the unruly black enslaved), but also a sexualized display of the black body that reified and circumscribed the tensions of power, gender, race, sex, and desire in the city; a consumption culture that continues to haunt Afro-paradise today. Although slavery was a racial institution, it was a gendered and sexualized one as well, where the sexual exploitation of the black body was as much a part of the biopolitical economy of oppression as the exploitation of the body for physical labor. It was common, for example, for white masters and mistresses in Brazil, particularly those who were not wealthy, to pimp enslaved black women to turn a profit (Freyre 1973). In addition, we know that the sadistic consumption of the black body for pleasure was a cultural aspect of the institution of slavery (Glymph 2008; Sharpe 2010). In essence, slavery was a pornographic enterprise. Debret's painting encapsulates this pornographic nature and that of the pelourinho as torture device as well.

In using the word *pornography* I want to invoke Audre Lorde's definition of an absence of the erotic, or specifically, an emphasis on "sensation without feeling," obscenity, and the "abuse of feeling" (Lorde [1984] 2012, 54).[19] The pelourinho was an obscene display of sensation without feeling. The subtle implication of disavowal in Amado's description reminds us that the torture and display of the black body in slavery could not be dissociated from the sexualized nature of racial domination within this institution in the Americas. We need only return to Saidiya Hartman's (1997) analysis of Frederick Douglass recounting the whipping of Aunt Hester, or the sexual nature of inspection on the auction block throughout the black Atlantic, to be reminded of these inescapable undertones. Amado's reference to patriarchy and gender domination in all of this also brings us back to the gendered, racialized, and sexualized nature of the emerging Brazilian social structure. The "little mistresses" are purposefully positioned inside the home, implying their own subordination within the patriarchal system as they watch from their windows the black body, naked and tortured, on display.

Even Debret's graphic painting displays an ironic absence of detail that produces an important moment for pause and reflection. For example, in the gray zone, two men lie on the ground beside the one being currently punished; ordered to lie down, say Debret's notes, so that the blood will not run from their wounds and lead to infection (Bandeira and Lago 2007).[20] Although I have included a description of some of the pelourinho's gruesome details here, instead of continuing to list the often-hideous particulars of how black people were repeatedly tortured, frequently to death, on the pelourinho, I suspend my analysis in order to focus on the ghostly hauntings that the absence of further details leaves in our minds.[21] The lingering absence of our knowledge about the horrors that went on for almost three hundred years saturate the city of Salvador and Afro-paradise.

As mentioned previously, Salvador is not the only site in Brazil where the pelourinho was an organizational marker of the colonial city. Nearly every urban city in Brazil had one—from Rio de Janeiro to Natal. A 1940s debate in the city of Natal reveals much about the political significance of pelourinhos in the making of the nation. In the 1940s, Natal entered into a heated dispute over the reinstallation of that city's old pelourinho as a monument in the historic Praça André de Albuquerque (also known as Praça Vermelha). Although many citizens and the city legislature rejected the idea, the mayor and the conservative elite passionately defended it (Souza 2001). Notable anthropologist, essayist, and writer Luis da Câmara Cascudo argued the case in favor of the pelourinho (Cascudo 1950). He wrote a series of articles for the local paper "explaining" the true meaning of pelourinhos to the Brazilian masses, emphasizing the symbolic value of the pelourinho as an instantiation of the Portuguese social contract that would become the Brazilian social contract. He writes, "What is the pelourinho? The insignia of the town! [It] is your heraldic sign of independence and notorious, government autonomy" (1950, 1; my translation).[22] The pelourinho is the emblem of the order of the Portuguese kingdom and, by extension, the naturalization of its colonial subjects as citizens, justice, sovereignty, and municipal organization. It is the performative instantiation of the rule of the metropole in the colony and the conveyance of the natural sovereignty of the space as a space and its citizens' inalienable rights under the Portuguese Crown. Whether we agree with Cascudo's very conservative and colonialist interpretation of the pelourinho, his reading docs allow us to think about the memory of its presence in the strictest of Portuguese loyalist terms: the pelourinho was the symbol of sovereignty, justice, and liberty for the colonial state and Brazilian elite, and had everything to do with the consolidation of the metropole's influence in the colony—the social contract.

Understanding the pelourinho as a powerful symbol of the Portuguese social contract, and by extension the organizational moral fiber of Brazil, permits us to think about its layered meanings as well as its continued significance.[23] Although the theory of the social contract seems to have no overt references to race, gender, or sexuality, it is in actuality sexual (Pateman 1988) and racial (Mills 1997).[24] Consequently, the pelourinho is not merely a representation of the Portuguese-cum-Brazilian social contract. It is also a symbol of patriarchy and white supremacy/antiblackness. Afro-paradise, like the pelourinho, emerges from these logics.

A cross-temporal reading of the space of Pelourinho brings us back full circle to Bahia, the Afro-paradise. Between 1807 and 1835, the pelourinho was located in the square that now carries its name in the historic center of Salvador—Largo do Pelourinho. Historian João José Reis asserts that this was such an intense period of slave revolt in Salvador that the city became almost synonymous with slave rebellion in Brazil (Reis 2003, 68). The zenith of this moment was, without a doubt, the Revolta dos Malês in January 1835, which Reis characterizes as "the most serious urban slave uprising to happen in the Americas" (2003, 9; my translation).[25] From the night of January 24 through the morning of January 25, a conglomerate of enslaved and freed Africans occupied the streets of Bahia and confronted armed soldiers and civilians for more than three hours (Reis 2003, 9). The revolt was led by a group of Muslim Africans, most of whom were from the Hausa nation in what is now Nigeria, called Malês. Despite its relatively short duration, this would be one of the most successful slave insurrections in the Americas, and would have a lasting impact on the Brazilian social order for centuries to come. The volume of these uprisings, and their resilient, persistent grinding away at the colonial/slavery structure, pushes us to consider contemporary moments of state violence against the black body and militantes' responses to this violence as a continuation of this war.

We should interpret the placement of the whipping post in the Largo do Pelourinho for precisely twenty-eight years in conversation with this period of uprising. We should also acknowledge the dialogue between Bahia and the broader global politics of this time. As historian Franklin Knight observes, "the period between 1750 and 1850 represented an age of spontaneous, interrelated revolutions and events" (2000, 103). The Haitian Revolution in 1804 was the largest and most successful *social* revolution in the Americas (Knight 2000).[26] The leadership of enslaved Africans in that revolution sparked alarm throughout the colonial world, leading many colonies, like Jamaica, to change their laws restricting the movement of the enslaved (Curtin 1968). There were also changes in Europe that shaped this moment. On March 25, 1807, Britain abolished the slave trade. In response to the British ban, Brazil took its slave importation underground, carefully hiding the continued importation of enslaved Africans that lasted well into the nineteenth century (Reis 2003). On August 1, 1834, Britain abolished slavery itself, affecting all of its colonies and encouraging other colonies to follow suit. The state's interaction with the black body and the legal practices that Brazil developed toward black people from 1807 to 1835 were framed by these transnational politics.

When in 1825 the use of the pelourinho was finally suspended, the city was already in economic and social decline. In 1763, the Portuguese had moved the head of the colony to Rio de Janeiro, displacing Salvador and signaling an economic downturn in the city that intensified with the decline of the sugar industry (Fausto 1999). Salvador's elite began to move out of the Pelourinho to places farther away, such as the neighborhood of Vitória, abandoning their homes and/or bequeathing their property to their servants, thus shifting the demographic of downtown Salvador from rich and mostly white to poor and mostly black (Butler 1998; Collins 2011; Perry 2013). Throughout the better part of the twentieth century, Pelourinho was the eyesore of Bahia, associated with poverty, crime, prostitution, blackness, and social anomie.

However, in the latter part of the twentieth century, the intellectual elite in the city, like Jorge Amado, became interested in the old historic center and invested in its revival (Félix 1995). This led to a series of efforts to revitalize the downtown area, culminating in UNESCO's backing in 1985. In the 1990s the state government of Bahia, in partnership with the city and international forces like UNESCO, began to gentrify the Pelourinho into a gritty but Disney-like tourist haven.

The gentrification of Pelourinho also led to a new, reformed cultural identity for the neighborhood. Instead of being a representation of the Portuguese gentry it once had been, or the rundown, crime-ridden underbelly of the city that it became, it turned into the symbolic representation of Bahia's Afro-paradise, a folkloric marker of blackness literally disassociated from the black bodies that had once lived there. This image of black Bahia—its authenticity, its cultural capital, and its global economic value—became one of the city's primary selling points and tourist attractions (Collins 2011).[27] A signal of this shift was the state tourist agency's hiring of mostly African-descendant black women dressed up as baianas to walk throughout the Pelourinho, greet guests, and take pictures for a fee. Like the inflatable baiana on UNESCO's website, gentrification efforts and tourism have cognitively dissociated black cultural representations from their original historical referents. This dissociation hides the painfully violent histories of the presence of black bodies in the center of the city. The correlation between the pelourinho, Brazil's social contract, and the memory of the black body in pain haunts Bahia's happy, smiling black faces.

Bahia, the Palimpsest

Cultural geographer Milton Santos once described the territory of Brazil as a palimpsest—a layered space of movement, epochs, objects, information, and ideas, actual, imposed, and superimposed (Santos and Silveira 2001).[28] Within that territory, Bahia is a black geography where "physical geographies are bound up in, rather than simply a backdrop to, social and environmental processes. . . . [T]he materiality of the environment is racialized by contemporary demographic patterns as shaped by historic precedents. . . . Often hidden from view . . . black histories, bodies, and experiences disrupt and underwrite human geographies" (McKittrick and Woods 2007, 3, 4). Forgotten and hidden histories tacitly shape the material environment in Bahia. Afro-paradise is forged in blood and its invisible mist permeates the air.

Bahia is layered, revealing and concealing the violence that produces its spatial reality. Afro-paradise is itself a palimpsest, an extension of the state's spatial project (Santos 1995).[29] The positioning of the Pelourinho as the geographic, cultural, and historic center of the city locates the tortured black body as that which is, and in many ways always has been, the nodal point for delimiting Salvador. The inflatable smiling black baiana sitting in the middle of what was once a slave market, near the spot where slaves were tortured, is one such scene of hardly discernable, invisibilized terror. The celebration of black culture etches over historical violence—a metaphor for the region and the nation writ large.

The analytical framework of the palimpsest disrupts conventional notions of time, space, and the nation-state (Alexander 2006; Mbembe 2001; Shohat and Stam 1994; Thomas 2011). M. Jacqui Alexander employs it to consider time in terms that are "neither vertically accumulated nor horizontally teleological" (2006, 190). Her reframing of time encourages us to reconfigure the "here and now" by thinking of time/space in terms of transit, movement, change, and flux.[30] Deborah Thomas (2011) uses the concept of the palimpsest to think about the historical as "both analytic category and method, a way to parse the place of the past in the present" (2011, 11). As anthropologists, we can think of palimpsestic time as an approach to analyzing violence in regions where we assume it "is part of the fabric of everyday life" like Latin America and the Caribbean (2011, 10). Our stereotypes emerge from the racialized political history of this region and their unique relationships with both slavery and colonialism.

Yet violence is also a diverse cultural form (as opposed to that which lacks history or rationale) that requires an analysis that not only incorporates "the histories that generate these forms . . . but also the representational spheres through which these forms are aestheticized" (2011, 11).[31] We must use both historical and aesthetic analytical models to create a methodological approach that prefaces engagement with historicity and aesthetics, and disrupts colonial tropes of black nations/regions/spaces that adhere to strictly linear, Cartesian notions of time, space, the body, and subjectivity (Roach 1996).[32]

Even after Brazil became independent, first under the imperialist rule of the Portuguese Crown (1822), then under the oligarchical rule of the large landholding elite (1887), the social conditions of colonialism persisted, buttressed by slavery. The racialized, elite position of the original Portuguese settlers was eventually taken over by their Brazilian-born children. Indigenous people continued to be colonized, and Africans and their children, because of their roles as slaves and ex-slaves, continued to be colonized as well. This caste system—a holdover of colonialism and slavery—still informs the social structure of Brazil (e.g., Gonzalez and Hasenbalg 1982; Nascimento 1979). Racialized conditions of oppression divide the nation, not necessarily along a strict line between black and white, but along a political line between colonizers and the colonized, even in the postcolonial context, as I discuss in chapter 2. But when thinking about the relationship between the colonial and the present, it is even more imperative to avoid teleological models of time that rely on "hypervisible practices of racialization and (hetero)-sexualization" (Alexander 2006, 191). Colonial practices are "neither frozen nor neatly circumscribed within temporalities" (ibid.).

Reading Bahia as a palimpsest fleshes out the uniquely (post)colonial politics of Brazil. Achille Mbembe uses the term *entanglement,* the "combination of several temporalities" into one age, to define the postcolony—the contemporary age of Africa (2001, 15). The term *postcolony* is applicable to Brazil as well, presenting an added dimension to the discussion of the palimpsest (Comaroff and Comaroff 2006). Time "is not a series but an interlocking of presents, pasts, and futures that retain their depths of other presents, pasts, and futures, each age bearing, altering, and maintaining the previous ones" (Mbembe 2001, 16). The Bahian palimpsest constructs the state as a scrambled space, interweaving the past, the present, and the future into simultaneity. The cultural logic of antiblack state violence in Bahia emerges from Bahia as a space of entanglement.

The pelourinho haunts the city of Salvador, Bahia, and the nation with the screams of slavery. The black body, sentient and incontestable, is the ironic juncture where Afro-paradise becomes knowable.

The Black Body in Pain

In 2012, I sat down with Hamilton Borges dos Santos, lawyer, longtime militante and cofounder of the React or Die!/React or Be Killed! campaign and Quilombo X. In that interview, Santos noted that what in part motivated the emergence of React or Die! in Bahia in 2005 was the lived experience of state violence for black soteropolitanos: "The reality [of violence] was destroying the communities where we lived, and so we decided to return to our roots, to the communities where we lived, or, as it is said in street language, '*onde o chicote estrala*' [where the whip tears]." The phrase *onde o chicote estrala* is a slang expression that urban youth use in Brazil to articulate that place where the materiality of life becomes stingingly real. It literally refers to the point where the whip cracks, or that place where the whip tears the flesh as it hits the skin. Hamilton's use of the phrase to describe the site where the black experience with violence becomes material and knowable, and to articulate that juncture as the birthplace of React or Die!, presents a powerful, symbolic entryway for understanding the impetus behind the antigenocide movement and its political claims, and the connections between this contemporary moment and the ghosts of the pelourinho. When urban youth employ the phrase *onde o chicote estrala* to refer to the real, they invoke what novelists Toni Morrison (1987) and Conceição Evaristo (2003) might call a "(re)memory" of slavery and colonialism, or the almost imperceptible ways that the dead and the past come to haunt our understanding of our lives in the present. Where the whip tears the flesh is a culturally specific reference that resonates across time and space, and that frames the black body in pain as the mark of what it means to be alive and sentient. Sentience here is not only the physiological ability to perceive or feel things; it refers to our ability as beings to feel as a mark of our humanity for ourselves and the measure by which other people determine our humanity.[33] *Onde o chicote estrala* is where life becomes real for urban youth and where the black body in turn becomes the referent for material reality in Brazil. This reality invokes the pelourinho, Bahia as a palimpsest, and the irony of Afro-paradise.

The flesh that is torn by the whip is both hyperreal and hyperinvisible. It is hyperreal because the oft-repeated statement reminds us that we know the body through pain, and by extension we know what is real by feeling pain. It is also hyperinvisible because despite that knowing, the use of the term cognitively dissociates its original referent (the black body being whipped) from the reiteration of this moment as a metaphorical reference for raw life. *Onde o chicote estrala* encapsulates the pain once felt by tortured black people in the past (pelourinho) and its resonance with the daily experiences of survival in the present (carnival, Afro-paradise). It translates the memory of pain into a passing reference that articulates the critical juncture of the real—a juncture haunted by ghostly echoes.

Where the whip tears the flesh is not just a metaphor for the critical points where life itself becomes immediate. It is also a transtemporal, racialized conjuring that calls upon the memory of the black body to *define* contemporary urban *reality*. As such, the slang phrase is an opportunity for reflection, to stop and think. If the modern is, as Baudelaire suggests, that which is fleeting, ephemeral, and elusive, then the tortured black body is the oppositional point against which Brazilian modernity articulates itself, and therefore the birthplace of the nation. In other words, it is the concreteness of blackness, the sentience of the black body, and the reality of black suffering that give the modern Brazilian nation-state—in all of its racial fluidity and hybridity—its meaning. And this emerges vividly in the space of Bahia.

Elaine Scarry observes, "To have pain is to have *certainty*; to hear about pain is to have doubt" (1985, 13). The body in pain is a powerful referent for the real in the human imagination. The tortured black body is what Scarry might call a *transfer point* for the disembodied cultural fiction of Bahia's racial democracy: Afro-paradise. The incontestability of blackness (as it is felt and known through the black body in pain) is the cultural affirmation of Afro-paradise.

According to Scarry, one of the outcomes of war is "a process of perception that allows extreme attributes of the body to be translated into another language, to be broken away from the body and relocated elsewhere at the very moment that the body itself is disowned" (124). Translating the body into a language of something located outside of the body itself is a transfer point. It is the process of transference that confers reality onto something, specifically an idea or value. This process of transfer translates the "*incontestable reality*" of the body in pain into an issue or idea that "*has no independent reality of its own*" (125; my emphasis). In other words, invented cultural ideas, thoughts, and values become concrete in our minds when we associate them with the incontrovertible truth of the body in pain. Things that are intangible, fluid, nebulous, or otherwise difficult to grasp become experienceable when we can conceive of them in the material terms of the body. We touch the hurt body of a person, juxtaposed to a disembodied idea, and experience the reality of the disembodied idea through our sensorial proximity to the hurt other body (125). The virtual experience of the tortured black body in Salvador, "felt" through the Pelourinho as a tourist space and the ghostly presence of black suffering and torture throughout the center of the city, leads soteropolitanos and tourists to believe, paradoxically, that they have experienced a mythical black reality. However, as tourists walk through the Pelourinho, learning of the colonial history of the space or dancing to music and drinking cocktails during carnival, the pleasure that we feel of Bahia is in actuality mediated through the black body in pain.

The fact that Afro-paradise is made real through the black body in pain reminds us that "the body tends to be brought forward in its most extreme and absolute form only on behalf of a cultural artifact or symbolic fragment that is without any other basis in material reality: that is, it is only brought forward when there is a crisis of substantiation" (Scarry 1985, 127). Afro-paradise, a disembodied cultural fragment, is fluid but its body anchor is not. It is the materiality and incontestability of the black body, not its inexactness, that the rhetoric of Afro-paradise requires to substantiate itself.

The black body in pain is the anchor not only for Afro-paradise but also for the myth of racial democracy that is its backdrop. Thus, blackness, not racial fluidity, is that which constitutes Afro-paradise and Brazilian racial democracy. Logically, the black body should be used to anchor the idea of blackness (as a parallel notion associated with the body itself). Yet the sacrifice of the black body involves the transfer (which Scarry reads through torture) of the material fact of the body into a disembodied cultural fiction (1985, 126). In Bahia, the racial harmony of racial democracy and its happy blackness goes through a "twisting of terms" in which "the attribute of the body before the translation is the opposite of what the attribute is called after the translation" (1985, 126). Racial democracy, the cultural appropriation of blackness, its folkloricization, and the dissociation between these processes and the black bodies that produce them constitute Afro-paradise in conversation.

Ironically, the materiality of the black body in pain also anchors the myth of the fluidity of blackness in Bahia and its political consequences.[34] The black body in pain is that which the state brings forward, in its most extreme form, to substantiate the symbolic fragment of racial democracy, a cultural artifact that requires the black body to anchor it in material reality because it has no tangible basis of its own. In fact, Afro-paradise and racial democracy suffer from a crisis of substantiation—the crisis that Carlinhos Brown brought our attention to with his declaration. The purported fluidity of race and intangibility of blackness in Brazil that decades of scholars have argued exists[35] stands in contraposition to the material reality of the lived experience of suffering, encapsulated by the effaced traces of the spectacle of the black tortured body in the heart of Bahia.

The Performatic Nature of Violence: Framing the Theater

If the conditions of Afro-paradise are the black body in pain, then what are the political possibilities for black people in the face of this seemingly unconquerable reality? Afro-paradise is not only always in tension with its paradoxical frame, but it is also always in tension with the very black people that it attempts to both exploit and erase. Nowhere has this tension been laid bare more vividly than through theater and performance.

At least since the 1940s, some of the most critical and biting critiques of race, nation, and the state in Brazil have come from black theater. The theater has been a key site of black political mobilization. In 1944 Abdias do Nascimento, the very activist, scholar, and politician who would later describe Brazilian racial democracy as antiblack genocide, founded the Teatro Experimental do Negro (TEN) (Black Experimental Theater) (Nascimento 1961). For more than twenty years, until Nascimento's exile during the military dictatorship, the Black Experimental Theater charged the stage and questioned the myth of Brazilian racial democracy. Plays like *Sortilege* (Black Mystery) and *Anjo Negro* (Black Angel) were deeply critical plays that decried Brazilian racism directly and unabashedly (Nascimento 1966; Nascimento 2004). Their frequent censure by the Brazilian government demonstrated the theater's political and symbolic import.[36] What happened on the stage mattered to the integrity of Brazilian national identity, and the response by state censors ironically hinted at the fact that TEN struck a nerve of truth in its critiques. Nascimento understood the power of the stage to challenge the ideological foundations of the state. He also understood that the violence of racial democracy is itself a performance that can only be fully comprehended through its performatic reenactment on the stage.

Black theater is also part of the genealogical history of black resistance to the racial apartheid of Bahian carnival. Beginning in the 1970s, black Bahians began organizing Afro-blocos—Afrocentric carnival groups that emerged from community organizations—to directly challenge the racial apartheid of Bahian carnival (Crook and Johnson 1999; Dzidzienyo 1985; Fontaine 1985; Gonzalez 1985; Rodrigues 1999).[37] In 1974, in the middle of Brazil's military dictatorship, two black men, Antônio Carlos (affectionately known as Vovô, grandfather) and Apolônio de Jesus, established Ilê Aiyê (House of Life), an Afrocentric carnival group. The group was a response to the de facto racist policies of elite carnival groups that prohibited blacks from parading during carnival. In turn, Ilê Aiyê forbade whites from participating in their carnival processions, valorized the black aesthetic, and celebrated Bahian political and cultural connections with African heritage, like candomblé. Carlinhos

Brown's afoxé carnival group, Timbalada, can be read as an outgrowth of this Afro-bloco movement, and his political statement in 2007 was part of a legacy of black performance protest against the racism of carnival and Bahian society.

The Afro-bloco movement made a tremendous impact on the country, particularly in Salvador (Perrone 1992). Ilê Aiyê became a fervent political black cultural organization and Bahian carnival went through a period of "re-Africanization" that made black culture and music the hallmark of Bahian carnival (Dunn 1992; Risério 1981). In many ways, the founding of Ilê Aiyê, in fact, marked a new phase in black political organizing in Brazil that rekindled earlier moments of black cultural-political protest like Abdias do Nascimento's TEN (Crook and Johnson 1999; Fontaine 1985). An education organization, Ilê Aiyê focused on community outreach and "black advancement" (Perrone 1992, 46). And although the Afro-bloco movement distanced itself from explicit involvement in politics or militancy per se, it did inspire generations to assume a political black identity and boldly confront racism.

Following Ilê Aiyê, Neguinho do Samba founded Afro-bloco Olodum in the neighborhood of Pelourinho in 1979. A wildly popular neighborhood Afro-bloco, Olodum tapped into the political pulse of Pelourinho's black community and created a space where the "outcasts" of the historic city center could celebrate carnival, critique the state, and be themselves (Perrone 1992). In 1990, afro-Afro-bloco Olodum founded Bando de Teatro Olodum (BTO) (Olodum Theater). Olodum recruited former student activist and theater director Marcio Meirelles to be the theater group's first director.[38] Black theater made a reappearance on the national scene with BTO. Not since TEN had there been a nationally known black theater group that used the stage to explicitly deconstruct Brazilian racism. Like TEN decades earlier, BTO charged the stage with controversial plays that directly challenged the myth of racial democracy. A signature example would be the play *Cabaré da RRRRRaça*, a satirical piece about racism in Brazil that won international attention when BTO decided to charge black and white theatergoers different prices to see the show (Meirelles and Bando de Teatro Olodum 1995; Sterling 2012; Uzel 2003). BTO's radicalism was not only its ability to deconstruct Brazilian racism, however; the troupe also took on the unique politics of the black experience in Salvador directly.

In 1992, when the Bahian government decided to "recuperate" Pelourinho, black residents fought back. Although Pelourinho was a poor and crime-ridden neighborhood in the vision of the state and mainstream society, for many residents it was also one of the oldest black neighborhoods in the city and the cultural heart of the black arts community. Employing a research to performance methodology, BTO partnered with residents from Pelourinho to produce three plays about the government's expulsion of residents from Pelourinho: *Essa é Nossa Praia, Ó Paí Ó,* and *Bai Bai Pelô.* BTO brought the pedagogical theater approach of Brazilian theater activist Augusto Boal (1979) and the philosophies of Bertholt Brecht (Willett 1964) to the stage. However, the troupe also drew inspiration from the uniquely black theater legacies of both TEN and the work of Solano Trindade. The trilogy took an ethnographic look at the lives of the residents of Pelourinho as they were faced with the looming, seemingly inevitable threat of forced removal (Meirelles and Bando de Teatro Olodum 1995). The result was a tragic comedy that was both satirical and audaciously critical of the state government and the international neoliberal politics that produced this moment. The Bando brought attention to Afro-paradise by revealing the relationship between the state's plan to turn the Pelourinho into an exotic playland and structural (gentrification) and physical (police abuse) violence against the very black residents who inhabited that space. The actors performed the trilogy for residents of the neighborhood and the city at large. The result was a raw counternarrative that was told in real time, on stage, literally as the state dismantled the community.

We can understand theater anthropologically as not only a process but also as a social and cultural event within a political and historical context (Fabian 1990; Kondo 1997; Madison 2010). Throughout the world and throughout history, marginalized people have used theater and performance as platforms for organizing and rallying around a common cause. From the work of Wole Soyinka (1976) in Nigeria to that of Amiri Baraka and Luiz Valdez in the United States (Elam 1997), people have used the theater to critique raced, classed, and gendered hegemonies. This use of performance is often tied to a social or political movement (Elam 1997). Theater has been, and continues to be, a barometer of local and national politics. In this sense the theater is not just bound, staged performance but also a creative and ephemeral work that temporarily disrupts a given political moment. The theater, in its reflection (and refraction), holds the power to critique local and global social processes as they occur, producing counterhegemonic narratives to the metadiscourses of pain and violence that characterize political realities like Afro-paradise.

According to Dorinne Kondo, the theater can be a site for "aesthetic/political contestation" (Kondo 1997). Although performing on a stage does not completely undermine oppressive social orders, it can, when mobilized, become an arena for subversive resistance. The theater allows people "on the margins" to "[disrupt] generic conventions" (1997, 19). However, with the creation of a counterhegemonic space also comes the reification of hegemony.

For example, despite the efforts of Afro-blocos, the habitus of Bahian carnival is more social microcosm than social inversion. However, what counts in performance is a *momentary* disruption of our regimes of truth (Kondo 1997). It is tempting to measure the extent to which the theater affects the daily lives of those who have witnessed it in order to gauge its efficaciousness, to measure its success according to its ability to raise the consciousness of audience members and/or directly impact their lives. But this is an ineffective way to assess the totality of political impact (e.g., Elam 1997; Kershaw 1992) because social protest theater is often a sign of a community under duress (Elam 1997; Kershaw 1992; Reinelt 1998).[39] Thus, its impact must be measured according to the whole social process of a generation rather than individual mind changes. Social protest theater is therefore a way to gauge a political moment and interpret its meaning. Theater and performance are social barometers we can read for theoretical, social, and political insight.

One of the reasons that theater and performance have played such a vital role in black politics in Brazil is their ability to unmask racial violence in a racial democracy. TEN's early portrayals of racial democracy's violent overtones opened the door to discussions about the relationship between racial democracy and the black body in pain. Culture Shock is part of its legacy.

BTO laid the foundation for contemporary black theater in Salvador.[40] Smaller, lesser-known troupes like Culture Shock are the new legacy of black arts politics in Brazil. These troupes use the theater as a form of cultural and social outreach while seeking to uphold a high artistic standard (albeit with little resources). Black youth groups, community organizations, and grassroots projects continue to employ the theater to challenge hegemonic social structures. And although I do not want to present Culture Shock's work only as social protest theater, it has emerged in response to the urgent paradox of Afro-paradise. The stage has long been a forum for contesting hegemonic racial social structures. Performance is one of the many layers of Bahia, the palimpsest. The play continues . . .

INTERLUDE II

"The Berlin Wall"

Actors run quickly back and forth on the "stage" inside the circle of onlookers made up mostly of children and adolescents from the neighborhood of Fazenda Grande do Retiro and theater festival participants. They crouch and point to their heads while looking at the audience, shouting as they run around the stage/circle. Their gestures and their words tell the audience to "stop to think":

ACTORS: Stop to Think! Stop to Think! Stop to Think how it's going to be!

MC: A guy with a big beard named Osama bin Laden, that until today no one has been able to catch.

The actors make wide-armed gestures of chasing and being caught and pretend to fall backward and forward as the MC lists fallen and sinking monoliths of world history:

Hitler fell . . . The *Titanic* sank
and the Berlin Wall today exists in Salvador.
The Berlin Wall today exists in Salvador.

The shift from the demise of Hitler, the *Titanic,* and the Berlin Wall to the ironic persistence of the Berlin Wall of Salvador indicates that the great, seemingly timeless monoliths of history fall but then pop up again in a different form and with different political ends in new places. History repeats itself. Three actors (actor 1, actor 2, actor 3) link arms to create a human wall. The

MC walks toward the wall from behind and leans on the actors' arms. At this point the human wall becomes a representation of both the physical wall itself and those who guard it. As the MC leans gently, he asks politely and calmly to pass through the barrier.

MC: Excuse me here, let me pass here.

The wall gives the MC an abrupt, aggressive shove backward, a sharp contrast to his calm, polite request. Actor 4 of the human wall shouts as he pushes:

ACTOR 3: No negão!

Actor 3 continues to purse his lips and shake his head "no" at the audience. The MC replies,

MC: But how can you? In the Brazilian university, 2 percent of students are black. This means that 98 percent are white? I'm going to enter right here.

With more pep in his step this time, the MC approaches the wall with quick strides from the left as if he is trying to catch it unexpectedly so that he can push through more easily. When he reaches its arms he pushes harder than he did the last time, grabbing the middle actor of the wall with his right arm and trying to press through the link with more force by putting his left arm over the wall and pushing with his left rib cage. This time, he meets another resigned and firm rejection. The wall squats slightly and plants its legs firmer into the ground as it shoves the MC, shaking its heads and looking back over its shoulders at him as he makes his attempt. The wall's movements are forceful and abrupt.

ACTOR 2: You're not entering here! No negão!

Actor 2 looks over his shoulder with disdain and sucks his teeth as he and the actor to his left, both part of the wall, look back at the MC again.

MC: But how can you? I turn on the television [the MC turns to the people in the crowd and points] and I don't see you, I don't see you, . . .

MC: I don't see me, a negão! [He points back at himself]

The MC once again returns to the wall to try to break through. This time, he pushes with even more determination.

MC: I'm going to enter and it's going to be right now!

As he speaks, the MC stands firmly erect, feet planted. He raises his right arm in the air and pounds his fist twice as he speaks. He is not standing too far from the wall. Once he finishes speaking, he turns around, takes a step, and tries to push his body through the human chain again; again the wall responds with a hard thrust backward. The wall shouts,

WALL[1]: No negão!

Actor 1 turns around while he still has his arms linked with actor 2, and, looking menacingly at the MC, yells, "What a wack guy!" The MC huffs and begins another complaining rant as he stands back looking at the wall and the audience that surrounds him.

MC: But how can you? On the television I flip to channel 4, I flip to channel 5, I flip to channel 7, I flip to channel 9, I flip to channel 11, I flip to channel 13, 28, 44. There's not one children's program host who's black in a country [sic] in which 85 percent of the population is black.

The MC tosses his right and left hands alternatively as if counting as he lists all of the public television channels that are on the air in Bahia. Once he gets through the list, he holds up one finger defiantly as he makes his point. Among all of the public television channels, there is not one black children's program host. As he makes this revelation, he looks intently at the audience once more, purposefully making eye contact as he makes his point and pausing slightly to peer into the audience's eyes to emphasize the seriousness of the matter.

MC: Now you're going to see. It's going to be now!

The MC runs toward the wall and tries to jump through the linked arms with another aggressive attempt to pass. As he jumps, he flings his arms over the linked arms of the wall. It catches him and blocks his passage, and as with the previous encounters, his escalated forcefulness is met with an equally escalated level of force. This time, the wall pushes him back so hard that he flies across the circle and almost falls down. Actor 1 then takes his hand and pushes him backward even further and actor 2 kicks his foot back at him as if to make sure he does not try to get right back up and come back.

WALL: The answer again is "no negão!"

The actors portraying the wall resume their calm, protective pose as they glance around the audience circle, appearing vigilant and scowling slightly. Calmly, and a bit more softly, the MC, now standing back, begins to speak again.

MC: But wait a minute. If I pay 200,000 reais,[2] can I enter there?

The MC smirks and smiles as he makes his offer. The wall changes its demeanor completely and starts to be welcoming. Actor 1 opens his mouth in a surprised, gaping smile. The actors raise their arms as if rejoicing and then pull their arms back down in welcoming bows. They bend over low and begin gesturing the way through the "wall," which is now invisible because they have broken their poses. As they bow low, they also gesture as if brushing off and kissing the MC's feet.

WALL: In that case, yes! Welcome!

The MC looks down at all of the commotion and begins to speak again, this time with mocking inflection.

MC: Is that so? Then what you're saying is that you don't discriminate against my money, huh?

The MC gives actor 2 a slight shove as he turns to the audience to remark on the irony. Then he changes his tone of voice and begins to shout defiantly again, picking up his right hand and slamming it down hard through the air three times.

MC: I'm going to enter there and I am not going to pay anything and it's going to be now!

In one last antagonistic effort, the MC runs toward the wall.

It is now scattered from breaking form in order to welcome the MC's money offer. The actors scramble back to take a defensive posture. As the MC tries to make it through the wall again, it struggles to maintain its charge of blocking his passage. This time, all of the actors onstage, including the MC, erupt in a physical struggle. Actor 2 throws the MC to the ground.

WALL: No negão! (Vai viado)

The MC turns to the audience as the struggle ends and slightly chuckles. All of the actors are now on their feet. They very briefly pause as the MC begins to speak again, marking transition out of this vignette into the refrain.

MC: You see now that the Berlin Wall exists in Salvador?

All the actors walk around inside the circle gesturing with their hands wide to the audience and then pointing back to their heads as they chant the refrain.

ACTORS: Stop to Think! Stop to Think! Stop to Think how it will be!

Scene ends.

2 The Paradox of Black Citizenship

> The settlers' town is a strongly built town, all made of stone and steel. It is a brightly lit town; the streets are covered with asphalt, and the garbage cans swallow all the leavings, unseen, unknown and hardly thought about. . . . The settlers' town is a town of white people, of foreigners.
> —Frantz Fanon, *The Wretched of the Earth*

In January 2007, photos of a black man lying prostrate on a beach while a police officer pressed his boot down firmly on the back of his head circulated like wildfire among militantes. In a series of fourteen photos (one of which is pictured in figure 2.1), a white policeman straddles a black man, steps on his head with his boot, and points a gun to his back, the foaming waves of

Figure 2.1. A military police officer steps on a vendor's head on Ondina Beach, Salvador, in January 2007 (photo from *A Tarde*).

the ocean lapping the shore behind them. In subsequent shots, a tanned white man wearing a khaki hat, yellow Speedo, and sunglasses comes in and peers as the policeman asks the prostrate man questions. Two black male beachgoers walk up and watch from a different direction. Three more come to look. A crowd begins to gather. A white blonde woman wearing bulky jean shorts, a white bikini top, and a cloth headband enters the scene and begins talking with the tanned white man with the tan hat and yellow Speedo. The images, the file names that accompanied them in an e-mail thread (which I read as captions),[1] and the narrative that emerged framed the moment as an archetypal instance of racially discriminatory policing in Salvador.

The altercation at Ondina, just blocks away from Joel's neighborhood of Nordeste de Amaralina, happened just before carnival in 2007. A white Spanish female tourist was robbed on the beach, and a police officer approached a vendor as a potential suspect. I first learned of the brouhaha when I received this and a series of sequential photos of the incident taken by the same photographer through React or Die!'s listserv. The episode had already ignited protests and a series of public debates among militantes, who tied it to the fine-tooth-comb operations the state periodically does in order to "curb crime." The compound injustice of the scene and its raced, gendered, sexualized, and classed implications incensed black movement organizers: A white female European tourist (noncitizen), feeling threatened by a black man ("citizen"), is quickly protected by the state (the police officer standing in as its proxy as protector and patriarch), at the expense of a tax-paying soteropolitano. The series of images and the story captured the lived reality of racial apartheid and police harassment in Bahia in high relief. Ironically, the antiracism initiative, Dial Racism (Disque Racismo), was to hold a public meeting with the secretary of public security titled "Police Violence during Popular Festivals" the next day.

One of the first vignettes of *Stop to Think*, "The Berlin Wall" (transcribed in the second interlude) is an allegory of racial apartheid in Bahia. According to Faye Harrison, "Apartheid is a policy of enforced separation between races, but the term is also used to characterize any invidious structure and practice of racial inequality—intended or unintended" (2008, 220). When we think of apartheid, we tend to think of South Africa. Yet Brazil also adheres to colonial logics of racial apartheid. Although Brazil never experienced the legal segregation that defined South African apartheid, it has historically been defined by a de facto racial segregation that subtly divides the nation according to race.[2] And this de facto racial apartheid is also closely intertwined with the question of citizenship.

Culture Shock portrays Brazilian racial apartheid as a living, breathing Berlin Wall that exists in the city of Salvador. Satirical, funny, and lighthearted on the one hand, and utterly painful on the other, this vignette is one of the play's strongest attempts to argue that we cannot understand racism in Brazil without first acknowledging that it is not necessarily what is said but what is enacted and embodied that constitutes racial prejudice and discrimination within the nation. When the troupe performs this comedic vignette, the audience is typically rapt. Despite its serious topic (racism), the performance is funny and lighthearted, encouraging people to laugh out loud throughout. At Fazenda Grande do Retiro, the crowd that gathered to watch chuckled throughout the presentation, myself included. The exaggerated imitation of everyday racism strikes a chord with onlookers. One young woman, Ana, told me after one performance that the scene works well because it makes you laugh at yourself. The humor allows us, the audience, to see that racism functions in nonverbal ways and is adaptive, malleable, and cunning. Racism is performative; it literally enacts the very conditions it articulates. In this way it is spatializing. It defines the topography of the city of Salvador, marking some spaces as black and expendable. The irony of it all is that the people who personify the angry, determined wall in real life are often the very people that the wall intends to exclude, like the black police officers and the cordeiros discussed in chapter 1. Black people confront visible and invisible human walls in their everyday attempts to access resources and dignity in the city, and these walls are often subtle, elusive, and guileful. The police and other residents tasked with maintaining security act as a border patrol that delineates the boundaries of the moral racial social order. Spatial practices of race performatively and theatrically press the black body to the margins of national belonging like the military police officer's boot on the black vendor's head or the police batons that push the pipoca during carnival. Through these embodied practices, the state produces national frontiers of belonging along the cartographic lines of a racial hierarchy. This process is macro as well as micro. The maintenance of racial democracy as a *national* ideology depends on the diffuse, mundane repetitions of violence in states, cities, and neighborhoods as well as the more spectacular moments of state terror that we associate with police violence.

These practices present yet another duality: they mark black bodies as national subjects while excluding these very bodies from citizenship rights. Citizenship is also the production of violence. This is the paradox of black citizenship: the state relies upon blackness as a cultural reference, requires that black people adhere to the laws of the land (pay taxes, register for identity cards, and vote in elections),[3] subjects black people to intense surveillance and aggressive policing, but does not, in practice, extend black people equal protection under the law, provide equal access to state services, or allow black people to participate in civic and cultural society unhindered.

Citizenship is a political relationship between a state and its people. Aihwa Ong argues that citizenship is "a cultural process of 'subject-ification,' in the Foucauldian sense of self-making and being-made by power relations that produce consent through schemes of surveillance, discipline, control, and administration" (1996, 737). And in Brazil, as in many liberal democratic societies, the task of "instilling proper normative behavior and identity" (1996, 738) in the populace is not just a state matter but also a civil matter. However, in the case of black Brazilians, I would argue, the state and civil society engage in cultural processes of subjectification in order to produce black people as objects of the nation without subject-citizen status. This brings us back to the precarious relationship between biopolitics and necropolitics. In other words, the biopolitical practices of subjectification occur in order to pacify and control black bodies but not necessarily assimilate them into the nation-state. If we read the process of subjectification in conversation with the necropolitics of the horizon of black death (Ferreira da Silva 2009; Mbembe 2003), then the production of black docile bodies (to draw on Foucault) perpetuates the machinery of the state by managing life in the service of death (Foucault [1977] 2003; Foucault 1978).[4] This chapter focuses on that aspect of managing life.

Through a close reading of "The Berlin Wall" vignette, React or Die!'s campaign efforts, and black soteropolitanos' reflections on citizenship, this chapter examines how Bahia produces antiblackness. During the "quieter" hours—when carnival is over and the streets have been "cleaned up," in between the more spectacular moments of violence like police raids and death-squad murders—what are the micropractices of racism that sustain antiblackness?

Black Citizenship

The global politics of black citizenship have been a contentious issue for scholars (Basch, Schiller, and Blanc 1994; Clarke 2013; Gilroy 1987; Schiller, Basch, and Blanc 1992; Thomas 2004). Black people do not enjoy citizenship in the Americas, or so black radical thinkers have long argued. From Martin Delany ([1852] 2004) to W. E. B. DuBois (1948), Queen Mother Moore (McDuffie 2011) and Kwame Ture (Carmichael 1967), the condition of black people in the Americas defies the idea of black American citizenship (in the national and hemispheric sense of the word). In the United States, laws and legal decisions such as the Fugitive Slave Act (1850), *Dred Scott v. Sanford* (1857), and *Plessy v. Ferguson* (1896) explicitly declared black people sub-human and noncitizens. And despite the more inclusive language on race later adopted with the Civil Rights Act of 1964, the idea that blackness and citizenship are mutually exclusive continues to haunt the U.S. legal system. A precarious relationship between black people and citizenship also plagues the African diaspora. As Carole Boyce Davies and Babacar M'Bow observe, "For many years the status of African diaspora peoples in various nation-states has entailed a recognition that they are always a 'deportable' subject. . . . Africans often did not have access to the basic rights accorded citizens in many locations prior to civil rights and other anti-colonial movements" (2007, 19). From England (Gilroy 1987) to India (Davies and M'Bow 2007), black people have found it difficult to be fully recognized as national subjects in the modern era.

In Brazil, similar dissociations between blackness and citizenship have also occurred historically, albeit in less explicit legal ways. For example, during the period of intense slave revolt in Bahia from 1807 to 1835, the state often used deportation to punish rebels of African descent (Reis 2003). At the dawn of the new nation, throughout the nineteenth century, black citizenship was always conditional and shaky. Not only did government officials intensely debate the extent to which free, Brazilian-born blacks could be full citizens, they *actively hid* these debates in order to construct a rhetoric of national homogeneity and racial harmony that we would come to call *racial democracy* (Chalhoub 2006). And although this explicit language of racial exclusion is no longer documented, its historical reverberations continue. Contemporarily, black citizenship is often hollow—black people rhetorically have rights that do not manifest practically.

For decades black Brazilian scholars and their allies have argued that black Brazilians do not enjoy full access to citizenship despite being legal subjects of the nation (e.g., Andrews 1991; Fontaine 1985; Hanchard 1994; Hanchard 1999b; Hasenbalg and Silva 1988; Mitchell and Wood 1999; Reiter 2009; Skidmore 1985). This argument has focused on black people's marginal status, however. Yet in asserting that black Brazilians are marginal citizens, we miss a key aspect of the relationship between blackness (as a historical, social, political, and racial category) and the state. Black people do not experience equal protection under the law or equal access to national territory, rights, and resources.

To be sure, Teresa Caldeira and James Holston have argued that Brazil is a "disjunctive" democracy where citizenship is a dicey category for all Brazilians

(Caldeira 2000; Holston 2008; Holston and Caldeira 1998). In the aftermath of the authoritarian regime (1964–85), Brazil instated political democracy but maintained an ex post facto, de facto authoritarianism. Consequently, while Brazilians enjoy political citizenship, the state, both directly and indirectly, denies most citizens civil citizenship, better defined as *social rights* (e.g., Dagnino 1994a; Holston and Caldeira 1998; Mitchell and Wood 1999). Intense class stratification and social hierarchy have guaranteed that citizenship has never implied the equality of all Brazilians (Baierle 1998; Estanislau 2000; Holloway 1993). However, when we pay close attention to the routine interactions between the state and black Brazilians in the new democratic period, we notice that black people are denied not only social rights but also the right to life—not only a constitutive part of the definition of *citizenship* under any democracy but also a fundamental human right that transcends the rhetoric of civil rights that we associate with political democracy. Even if Brazil is a disjunctive democracy, blackness still sits symbolically outside of this reality.[5]

If blackness in Brazil is caught somewhere between biopolitics and necropolitics, then the state's project is not to produce black citizen-subjects but rather black national objects, and to exclude black people from the nation rather than incorporate them into the citizenry. As national objects, they are a territorial extension of the national landscape. This creates a paradox: black people are at once nationals and noncitizens.

We can observe the dissociation between blackness and citizenship readily in the practices of de facto segregation in Salvador. Policing practices—practices of control—demarcate the boundaries of citizenship. Race greatly defines where Brazilians can go and how they will be treated when they get there (Gonzalez 1983). Moreover, the state itself restricts black movement, and the legal system limits the extent to which black people can seek justice through the courts by making it nearly impossible to prosecute laws that were meant to eliminate racial discrimination in the nation, like the constitutional law that criminalizes racism (Guimarães 2003). At the same time, the same state—as represented by the police forces and death squads—also kills black people with impunity and makes it almost impossible for black people to seek a remedy for these injustices within the legal system as well. This denial of citizenship rights is not, however, *in spite of* a functioning political democracy. Rather, it is *constitutive of* democracy. The state defines citizenship and national belonging in contraposition to blackness. Thus, blackness is the stage upon which the nation performs itself. This chapter examines the policing practices, from the spectacular to the mundane, that maintain this racial social order and how they produce the city of Salvador.

Appealing to Justice

The few months after the vigil of 2005 were a time of intense discussion and action for the new React or Die! campaign. I participated in a couple of early planning meetings and volunteered to support the campaign through international outreach, including, first and foremost, translating the manifesto from Portuguese to English. From then on, translation and transnational communication became one of the ways I would contribute.

On May 15, organizers inaugurated React or Die! in the city of Feira de Santana, a suburb of Salvador. Shortly thereafter, on June 14, world-renowned hip-hop artist MV Bill launched his book *Cabeça de Porco* (Soares, MV Bill, and Athayde 2005) in Feira de Santana in homage of the initiative, and then continued his tour of Bahia with a visit to Salvador to help inaugurate React or Die! at the Federal University of Bahia (UFBA). MV Bill's fame brought celebrity status to the campaign, and the city and the nation were soon buzzing with the phrase *React or Die!*

In July, militantes demanded that the state of Bahia hold a public hearing on antiblack genocide. Held at the state legislature office, the resulting meeting included the president of the Human Rights Commission of Bahia, a representative of the public prosecutor's office (Edmundo Reis), and federal representative Luiz Alberto. Various people from the community who had been victims of state violence testified, including many women who had lost their children, partners, and family members to death squads and the police. The diversity of the testimonies, and the critical role that women played in the denunciations, helped to define the complex matrix that the campaign sought to confront: it was not just that the women who testified had lost a loved one as a result of state lethality, but they were also victims of this violence as well. They had come under the direct threat of violence either because they had reacted to the use of force against their loved ones in the moment of the aggression, or because now, after the fact, the same aggressors who had killed their loved ones were seeking revenge on them. As the campaign reminded us, a kind of state-sponsored domestic violence situated the police as representatives of a patriarchal state that had been authorized to terrorize women in a uniquely gendered and sexualized way (Mann Carey 2014).[6] The women made their testimonies under the risk of torture and death.

State-sponsored public hearings should not be read as the state's agreement with or acceptance of the campaign's denunciations. One public official's statement after the hearing at the state legislature represented the dominant view on the conversation around antiblack genocide at the time. A representative from the state prosecutor's office, Edmundo Reis, stated that there seemed to be no tangible connection between racial discrimination and police death squads in Bahia. Instead, he posited that the racial makeup of victims of death squads could be attributed to (1) the tendency for death squads to be active in the poorer, peripheral neighborhoods of Salvador where the majority of black residents *happen* to reside; and (2) the fact that 85 percent of Bahia's population is of African descent (Ramos 2005). Reis's argument completely sidestepped the question of structural racism and ignored the hegemonic effects of white supremacy that require us to conceptualize racism beyond individual actions by white bodies against black bodies. Although the public hearing demonstrated the state's willingness to hear the complaints of the community, the response of Edmundo Reis underscored the work that needed to be done to get the state and society to recognize that state violence against the periphery was a specifically racialized violence and antiblack.

Except for politicians like Luiz Alberto (the clear exception to the rule),[7] local and national government representatives read the accusation of genocide against the state as ludicrous. Not surprisingly, part of their blanket dismissal of the idea was anchored in racial democracy and the image of Bahia as "Black Rome"—a black cultural mecca and majority black space (Dunn 2007). A few weeks after the hearing, I went with some of the campaign's members to a book launch for renowned sociologist Gey Espinheira. The book, *Sociabilidade e violência: Criminalidade no cotidiano de vida dos moradores do Subúrbio Ferroviário de Salvador* (2004), examines the phenomenon of violence in the Subúrbio Ferroviário region of Salvador. It directly addresses the very issues that the militantes were seeking to denounce. Four of us sat in the front row of the packed lecture hall that day listening to Espinheira and his team present their work. When we came to the question-and-answer period, one of the React or Die! members, Zumbi, raised his hand to ask a question. Knowing a bit about the background of the project and its racial politics, Zumbi provocatively asked Espinheira about the impact race has on the police violence that plagues the suburbs. In response, Espinheira noted candidly that if one were to correlate police violence with racism, then in actuality the picture would resemble something more like black-on-black violence than white violence against black people because of the high percentage of black police officers. Indeed, as Sílvia Ramos and Leonarda Musumeci find in their work on race and policing in Rio de Janeiro, state policing "is an institution with a strong black presence, not only in the lower ranks but also in the upper ranks and even in high command posts. Yet . . . instead of this opening a door to open debate on the issues of race and racism, it often serves as a pretext to avoid the subject" (2005, 44). The existence of a high percentage of black police officers is frequently the pretext for not addressing the issue of racial discrimination in policing. However, this excuse ignores the issues of structural racism that React or Die! was seeking to address.

Campaign organizers visibly tensed with anger. Many people in the room, including several of the black graduate students who had worked as research assistants on the project, began to shift nervously in their seats. We all could feel the tension in the air. And the look on the faces of the members of React or Die! said one thing: How could something so painfully obvious to some be so outlandish and invisible to others? It was as if the representatives of the movement were trying to combat a devil that only they could see.

Faced with the state and society's refusal to acknowledge the credibility of their claims, the campaign decided that the next best step was to redress state violence from the outside: international human rights appeals. In July, React or Die! took two important steps in this direction. First, they appealed to United Nations special rapporteur Doudou Diène, then visiting Salvador. His focus at the United Nations from 2002 to 2008 was contemporary forms of racism, racial discrimination, xenophobia, and related intolerance. During his visit, React or Die! organizers managed to deliver the campaign's dossier outlining the crisis of death squads, police violence and torture, and the racial implications of this violence to Diène. Second, shortly thereafter, organizers connected with the Inter-American Commission's rapporteur on the rights of Afro-descendants and against racial discrimination, Sir Clare K. Roberts, who also traveled to Salvador via the Organization of American States (OAS).

Roberts participated in an open forum on police violence and racism in Bahia in the auditorium of the Brazilian Bar Association (OAB) headquarters downtown. I attended that forum with the movement organizers. The principal topic of discussion at the forum was death squads. Family members of victims testified in front of a panel of state government representatives and black movement activists. The room was packed with people, most of them local people from the black movement who I recognized from other, similar political events. Jussara was an older woman, heavy-set, with beautiful smooth skin and a round face. She spoke passionately and eloquently when they called her up. As she stood at the podium, her dark skin glistened under the heat of the bright lights of the auditorium. She was a grandmother who had lost her grandson to police violence during a raid on her home. He was dragged out of her house in the middle of the night and assassinated by police officers shortly thereafter. She did not say much about the details of his death or the invasion. Instead she spoke of her love for her grandson and the need for justice for the community. "O que nós queremos é justiça"—what we want is justice, she said. Her voice was strong, penetrating, and firm. Tears welled up in her eyes but did not fall. She refused to break down in front of the very people who had taken her baby away. I struggled to focus on what she was saying. Her story was similar to countless others that I heard during my time living in Bahia and it caught me in the throat and clutched my heart. No matter how many times I heard these stories I could never, and did not ever want to, get used to hearing them. Her pain and suffering were palpable, and I looked around nervously trying to avoid making contact with it so I could also avoid coming to grips with the unspeakable pain that permeated the air.

I was distracted from her testimony not only by my emotions but also by watching the panel, representatives of the state's public security office and the Inter-American Commission. I found myself constantly assessing their facial expressions. The representatives of the Bahian government stood out in this room filled mostly with black people—they were the white people in black suits at the long folding table covered in white cloth, with glass pitchers of water strategically placed. These government officials looked vacantly at Jussara as she spoke or they looked down, "taking notes." Sir Clare Roberts, the Inter-American Commission representative, watched her attentively as he listened to his interpreter. Under the hot lights, with the government officials to her right jotting down her words, it seemed like Jussara was on the witness stand or in a police interrogation. As a member of the audience I felt like I was doing police work; as an anthropologist I felt implicated in the consumption of Jussara's "story" (Angel-Ajani 2008; Malkki 1995).[8] What purpose—whose purpose—were we serving?

The goal of the afternoon was not for the state to gather information or details of these cases of state terror. The state was barely interested in Jussara's story, and it only symbolically investigated the death of her grandson after that point—making promises to look into it but no headway, just shuffling papers to make it look like work was done. Rather, the purpose was to perform state accountability for an international audience—the OAS. The hearing was a choreographed performance. The long walk to the podium, the flushed face filled with tears, the government officials in dark suits and white shirts looking intent but hearing nothing, in front of an audience that had heard it all before.

Jussara spoke for about ten minutes, not just about her grandson but also about the general conditions of her community (which I do not name here in the interest of anonymity). "My grandson died because our community is abandoned. The children do not have proper schooling. We do not have sufficient water and energy in our community. We deserve respect and we demand respect from the state." Jussara recited a litany of concerns that tied her grandson's death and the question of "public safety" to the lack of social services in the periphery, absence of adequate infrastructure, insufficient education, and the need for better services from the government. She sounded like other soteropolitanos talking about the violence they experienced. When asked to speak about one injustice, people often and quickly spin off into a conversation about another. One experience with injustice melds with the next. There is no material disconnect between the spectacular and the mundane. The police invading their homes at night and killing their children and the state refusing to keep up the roads are part of a genocidal assemblage. This takes us back to React or Die!'s definition of *genocide*: a historical and experiential cluster of experiences that links one moment to the next and one body to the next. The framework of intersectionality is not sufficient enough to describe assemblages (Puar 2007). Assemblages imply transnational entangled time, connections, and clouds and clusters of interdependence and crossing. To talk about spectacular experiences with state terror in Bahia necessarily flows into other discussions of related, connected violence elsewhere at other times. Everyday experiences with racism and discrimination—violence in the "quieter" hours—are extensions of the spectacular just as the spectacular is an extension of the everyday.

Because Roberts was a guest of the state, city officials kept a close watch on his interactions with local residents, making it difficult for the campaign to get his ear. But the campaign, taking advantage of my presence at the meeting and my English proficiency, got me to approach him after the forum, introduce the militantes from React or Die!, and establish contact. This move later facilitated their submitting the React or Die! dossier to his office.

The internationalization of React or Die! after its founding is what, in part, catapulted it to national and global recognition. From this point forward, the campaign would continue to investigate cases and submit denunciations to the United Nations, solicit audiences with state police and public safety coordinators regarding the issue of antiblack genocide, and use the multileveled tactic of agitation to address the black community's concerns. On March 20, 2015, React or Die! coordinator Hamilton Borges dos Santos traveled to the OAS in Washington, DC, to testify against the Brazilian state on the genocide of black youth in front of the Inter-American Human Rights Commission (IAHRC). At the hearing, Brazilian government representatives admitted the existence of *extermínio da juventude negra* (extermination of black youth) (Justiça Global 2015). Subsequently, on February 28, 2015, representatives from React or Die! testified on antiblack genocide in front of the Comissão Parlamentar de Inquerito do Exterminio no Nordeste (Parliamentary Commission of Inquiry into Extermination in the Northeast—CPI) of the Brazilian Parliament (Azevedo 2015). Using their partnerships with human rights organizations, React or Die! has been able to thrust the question of antiblack genocide to the forefront of international human rights debates and national political attention.

Not only is the black body the backdrop against which the state defines itself conceptually—illustrated in chapter 1 with the discussion of the black body in pain—but the further relationship between the Brazilian social contract and the black body in pain inevitably locates black people outside of the national boundaries of citizenship as well. In other words, the use of the black body in pain as an ironic transfer point for defining Afro-paradise renders black citizenship (read also as black national belonging) impossible. Consequently, black organizers find little recourse with the state in their appeals for justice. Spectacular acts of state violence performatively mark the black body as that which sits outside of the social contract. And everyday practices of policing, from the spectacular to the mundane, not only maintain this relationship but also structure the national space itself, spatializing racism into racial apartheid.

Everyday Citizenship

For International Theater Day, March 31, 2004, *O Movimento de Teatro Popular do Subúrbio* hosted a march through the suburbs. Culture Shock invited me to participate, so I could film it. Much like the theater festival at Fazenda Grande in 2003 (where the troupe had performed "The Berlin Wall"), clowns, children, and various theater groups paraded through the streets. The movement was able to get a small trio elétricos to lead the parade, and I climbed on top of it in order to film. Rogério from Culture Shock, one of the members who knew the suburbs the best, rode with me. He had grown up here.

As we moved along the parade route, people came out of their houses to wave to us. We laughed and joked, singing songs and chanting phrases supporting popular theater, like "*abre alas eu quero passar, sou popular não posso negar*," which I would roughly translate as "make way and let me pass, I am of the people and I cannot deny it." The term *popular* is a reference both to the idea of being from the masses and to the title of the theater movement.

It took us about three hours to travel the entire parade route, and we did not even travel through all of the neighborhoods in the suburbs. As I watched the houses while I went by, I noticed how different the suburbs can be from the center of the city. Here there was more space. The houses were clearly working class and modest, but it felt more like the countryside than the urban hustle and bustle of the city. In fact, Rogério was very involved in the environmental justice movement in the region. At one point during the parade, he asked me to get down from the truck and walk with him. He took me to the side of the road where there was a creek where two boys were fishing. He asked me to film. Looking at the camera passionately, he began to explain the poor environmental infrastructure of the suburbs. The boys were fishing in a polluted area, not to be defiant, but because this was one of the only sources of food and income. The state's neglect of the environment was also one of Culture Shock's political concerns. For them, the question of citizenship and belonging could not be separated from the historical processes that have disenfranchised black residents from the right to enjoy and live off the land; to fish, swim, drink clean water, and live in a nonpolluted environment. Environmental degradation is another spatialized dimension of racial apartheid in Salvador and an aspect of the genocidal assemblages of citizenship that Jussara spoke about in her testimony (Smith 2009).

Indeed, their memories of home were closely tied to the environment. Later that year, Sobrevivente, Culture Shock's founder, asked me to work with him to produce a tenth-anniversary video for Culture Shock. The goal was to create a historical archive for the community of San Martins. This video included brief interviews with residents, particularly elderly residents, and reflections from former members on the work that the troupe has done over the years. It took awhile to get our schedules coordinated, but on September 20, 2004, in the late morning, braving the rain and the mud, we set out. As we walked around from house to house, Sobrevivente told me about the politics of San Martins and Culture Shock's involvement with them: the lack of a local health clinic, poorly maintained roads and drainage systems, criminality, drugs, teen pregnancy, and political corruption. Having grown up in San Martins, Sobrevivente knew the older residents in the neighborhood. They were all generally happy to see us and hear about the project. They welcomed the chance to sit down and reminisce about the old days of the community.

Our interviews with residents were fascinating. There were moments of light laughter punctuated by points of heavy silence as we spoke with neighborhood elders about their memories and thoughts. Older residents expressed both nostalgia and disappointment to us about the environment of Fonte do Capim (Grassy Springs). The town had started as a community of settlers drawn to the location for its freshwater reservoir. The spring was surrounded by a grassy field (hence the name), and it was the main water resource of the community for years. Only one resident we met still had an old well behind her house, however, and the water was too stagnant and polluted to drink. Residents' stories of the freshwater of the past stood out in contrast to the gaping muddy holes that pockmarked the streets that day, exposing water and sewage pipelines. Dirt roads wound throughout the lower portion of the neighborhood.[9] The main road, where the community school was located, was under construction and it had large pits. When it rained, as it did the day we conducted the interviews, the mud made it difficult to walk through the streets and forced pedestrians to hug tightly to house entrances to avoid falling off makeshift wood bridges across construction holes. A lone worker was out raking dirt into the openings that day. In a few weeks the pits would be filled and the streets paved, just in time for the community to cast its votes—evidence of the corruption and manipulation that accompanies election years in Bahia.

Many residents were happy to talk about the years that they had spent in the community while some were uninterested. All of them had a lot to say about the violence in the neighborhood, as well as the criminality and youth's disrespect for elders. Their consternation with the upcoming generation of young people sounded familiar, similar to the conversations I had had with older residents of my own community in the United States. The politics of violent policing in the periphery are complex; ironically, even the residents whose neighborhoods are the targets of violent repression are at times in favor of these harsh measures. One resident even spoke of the need to do a *limpeza geral* (clean sweep/general cleaning) of the neighborhood, rounding up criminals and roughing them up, in an echo of the state narrative. His tone reminded me of the "talk of crime" that Teresa Caldeira documents in everyday discourses of public safety in São Paulo (Caldeira 2000).

The elders' comments were also about citizenship, in that they expressed the complex emotions and politics involved in the desire to live in peace and security at the periphery. Indeed, black Brazilians repeatedly and adamantly talk about citizenship, nationality, and national belonging, laying claim to the "right to rights" (*direito a ter direitos*) (Dagnino 1994b, 107), particularly in grassroots politics. Let's think back to Jussara's testimony for a minute. Her invocation of genocidal assemblages—the matrix of violence from police aggression to the lack of social services in her community—was also an appeal to the discourse of citizenship. Her rights and those of her community are not being met. However, within their ideological investment in nationality, I argue, black soteropolitanos consistently recognize a racialized, parallel national status that differentiates their position within the nation from that of nonblack Brazilians. In general, one does not find the sense of "statelessness" in Brazil that we often identify in the United States among black people. However, black people often invoke the topic of citizenship even when they feel alienated within the nation-state. Their complaints are certainly a racial critique of Brazilian citizenship. My conversation with an actor from Culture Shock demonstrates this. Rafael defined *citizenship* for me:

> Wow. Chris, there are so many things . . . don't throw trash on the ground because if you do that the trash will clog the city sewer . . . stuff like that . . . help people who do not have resources . . . do you understand? Historically the church practiced citizenship by helping the poor and such . . . but nowadays they just build castles. . . . I think the theater . . . hip-hop is very involved in citizenship, you get me?

Here, Rafael articulates a vision of citizenship that is more akin to civic responsibility than a reflection on national belonging and the traditional liberal democratic definition of the term. Indeed, throughout my time conducting field research, I often found that people in the periphery defined *citizenship* in this way, articulating it as a conscious act of social responsibility.

Rafael also articulated *citizenship* as the freedom of movement, speech, and the power to demand civic freedom. Rafael again:

> After I came to recognize my Afro-descendant history . . . I practice citizenship whenever I can. If I am in the street and I am sad, I have a certain freedom of expression and I don't have to care about anyone else, you know? If I'm on the street and I want to scream out, I scream out. Whoever wants to look at me funny can do so [but I have the right to freedom of expression] . . . this power I will take with me . . . until death.

Rafael articulates citizenship as the right to freedom of expression, freedom of movement, power to act, and a social responsibility to self and others.

This rhetorical appeal to citizenship, however, does not align with a social and legal access to national belonging and rights. Rafael's ability to walk in the streets and express himself is greatly limited by policing practices, as he himself indicates in other moments during the interview.

> I've suffered a lot due to discrimination for being black, for having tattoos, these things also. . . . If I were a "white boy" I wouldn't suffer certain discriminations. For example, yesterday when I went to work, I arrived in the morning and caught the security guard that works at seven in the morning instead of the regular guard I catch when I get to work at night. He barred me from going into my job saying, "Look, this is no place for someone who has a tattoo. People who have tattoos are thieves." I lowered my head and said, "Hey man, you say people who have tattoos are thieves but I'm not a thief." Then I went to the director, talked to him, and he asked me if I wanted to file a case with the police [alleging racism]. I said no, I'll leave quietly and I think I'll bring my theater group here to help educate the staff.

The security guard stated that he did not want to let Rafael in because he had tattoos, and "people who have tattoos are thieves," but Rafael understands this as a coded excuse for excluding him because he is black. If he were a "white boy" with tattoos, the story might have been different.

There is a tension between Rafael's assertion that his citizenship affords him the freedom of expression and movement, and the restrictive realities he often experiences because he is black. Despite being outraged, Rafael refused to file a formal complaint against the security guard with the police. In actuality, in everyday conversation across Brazil, people frequently use the phrase "What do you want to do, file a complaint?" facetiously, the way that people in the United States say "Sue me." But the words carry another meaning, for one really can file a complaint in Brazil because racial discrimination is illegal and unconstitutional. Rafael's boss was in many ways legally responsible for the behavior of his employee, the discriminating security guard, so he could have felt some pressure to present the option of legal action to Rafael. But instead he escalated the situation immediately to the level of legal action, which implies that he felt that this was Rafael's problem. All parties would have known, moreover, that racial discrimination is rarely prosecuted in Brazil. When it is, the accused are rarely convicted. And when they are, they rarely complete their sentences, either by appealing the conviction or by achieving a reduction in fines and/or prison time (Guimarães 2003).

The category of "marginal citizen" does not adequately explain the extent to which black people have been excluded from the nation during the past four hundred years. Whereas Brazil is, as Holston and Caldeira (1998) argue, a disjunctive democracy, black people experience a special, racialized relationship to the nation-state that locates black people *outside* of that democracy. Although black people are located within the political structure of the nation—even, at times, ascending to high-status government roles like governor (Benedita da Silva) or justice of the Supreme Federal Court (Joaquim Barbosa)—the nation-state itself is defined *in contraposition to* blackness. Black people may be able to vote, use the public health system, go to public schools, be issued a national identity card, and work, but black people do not have access to equal protection under the law and do not enjoy the equal access to civil and legal rights that would truly integrate them into the nation's fold because of the interpersonal and structural racism that conditions their civil and legal experiences. Instead, blackness is the synchronic, folkloric past against which the nation is defined.[10] Blackness is constitutive of the nation as a cultural identity, but this cultural appropriation of blackness in actuality necessitates the death of black people both symbolically and literally.[11]

"Suspicion (like doubt) occupies the space between the law and its application" (Asad 2004, 285), Talal Asad reminds us:

> The principle of *legal* equality doesn't depend on attitudes of "concern and respect." Nor, conversely, does the expression of concern and respect presuppose the principle of legal equality. On the contrary, the strict application of the principle requires that citizens be treated with absolute *indifference*" (2004, 282; italics in original).

Yet as Asad also observes, in practice, the application of legal equality and citizenship plays out in the differential, subjective treatment of individuals by state agents and/or society. In other words, although citizenship *sensu stricto* would imply the impartial and indifferent treatment of all nationals, "the structure of bias" leads to differential treatment and therefore the exclusion of certain bodies.

A 2005 incident that happened to a friend and militante from the MNU Women's Group in Salvador illustrates the ways that everyday policing practices demarcate not only legal and civic but also cultural citizenship (Ong 1996) by declaring where black people are welcome and where they are not welcome.

Luciana Cruz Brito was shopping at the popular department store C&A with a U.S. African American friend in downtown Salvador when the store's security guard harassed them and accused them of stealing. They were verbally abused and eventually ended up at the local police precinct. In an open letter that Luciana wrote on September 13, 2005, she outlined the experience of discrimination and the gendered, racialized ways that civil society (in this case, a department store) routinely dissociates black people from cultural citizenship and civil rights in the nation. She chronicles being followed around the store by a security guard, cursed at, and ultimately publically humiliated. Because she and her friend had a bag of laundry with them when they entered the store, they were accused of stealing and called "bitches." When they subsequently complained about their treatment at a local police precinct, they were then subject to a series of racial microaggressions by police officers.[12] Instead of investigating their claims of having been the victims of racism, the police assumed that they *were indeed* thieves and treated them as criminals.

Luciana's story describes the theatrical ways that everyday police practices—performed by civilians (security guards) or the state (the military police)—mark black people as noncitizens in gendered, racialized, and classed ways. Obvious changes in the landscape of racial politics in Brazil have not eliminated formal and informal civil practices of racialized policing and discrimination, particularly in commercial spaces like stores and malls.

Luciana's story also highlights the internal tensions of Afro-nationalism. Both Luciana and her U.S. friend are university educated and told security guards and police this in response to their harassment. Nevertheless, this knowledge, and the fact that one woman is a U.S. African American and not Brazilian, only temporarily suspended the ill treatment they received. At one point Luciana began to speak to her friend in English while in the store, explaining the situation. In response, the department-store security guard immediately changed his demeanor, but only for a short time. Their speaking English briefly marked them as "exceptional," motivating the security guard to recant his accusations and temper his tone. Ironically, assumed "citizenship" (read in this instance as Brazilian national belonging) is what actually marked the two women as violable. Because the security guard initially believed that the two women were black *and* from Brazil, he assumed that he could violate their rights with impunity. In other words, being black Brazilian women would mark them as noncitizens who could be toyed with and verbally and psychologically abused even in violation of the constitution. This extends beyond the normative delegitimization of civil rights within Brazil's disjunctive democracy. Instead, Luciana and her friend (American but assumed Brazilian in this moment) were not only presumed to be people without civil rights, but also presumed to be criminals—a step beyond dysfunctional democracy.

In December 2013, working-class youth from the peripheries of São Paulo and Rio de Janeiro began to engage in *rolezinhos do shopping*—planned social gatherings at shopping malls. Young people would coordinate meetings at malls in order to socialize, flirt, eat junk food, gossip, take pictures, and just generally hang out. These groups were culturally tied to the funk movement in São Paulo—a subversive music genre that was "outlawed" in Rio de Janeiro in 2009 (but never really went out of practice) and was greatly restricted in São Paulo in December 2013. The military police assaulted a rolezinho of three thousand youth at Shopping Metro Itaquera in eastern São Paulo on January 11, 2014, using rubber bullets and tear gas to break up the crowd. Outside observers, from the news media to the academy, tied the rolezinhos to the lack of public leisure space for working-class youth. Some were quick to classify these gatherings as political demonstrations—young people asserting their rights to the city. But others said that young people were only hungry for attention and playtime ("Brazil's Rolezinhos" 2014). Regardless of our interpretation, the idea that black youth are a threat and are dangerous in spaces like shopping malls (either because they hold the potential to be violent or because they are potential thieves) has been circulating much longer then the rolezinhos of 2013 and 2014, as Luciana's story reminds us.

What happened to black youth seeking refuge from police in a shopping mall in 2013 underscores the irony of police repression of rolezinhos and the pervasive perception that black youth are seen as out of place and a threat in public places. On Saturday, November 30, 2013, military police officers, including special forces like Rota and Batalhão de Missões Especiais, surrounded the Shopping Vitória in Espirito Santo when a group of working-class black youth sought shelter inside the shopping mall from a police raid on a local party (Belchior 2013). The young people had been attending a funk party on the pier next to the shopping mall when military police invaded the party and began to beat and harass the young partygoers. In response, a few of the young people fled to the neighboring mall. However, upon arriving at the mall, shopkeepers called the police, reading the gathering of young people as a threat. In response, the police surrounded the mall and apprehended any young person they thought fit the "funk type" (*padrão funk*), seating them cross-legged in a line on the floor with their shirts off and their hands behind their backs. Although the global media framed the rolezinhos that emerged in December 2013 and January 2014 as flash mobs that surfaced in response to the lack of leisure activities for youth in urban Brazilian cities, what happened in November 2013 reminds us that even when black youth do not purposefully organize in large groups to hang out, their presence is read as a threat.

Tensions around shopping are symbolic discourses on race, citizenship, and the right to rights. The politics of access to public-private space (malls, stores) and consumerism connects back to the topic of Afro-nationalism and the *negro permitido*. Afro-nationalism is built on an illusion of inclusion. Socioeconomically, black Brazilians have more buying power today than they have probably had at any point in national history. The Bolsa Família program reduced poverty by half in Brazil between 2003 and 2007 (Haddad 2008; Soares, Ribas, and Osório 2010). This has led directly to a growth in the middle class (Barros et al. 2010). The shift in the landscape in poverty has particularly affected Bahia. Specifically, the multidimensional landscape of poverty in Bahia has reduced significantly since the 1990s, and particularly during the early 2000s (Lacerda and Neder 2010). This has effectually meant that Bahians now have better living conditions (more access to basic sanitation, less-dense living quarters) and more buying power. Indeed, the public policies of the Lula and Rousseff administrations have cast the right to credit, the right to buy, and the right to live a decent life outside of poverty as *citizenship rights.* In other words, the social welfare policies of the Worker's Party have centralized the right to consume as one of the primary litmus tests of citizenship.

Malls and stores are, of course, not parts of the state apparatus. They are also not the public sphere (Habermas 1989). Yet they are spaces where civil society exercises practices of disciplining the boundaries of citizenship. Returning briefly to Ong, consumer power is an "important criteria of nonwhite citizenship in Western democracies" (1996, 739). And although Brazil is not a Western democracy, it is a BRIC (Brazil, Russia, India, and China) nation that aspires to Western standards of liberal democracy. "There is . . . a regulatory aspect to neoliberalism whereby economics is extended to cover all aspects of human behavior pertaining to citizenship" (Ong 1996, 739). Stories of discrimination while shopping are about more than just the economics of buying and selling. These spaces also reveal the existence of an invisible, racial dividing line in the nation.

Literal and symbolic dividing lines delineate the boundaries of citizenship across Brazil. The denial of citizenship is comprehensive disenfranchisement caused by a complex intersection of social conditions that situate black people at the bottom of the social hierarchy and limit their right to move freely and have equal protection under the law, even within the context of Afro-nationalism. And although this restriction is also about class and tied to the privatization of public space (Caldeira 2000; Holston 2008), it has distinctly racial dimensions that are not attributable to class, privatization, or the privilege of cultural capital. These racial dimensions are also difficult to identify because they are undeclared. Reading them as performative, performatic practices is therefore one way to know them.

Racial apartheid, as a spatial process, is theatrical. Embodied practices of policing from the spectacular to the mundane manifest the invisible dividing line that demarcates who belongs as citizen and who does not. Both the state and civil society enact these multisided politics, producing de facto racial segregation by regulating black people's access to privilege. This process defines where all black people, but particularly the working class and the poor, can and cannot go; do and do not belong: the Berlin Wall.

The Berlin Wall

Culture Shock's allegory of the Berlin Wall and critique of it are critiques of racism in Brazilian society. The deconstruction of the wall in the play is a theoretical analysis of Brazilian racial apartheid. When Culture Shock begins "The Berlin Wall" vignette, the actors enter with a whirlwind of energy, chanting the familiar refrain of the play, "Stop to Think! Stop to Think! Stop to Think how it's going to be!" From there they move into an energetic trans-national social commentary about the international circus hunt for the big beard named Osama bin Laden. In 2003, bin Laden's ever-elusive capture was the source of jokes and harsh critiques of U.S. imperialism. Culture Shock's satire of this moment puts *Stop to Think* into dialogue with other theatrical critiques post-9/11 around the world (Spencer 2012). Two actors run around the circle mimicking a game of tag where one person cannot quite catch the other, arms outstretched in grabbing reaches that capture nothing. The actors' poetic references in sing-song prose to other great feats around the world that seemed impossible but nevertheless came about, like Hitler's fall. The dialogue shifts from the U.S. war on terror to the iconic demise of one of the most demonized figures in history (Hitler), and then to one of the greatest tragedies of United States' history (*Titanic*), then back to a dislo-cated European symbol of the fall of the Cold War (the Berlin Wall), resur-rected and reconfigured in the contemporary context of racially stratified Salvador. Each reference invokes giant objects and personalities, seemingly impossible to capture, topple, and sink, that eventually came tumbling down. The implication is that the world builds monoliths, but time and resistance demolish them, only to have them reappear in another place and another time for the cycle to commence all over again. Each round of building and falling is important. This mental journey through space and time takes us, the audience, on a vertigo-inducing mind trip across political and transnational terrain. What is happening with the U.S. war on terror in Iraq and Afghani-stan is also behind state terror in Bahia. Cultural Shock's interpretation of the terrorist body approximates that which Jasbir Puar (2007) identifies in post-9/11 artwork,[13] not an overlap between bodies and experiences but literal morphing, bodies shifting into one another across space and time as if by transubstantiation. Afghanistan flows into Iraq into Salvador.

For Culture Shock, the Berlin Wall is the real-life system of oppression that divides the city between the haves and the have-nots along racial lines. Like the police and the cordeiros during carnival, embodied practices maintain apartheid despite the absence of legal segregation. These embodied practices literally and symbolically block black people from access to resources, due process, and dignity—in short, from citizenship—not with directly racist language or explicitly racist discourse, or even a literal concrete wall divid-ing a city, but through disciplining acts. Like the police officer who put his boot on the head of the vendor on the beach in Ondina, these disciplining acts inscribe blackness onto the body and the landscape, producing the to-pography of the city according to racial antagonisms.

The collage of historical and political associations tie the racist alter ego of racial democracy in Brazil to transnational imperialist politics. The actors frame Brazilian racism as another world crisis. This is the first time in *Stop to Think* that the play begins to connect global politics with local realities. Here, the references relate the past to the present in a cyclical fashion, bringing us back to the concept of assemblage once again. The discussion marks the beginning of a longer series of associations between the war on terror and what is happening in Brazil's peripheral neighborhoods, a connection that is made more explicit as the play progresses.

"The Berlin Wall" illustrates the *lived experience* of the coded racial seg-regation that frames the black experience in Brazil; that is, it represents the simultaneous immateriality and physicality of this wall. The use of the body in the scene asserts that embodied practices, not necessarily discursive ones, uphold the moral, racial social order of Bahia. We cannot touch the wall or describe how it looks, but we know it by the things it does and the literal bodies that constitute it, keeping other bodies out to maintain the divide at all costs. The barrier itself (the wall, racism) is human. The protagonist in the play (the MC) must repeatedly use his body to try to push through this barrier in order to achieve equality symbolically, but that equality never comes. By representing the wall as embodied practice, actors show us how other embodied practices, like policing racialized space, create antagonisms and draw lines of citizenship and belonging. Bahian racial apartheid is an emphatically aggressive, conscious enactment of racial hierarchy that is orga-nized by a principle of antiblackness. The wall is alive and active, and enacted into being offstage in the everyday when soteropolitanos literally embody it.

The vignette is rebellious in its analysis. By invoking the Berlin Wall, it not only suggests that racism in Brazil is as monumental, as concrete, and as symbolic as that wall, but also that the demolition of this barrier is inevitable with time, even if the people have to tear it down bit by bit with their hands. "Spatial exclusion is at the core of gendered racial stratification in Brazilian cities, and this exclusion produces mass black political organization" (Perry 2013, xv).

Performance is a key step in the process of the wall's undoing. Because the wall cannot be seen, it cannot be torn down and tangibly carted home as in Berlin in 1990. The suggestion is that the politics of performance—read here as either theater or the deconstruction of the repertoire of actions that define the nation as a racial state—will also be key to tearing down racism in Brazil. It is not even a legally tangible wall, like the Jim Crow laws of the United States, motivated by the *Plessy v. Ferguson* decision in 1896. The Berlin Wall of racial apartheid in Salvador is camouflaged, though not invisible, difficult to locate, and difficult to chart, principally because it is a referent for racial discrimination in a context where the boundaries of race are widely assumed to be fluid and permeable. Therefore, to be seen, the wall must be allegorized. The actors have to perform racism as "The Berlin Wall" in order to concretize the divisiveness of the classed/gendered/sexualized structure of Brazil for an audience that may feel this reality but not necessarily know how to articulate it. This allegory thus allows the audience to make cognitive connections between social barriers that are not talked about or acknowledged and physical barriers that discriminate and segregate.

A tension exists between the pervasive belief that race should neither be talked about nor addressed in Brazil and the pervading presence of racial discrimination in the country. João Vargas (2004) calls this tension the "hyperconsciousness/negation of race dialectic." Robin Sheriff (2001) calls it a silence that emerges from trauma. Culture Shock, however, asserts in the play that people come to understand and know what race is and what it means in the implicit, nonverbal, enacted interstices of the duality between hyperconsciousness and negation. In other words, they know it when they see it. This space is not a void. Rather, it is a space filled with embodied practice and meaning—images, actions, sounds, and gestures. In this space, social actors make negotiations, pass messages, and form identities. By overemphasizing the verbal (how people speak about race) and glossing over questions of embodiment and the visual, we miss crucial elements that define how people interact with one another. Body language and implicit visual and corporeal conversations produce racial subjectivities as much as what is spoken. Violent encounters are one space where this nonverbal communication is most influential.

Diana Taylor (2003), following Michel de Certeau (1984), encourages us to divest ourselves from our overreliance on archives—written recorded knowledge—in order to pay closer attention to the repertoire—gestures, looks, touches, and repeated actions. Within the literature on race and racism in Brazil, there has been a notable overreliance on the verbal to diagnose racial tensions.[14] On all sides of the debate, researchers, journalists, and those casually interested in the topic routinely reference casual conversation, popular attitudes, and daily interactions (how people talk about race) to argue either for or against the importance of race in Brazilian society. Some have argued that Brazilians lack "robust racial subjectivity" (Bailey 2009, 40). Others note that Brazilians avoid talking about race and suggest that there is a code of silence that surrounds the question of race but not an absence of racial subjectivity, tension, and stratification (e.g., Hanchard 1994; Sheriff 2001; Twine 1998; Vargas 2004). But what of the meaning that fills the silences of racial discourse? There is a relationship between race, performance, and the lived political realities of blackness in the nation that fills this silence with meaning.

If we read the Berlin Wall as the plot of a play, a scenario of racial contact, there must be many real-life protagonists—members of society—who determine which people gain access to a university education and what faces are shown on public television. The scene also implies that *anyone* who actively seeks to maintain race/gender/sexuality/class boundaries, and thus prevents black people from entering into realms of privilege, embodies and enacts the wall as well. In particular, the police are real-life border patrollers who protect and enact the wall of racial apartheid, even when the police themselves are black and live in the very neighborhoods they terrorize.[15] Like the actors in the play with little discourse or dialogue, the police, security guards, soldiers, and other guardians of the social contract enact racism in performative and theatrical ways: performative in the sense that actions bring epistemologies and discourses of race into being; theatrical in that their actions are public, dramatic, and follow a script.[16] Through strategic operations, policing physically ensures that black people stay "in their place" in the city (Caldwell 2007; Gonzalez 1983).[17] This practice heightens when working-class black people come too close to the wall or try to pass through.

"The Berlin Wall" vignette makes three specific claims about racism. The first is that it is pervasive. Racial apartheid affects various aspects of Bahian society, from shopping to representation in the media. The second is that racism is aggressive. The wall is maintained by conscious, semiconscious, and unconscious human actions that are vehement and decisive. The third is that discriminatory speech—the transcripts of racism that we often use as a litmus test for determining whether racism has occurred, like the use of racial epithets—is the punctuation of racism, not its substance. Although spoken narratives do not always accompany racist attitudes and actions, utterances (brief verbal interjections that function like captions) are the exclamations that add expression to embodied practices of racism. These utterances emerge out of the excess of more hidden and subtle racist acts, yet they provide clues about the racialized meaning behind what otherwise appear to be innocuous encounters.

Racism is pervasive. Throughout the vignette, the MC tries to push his way through the human barrier of racism. Each time he makes an attempt to break through the wall, he is met with a harsh, physical, aggressive response, and the exclamation "no negão!" His responses to this rejection vary slightly each time, but several points remain the same. When the wall refuses him passage, he pauses and interrogates the situation with the phrase "But how

can you?"—emphasizing the injustice and irony of the situation. The infer-
ence is that given the racial politics of Brazil, this should not be happening
in a country where explicit racism is allegedly rare or nonexistent. The MC's
incredulity accents the fact that racism comes as a surprise to him. Each time
after the MC says "But how can you?" he breaks from his interaction with
the wall and turns to the audience, taking a step back from the scene and
making another time for the audience to *Stop to Think*. During these pauses,
the MC makes comments on the statistics of racial discrimination in Brazil.
These reflections link the allegory onstage to the structural racism of Brazilian
inequality. In the first pause, he mentions the discrepancy between black and
white enrollment in the federal university, in the second he discusses the lack
of black faces on national television, and in the third, he returns to inequality
in the media. Finally, he sarcastically offers to pay his way through the wall.
This last-ditch attempt draws the question of class directly into the conversation, implying that race and class go hand in hand. His critique takes things
a step further. Although black people with means seem to have the option
to pay for passage through the wall, the implication is that white Brazilians
would be able to cross regardless of their means. White supremacy is the logic
of social access in Brazil. This observation returns us to Afro-nationalism.
Despite black people's increased access to goods and services and posts and
privilege within the government, black people still must gain permission to
participate in the nation as "citizens"—*o negro permitido*. Afro-nationalism
is an economy of exception, not evidence of inclusion.

The fifth attempt to pass through the wall deserves special attention. Here,
the MC resorts to guile and asks a provocative question: "But wait a minute.
If I pay 200,000 *reais*, can I enter there?" As soon as this proposition is made,
the demeanor of the wall changes. It immediately becomes friendly and ac-
commodating, bowing graciously while saying, "In that case, yes! Welcome!"
This change in attitude makes two points. The first is a familiar one, as the
adage says, "money whitens" in Brazil. This adage has circulated throughout
the country for decades, and scholars who study race in Brazil repeatedly
cite it in discussions of Brazil's infamous racial fluidity (e.g., Degler 1971;
Dzidzienyo 1971; Schwartzman 2007; Telles 2004; Telles and Paschel 2014).
The saying proposes that, while de facto racial segregation exists in Brazil,
the realm of white privilege welcomes those with money. A black person
with means can therefore whiten herself simply by attribute of her assets.[18]
By implication, race is fluid. However, the critique is subtler, and rejects
the assumption that this is what "money whitens" actually means. A black
person could buy his way through the wall, yet this is an *illusion of racial
inclusion*. Money motivates the wall—or those who maintain and benefit

from it—to *overlook* race. Race is still there. This slight nuance counters
assertions that class, not race, governs Brazilian social relations. To be sure,
it is not that blackness is incompatible with middle-class status or class ascension (Sansone 2002). Black people do not become white through class
ascension. Rather, class bestows temporary and politically conditional access.
Just like poor black Brazilians, elite black Brazilians—those who enjoy the
conditional benefits of Afro-nationalism—stand outside the wall waiting to
be let in. In other words, those with economic and/or cultural privilege, like
university students, politicians, middle-class business owners, professional
actors, soccer players, or musicians, also require white permission in order
to pass through the wall. In the "real world" this often comes in the form of
sponsorship (getting someone a job, bringing someone to a party, godpar-
ents). The other irony of this reality is that the wall itself—security guards
and police officers—have no access to the realm of privilege because of their
status. Because they are the wall they cannot reside within the wall, so to
speak. *Negros permitidos* are only those who have the cultural or economic
capital necessary to gain temporary access through the wall; those scripted
as "acceptable."

   Racism is aggressive. The physicality of the embodied performance of the
wall is the most crucial aspect of the vignette. Physical aggression is essential
to the maintenance of the wall and its sustainability. Violence is integral to
maintaining its "security." Each time the MC attempts to pass, the wall meets
him with a pugnacious response. The intensity of the aggression varies. At
time he is pushed; at other times he is thrust backward, thrown, kicked, hit,
or punched. Regardless, even his calm and polite requests for equality are met
with violence. The wall's aggression emphasizes its physicality. The forceful
enactment of policing stresses that racism is not only felt but is also violent.
What is enacted is more important to understanding this process than what
is said. Each aggressive motion tells us, the audience, that maintaining this
wall is a weighty task that carries great import for those invested in its per-
manence (the actors who embody the wall, and presumably whomever or
whatever is motivating them to do their job, and those who are protected by
the wall on the other side). In the everyday, this looks a lot like the dividing
lines of carnival.

   Discriminatory speech punctuates racism but is not its substance. The embodied action of the vignette sheds light on the dialogue, and what is said
accents the action. Utterances become crucial meaning markers throughout
the play. For this reason, I think of speech as punctuation in this performance,
using the term *punctuation* to refer to something that marks the text of the
performance in order to clarify it. Two punctuations in the dialogue are

very important to the meaning of this vignette: the repeated interjection "no negão!" and a brief off-the-cuff utterance of the phrase "vai viado." Both articulate the intersections of race, gender, sexuality, and class.

The term *negão*, used throughout the scene, is a double entendre. In popular culture it is a term used to say "guy" or "man" with no explicit racial indications—any man can be referred to as a *negão* in Brazilian society. However, the etymology of the word is explicitly racial. The term *negão* comes from the word *negro*, and literally means "big black man." The suffix *ão* in Portuguese is used to indicate greatness in size in the masculine form. Thus, a black man, *negro*, plus big, *ão*, equals *negão*, a big black man. Race is embedded within its meaning, and this scene emphasizes that racial denotation. The MC is not particularly large in stature, or particularly dark-skinned, but his dark-brown complexion and masculinity signal the literal relevance of the term *negão*. His speech references clearly mark his character as black. When he recites the phrase "I don't see me, a negão," he intentionally invokes it as a racial marker and self-referent. His purposeful use of the article *um*, which means *a* in the phrase, is our clue. Here *a* is used to indicate his belonging in a group of which he is one of many *negões* (plural)—a semantic move that has the effect of invoking *negão* as part of a collective identity and not just a passing reference.

At first, though, race does *not* seem to be the point: everyone in the scene is black, and no one is visibly wearing any indictors (masks, costumes, etc.) that signify whiteness. As we watch the presentation, we are not sure of the intended racial classification of the wall itself. Is it white? Is it mestizo? Is it black? The ambiguity seems to be intentional, for in other scenes, actors don white masks to represent whiteness explicitly. Here the wall looks like the protagonist who is trying to pass through it. The point is that, offstage, from the police to the security guards at fancy malls and hotels, black men are frequently employed to patrol the boundaries of race and place in Brazil. These men are purposefully chosen for their gender, race, and stature. Stereotypes of black men in Brazil, much like in the United States, frame black men as hypermasculine, hypersexualized, strong, and brutish—the perfect mixture for security services.[19] In addition, in Brazil's urban spaces like Salvador, elite white patrons like to hire black male security professionals because of their assumed close ties to poor black communities and *bandidade* (banditry). Many people think that they are therefore better positioned to negotiate with criminals. The utterance "no negão" could therefore imply a certain level of familiarity and intimacy between the wall and the MC as well.

The repeated exchange between the MC and the wall is the only instance of dialogue in the vignette, and it is striking that it is a negative response.

Indeed, this may not even constitute dialogue, since there seems to be no real sustained conversation between the MC and the other actors; rather, "no negão" is an automatic response.

In addition to the repeated phrase *no negão*, one offhanded statement that the wall ad-libs in the performance of the vignette at Fazenda Grande do Retiro also returns us to the intersections of race, gender, sexuality, and class in Bahian apartheid. During one of the confrontations, one of the actors spontaneously inserts the phrase *vai viado* into his commentary, hurling a gendered, sexualized, and popular homophobic epithet at the MC. *Viado* literally means *deer*, but is used throughout Brazilian society as a demeaning slang expression for someone who is gay. Heterosexual men often use it, as they do many homophobic terms, to perform heteronormative masculinity. The masculinized aggression of the performance in this scene and the utterance of this phrase therefore seem to go hand in hand. Although the phrase is clearly and directly homophobic, it is so pervasive in everyday parlance that its harshness typically goes unnoticed by those who employ it as a casual expression; here the crowd meets it with laughter. The insertion of the term at this moment, stresses, albeit unintentionally, how discourses of gender and sexuality also unconsciously collapse into the practices of masculinity tied to racial boundary making, disciplining, and "policing" citizenship and belonging. Disciplining citizenship is not only a racial project but also a gendered and sexualized one that depends upon the heterosexist racial patriarchy of the state and society (Alexander 2006; Ong 1999). The nation is clearly imagined as not only a white space but also as a male, heterosexual space.

The utterance, punctuated by unprecedented violence—a last push that flings the actor across the stage and to the ground—shows us that embodied practices of racial hierarchy are overdetermined, masculinized, and sexualized. Once again, this allegory also references the everyday offstage. Policing, either by police officers or hired security, is also a masculinized and sexualized performance.

The vignette solidifies its meaning by drawing the audience into the scene. Throughout the play, actors literally and symbolically pull the crowd into the performance in ways that lead spectators to identify with it. In 2003, this was a radical move given pervasive taboos against talking directly about race. At that time, many people in Bahia refrained from talking about race and were uncomfortable with directly and openly identifying as black. When I interviewed two new members of Culture Shock in 2005, William and Douglas, they became visibly nervous and tense when I asked them about being black. They literally jumped in their seats a bit when I said it. After a few months working with the theater troupe, that tension faded, and they became more comfortable not only stating that they were black but also articulating a racial politics associated with that identity. It is not that they did not know they were black before joining the group, I would argue, but talking about being black—in an open, declarative way—made them uncomfortable. I say this because, at other moments in our conversations during that year, they clearly indicated a sense of black identity. However, it was their work with the theater troupe that got them to *assumir* (acknowledge) being black in a bold and shameless way.

The sliding-scale tradition of racial classification encourages many Brazilians to distance themselves from blackness as much as possible (Telles 2004; Twine 1998). When the MC begins to discuss the lack of black representation on television, he turns to the crowd and begins to point, saying, "I don't see you" two separate times to two separate people. He then turns his finger back to himself and says, "I don't see me, a negão." With these acts, he marks not only himself as black, but those he points to in the audience as well. By pointing to the crowd and directly indicating audience members, the actors invite the spectators to identify with and become outraged by racism, to see themselves as black, and to identify as victims of this discrimination. Thus, the final commentary on racial apartheid is a rebellious one.

It is possible that the initial politeness of the MC mirrors the way black Brazilians have attempted to traverse racial barriers by asking permission to integrate segregated spaces either directly or indirectly. The increasing anger and frustration of the MC as he repeatedly tries to unsuccessfully forge the wall represents the increasing frustration about racism mounting among black Brazilians. The last part of the scene, when the MC declares that he will not pay to gain access to the other side of the wall but will force his way through, is a breaking point. The last attempt he makes, using all his strength, also fails. The subtext is, therefore, that the next move is revolution: dismantling the wall itself, forcibly and violently.

Repertoires of Blackness

"The Berlin Wall" encourages us to think of racial formation in Brazil in terms of structural antagonisms. How we embody race, and how our embodied practices then define other racialized bodies in dialogue, defines racial positionality. Race is a spatializing process that divides society into the subaltern and the dominant according to a black/white binary.

Racial identification gets collapsed with class and social status in the Caribbean and Latin America. As discussed in the introduction, Sylvia Wynter employs the terms "metonymically White" and "metonymically Black" to refer to this "socio-symbolic calculus" (1994, 52). The concept of metonymical race recognizes that people act according to the logics of their social position and status. The agents of the Berlin Wall occupy a space of metonymical whiteness in that they are agents of white supremacy. Interestingly, however, this does not afford them all of the privileges of whiteness. Things are complex. They may be socially and phenotypically black, but their actions benefit whiteness. We can use a similar logic when we analyze those who personify the wall in the everyday, like the police. "Police services in racially hierarchical and ethnically conflictual societies increasingly incorporate citizens from historically stigmatized groups as officers or administrators" (Amar 2010, 577). Indeed, in Salvador, many of the police officers responsible for repressive policing are black and often from the periphery themselves, leading many to believe that antiblack policing is not a matter of racism. Since slavery, poor black Brazilians have sought employment as military personnel (soldiers, police officers) to obtain social mobility and escape the stigma and persecution of state violence (Holloway 1993; Sansone 2002). Today, the public image of confrontation between the police and "criminals" across Brazil is an encounter between black bodies (Sansone 2002, 520). Yet this does not mean that racism is not a factor in policing. Black police officers' active participation in antiblack policing practices actually encourages us to rethink our definitions of racism in structural terms (Ramos and Musumeci 2005; Wilkins and Williams 2008).

For Culture Shock, black police officers are agents of white supremacy. In this way, they are metonymically white. They are stand-ins for white supremacy when they enact violence and uphold racial apartheid. However, the racial politics of apartheid in a "racial democracy" are by definition messy, and this messiness makes performance an important deciphering tool. To reiterate, black police officers are not, themselves, whitened by their uniforms. Rather, the uniform allows the black police officer to defend the sovereignty of white power despite her or his individual racial classification. This job, like the uniform itself, is temporary. The black police officer loses his or her status when he or she takes off her uniform and goes home. Metonymical whiteness, like the whitening powers of class ascension, is a conditional "privilege."

The Berlin Wall allegory is not only applicable to race. In another performance of *Stop to Think* in the suburban neighborhood of Sofía in 2003, Sobrevivente stated in the question-and-answer period after the performance that the Berlin Wall refers to all groups that are excluded from society, including the LGBTQ community, the poor, gender communities, and so on.

However, the Berlin Wall embodies race in profoundly complex ways that are as mutable and yet as fixed as the wall itself. That wall is both insurmountable and fluid enough to reorganize itself to ensure the protection of white heteropatriarchal privilege.

Internal Colonialism

If black Brazilians are located outside of the Berlin Wall (our metaphor for social inclusion in the nation), then they are noncitizens, and the terms *citizenship* and *democracy* are not the frameworks that we should use to understand how blackness fits into the nation. A more appropriate, albeit controversial framework, I believe, is colonialism. Frantz Fanon (1965b) defines *colonial structure* as Manichaean, reflecting a diametric opposition between spaces of the colonized and the colonizer. This opposition produces an atmosphere of colonial violence, the habitus of the settler state and its politics. Unequal zones constitute the space of the colonial world: a space for the colonized and a space for the colonizer, distinguished by vast discrepancies in resources (1965b, 38). Like the Berlin Wall, the rule of law is division, and the state's surveillance and policing practices define the nation. The state's method for maintaining this atmosphere is terroristic police action, like raids and fine-tooth-comb operations. And subtle moments of violence uphold this dichotomy, like security guards policing black shoppers. Policing in all of its forms is a kind of border patrol that maintains an invisible partition between colonized and colonizer spaces. The wall is an apparition that is instantiated by its enactment, like the moment when the police officer stepped on the vendor's head at Ondina beach in 2007.

Bahia is haunted by colonialism, a temporally layered social dimension. By the early nineteenth century, the experience of slavery already defined Salvador as an intensely hierarchical city. Preabolition Salvador could be divided into four main social sectors, according to historian Kátia Mattoso (1978). Those at the top of the pyramid were the social and economic elite. These were, by and large, the slaveholding plantation owners, noble gentry, and government officials—a class that was almost exclusively European and white. For this class, prestige and whiteness were often more important than money. Plantation owners varied in economic status, with some having significant income and some being relatively poor within the broader social structure; who one was, to whom one was related, and connections meant everything. The commercial sector constituted the next step down. For these businesspeople, money was everything, and economic prowess defined the distribution of power. The next step down included artisans, street vendors, and semi-independent businesspeople whose jobs were not lucrative but afforded them a small semblance of respect in society. The bottom of society was, not surprisingly, the enslaved, the homeless, and vagabonds.[20]

Society almost exclusively associated black people with the social underclass in nineteenth-century Bahia. Bahian society was conceptually organized according to a clear racial binary that associated whiteness with elite states, and being enslaved or an ex-slave with blackness. As João Reis observes, "Africans, slave or freed, were a numerically significant part of the population of Salvador and were in the lower positions of the social hierarchy. Although [interracial] chances of social mobility existed, they were limited and may not be overstated" (2003, 43; my translation). The slight chance of social mobility between classes, regardless of race, was reserved for those in the middle of the social structure (businesspeople, street vendors, shopkeepers, artisans). Those at the top were almost exclusively white and those at the bottom were almost exclusively black. Reis also observes that "the status of freedom, liberated (former slave) or slave, internally separated Africans and African Bahians [Bahian-born Africans]. The whites escaped these last two conditions without exception, although occasionally reference is made to mulatto slaves that are so light-skinned that if they were free and more endowed, they could easily pass for white" (Reis 2003, 23; my translation). There was always a risk of downward mobility for black people, however. Robert Conrad (1983) chronicles some of the many cases when the state and society "misidentified" free black people (African and crioulo)[21] as slaves or (re)enslaved them simply because of their identity as black people. For example, one colonial law stated that "property of the wind"—objects without owners (like livestock)—could be claimed by those who wanted to confiscate them as property. Soon, black people without papers fell under this category as well, making free blacks' status tenuous (Conrad 1983, 322). Racial antagonisms and a ladder-scale social hierarchy shaped early Bahia, and shadows of this social structure remain.

The transnational black condition in the Americas is a political condition defined by the memory of colonialism/slavery and its continued resonance. Two observations predicate this approach to reading space in the African diaspora: (1) that colonialism and its conditions morph through time but do not change their fundamental, core Manichaean principles that divide the world between the colonized and the colonizer along the lines of race/gender/class/sexuality; and (2) this morphing occurs not only temporally but also spatially, appearing, disappearing, and reappearing at different moments and on different sites. The black body in pain is not only the site of the production of Afro-paradise, but it is also the sign of the colonial politics that continue to haunt Brazil. Blackness, within this context, is metonymically the colonial object of the state rather than its subject-citizen.

Colonialism did not end with the colony. The concept of internal colonialism (if not always the term itself) has been central to black radical scholarship across the Americas, defining the global condition of black people as a nation within nations (e.g., Allen 2005, Nascimento 1979).[22] Internal colonization has, this work argues, displaced, marginalized, and even disappeared indigenous people and people of African descent from within the borders of *Latinidad* and nationhood for centuries (e.g., Mignolo 2005).[23] This approach to understanding the black condition in the Americas is not only an intellectual one, but also a political one that deconstructs the racialized structures of oppression embedded in the modern nation-state. Employing this theoretical framework situates Bahia as part of the political continuum of Latin America, the Caribbean, and the African diaspora.[24] The concept of internal colonialism emphasizes the resonance of violence, oppression, and antagonism over time and space. It also permits us to conceive of racialized classes and social strata as internal processes of nation-states without relating to conflicts *between* nations as an analytical frame (Casanova 1965, 27). In the case of Bahia, given its history and its identity as a black space, this approach is particularly relevant.

The concept of internal colonialism and its use to define the global black condition has its roots in the work of Fanon (1965b) and his insight that the colonized black and indigenous subject (native) is and always has been an internal Other in the colony. The settler is the embodiment of the white European elite. The native is the embodiment of the indigenous colonized subject. There are moments when the native/colonized may be in a position of privilege slightly elevated in relationship to his or her colonized community, but this is not a change in the fundamental status/position. Rather, it is a game of power in which the native is temporarily afforded privileges in exchange for his or her service to the colonial system, an extension of the system of white supremacy (Fanon 1965b, 43). A constant negotiation between oppressor and oppressed on a terrain of violence defines the colonial state. Confrontations between the colonizer (who seeks to maintain the sovereignty, the social/racial/sexual contract, and the status quo) and the colonized (who seek to articulate their liberation in decolonial struggle) define this tension. Once again, the image of Ondina emerges.

Although theories of internal colonialism and global coloniality emphasize the conditions of colonialism in excess of the historical boundaries of the colonial period, and writers, particularly Fanon, emphasize the necessary element of repetition that the perpetuation of the colonial condition implies, I want to underscore it as a reiterative script that is played and replayed throughout time, albeit by different actors. The reappropriation of the term *colonialism* to apply to internal, domestic affairs not only expands the definition beyond its confines under internationalism, but also expands the definition with regard to time. If colonialism is a condition that can last even after the original settlers are no longer in place and independence has been achieved, then it is not simply a matter of creoles replacing settlers; it is also a matter of repeated action. In other words, in order to truly understand the political realities and consequences of colonialism, we must think of the phenomenon as a performance: a series of enactments defined by embodied memory. We must also read it as war.[25]

Applying the concept of internal colonialism to Brazil, the works of Brazilian scholars Lélia Gonzalez (1983; Gonzalez and Hasenbalg 1982), Clóvis Moura (1988), and Abdias do Nascimento (1979) have, in turn, strongly informed black-movement approaches to the antigenocide struggle, including the work of Culture Shock and React or Die! Gonzalez, Moura, and Nascimento analyze the black condition in Brazil in terms of the transnational politics of black subjectivity and its relationship to the colonial question, while at the same time acknowledging the unique problematics of the modern Latin American nation-state and Brazil's relationship to its black population (D. F. d. Silva 2007; J. R. d. S. Silva 2007). The React or Die! manifesto draws indirectly from Gonzalez's assessment of interlocking forms of race/gender/sexuality oppression, Moura's historicization of the black condition as a continuation of the condition of slavery, and Nascimento's intellectual contributions on genocide.[26]

Gonzalez, like Fanon, imagines the organization of Brazilian space in terms of a racialized hierarchy. She argues that Brazilian society spatially excludes black people from the social realm. This social contract is therefore a spatialized, racial contract wherein the center is white and the margins are black.[27] Clóvis Moura couches his deconstruction of Brazilian racism in a critique of what he terms Brazil's "colonial ideology" (1988, 35). Although he does not use the term *internal colonialism,* he reads Brazilian society as insufferably wedded to a colonialist mentality that is driven by Eurocentrism.[28] Abdias do Nascimento's thoughts on the genocidal effects of racial democracy in Brazil employ a pan-Africanist methodology and theoretical approach to understanding black Brazilians' place in the global black experience that also draws upon the theory of internal colonialism. He emphasizes the need to understand the subtle, nuanced, and hidden aspects of Brazilian racism that make black Brazil unique to Latin America, yet that resonate with a global black diaspora politics.[29] Their engagements define the black experience according to global resonances and the unequal relationships of power that define this global black experience. This includes, importantly, uneven confrontations with imperialism. Consequently, blackness is not only a common experience rooted in forced displacement from the continent of Africa, African colonialism, slavery in the Americas, and the antiblackness that emerged out of the twin legacies of slavery and colonialism. It is also the complex relationship between space, place, and power—the Berlin Wall.

De Facto, Post Facto

On May 13, 1888, Princess Isabel of Brazil signed the Golden Law (*Lei Aurea*), legally freeing all slaves in Brazil. In 1988, the black community took to the streets in protest of the government's celebration of the one-hundredth anniversary of abolition, choosing instead to take up the slogan Cem Anos sem Abolição (One Hundred Years without Abolition) (Crook and Johnson 1999, 2). Just prior to the protests and immediately after, social scientists in Brazil and abroad engaged in a series of debates about the politics of black citizenship in Brazil and the meaning of the one-hundredth-anniversary protests (e.g., Fontaine 1985; Andrews 1991; Movimento Negro Unificado 1988). The black community boldly rejected the image of the kindly princess having graciously and morally freed the slaves out of the goodness of her heart and instead asserted that, although legalized slavery ended in Brazil in 1888, the condition of black Brazilians had not changed. A state-endorsed system of racial discrimination veiled in the rhetoric of racial democracy remained, ensuring a de facto, post facto state of slavery—colonial racial apartheid.

The national rhetoric of racial harmony, explicitly expressed by the state in support of the idea of racial democracy, facilitated the political disempowerment of the black community for decades (e.g., Andrews 1991; Covin 2006; Crook and Johnson 1999; Hanchard 1999b; Hanchard 1994). This investment in racial democracy, increasingly fading to the background as the nation moves forward with its affirmative-action agenda, produced a utopic image of Brazil that denied that the country has distinct and isolatable racial identities, and instead affirmed the theory of a multiracial continuum. The official propagation of a racially harmonious national image worked as a deflecting shield, hiding the subtle yet exacting political and economic disenfranchisement of black Brazilians within a covert system of institutionalized racial discrimination. As a result, while blackness has overwhelmingly decided citizenship for generations, the discourse of racial harmony has traditionally made it extremely difficult to draw attention to this fact.

This is not to say that contestations to the paradox of black citizenship cannot or do not exist. Aihwa Ong affirms that "the cultural practices and beliefs produced out of negotiating the often ambivalent and contested relations

with the state and its hegemonic forms" often produce alternative articula-
tions of citizenship for subaltern people (1996, 738). Indeed, black Brazilians
imagine and reimagine their relationship to citizenship in dynamic, flexible
ways, particularly in relationship to transnational economies (e.g., Williams
2013). This is why black citizenship is truly paradoxical. Black Brazilians are
symbolically stuck at the Berlin Wall, constantly fighting to enter fully into
the very nation that they constitute with their physical presence, contesting
structures of power and the realities of apartheid. Yet these contestations over
citizenship are always in tension with what black Atlantic scholars call the
"tyranny of the nation-state" (Clarke 2013, 466). It is this tension between
blackness and the hyperterritorialized, nation-state vision of citizenship that
is often hegemonic in Brazil that I have examined here.

The epistemological effects of the association between "slave" and "black"
linger in ways that continue to haunt the African diaspora (Wilderson 2010;
Wynter 1995). Global epistemological frameworks of blackness continue to
locate black people outside the realm of the human, refusing to recognize
black people as coeval, dynamic, political subjects whose lives matter (e.g.,
Mbembe 2001; Wynter 1994). This broader ontological question pushes us
even farther beyond debates about citizenship. Black people become conceptually distant from citizenship in the popular imagination because they
are ghosts—invisible subjects relegated to the realm of either the dead or the
nonhuman.

In discussing the use of history to construct the modern nation, Benedict
Anderson (1991) notes that it has often been the practice of American nations (and here he is using the term accurately to refer to all countries of the
Americas) to "speak for the dead" in their memory project of constructing
a national history. Who the dead are is important here. Anderson observes
the practice of appropriating indigenous identity to the national identity as
part of the modern nation-state formation process. However, the appropriation of black identity is also applicable here. Speaking for the dead implies
that there are no more living people who can speak for the cultures that are
appropriated (indigenous and African). "Speaking for" in this sense declares
black and indigenous people extinct, existing only as a memory persisting in
a time separate from the present nation. The appropriation of black culture to
the national identity in Brazil in effect declares blackness dead, a synchronic
culture situated in another time.[30] This death certificate gives the state license
to speak for black people, denying them agency and, ironically, citizenship.[31]

INTERLUDE III

"Terrorism"

Actors begin to walk around the circle using their hands as imaginary guns, mimicking the police.

ACTORS: Terrorist attacks happen every day, in Brazil, in Salvador, principally in the Northeast.

Actor 5 walks deliberately across the stage/circle and points his hand, configured like a gun, at the head of an audience member.

ACTOR 5: Don't you run, you hear?
ACTOR 6: You [black] man! Where are you going?

Actor 6 walks to one side of the circle and grabs a black man from the audience by the arm. The man tries to pull back but the actor plants his feet in the ground and keeps pulling the audience member's arm, saying "Come back here, come back here" as they tug back and forth against each other. Many people in the audience start to laugh, including myself. Eventually the audience member stops pulling his body back and stands half-smiling and looking sheepishly at actor 6. He holds one of his hands up in the air in a half-mocking gesture of submission. Interestingly, he does this without anyone ever telling him to put his hands up. The MC walks up to the audience member.

MC: You [black] man, what do you want, a death certificate?

The MC turns back around and begins to address the crowd again.

MC: Many people think, many people assume, that terrorist attacks only happen in Iraq. Many people think, many people assume, that terrorist attacks only happen in Afghanistan. But terrorist attacks are much more than this.

ACTOR 5: Only 2 percent of the young people in Brazilian universities are black, *this* is terrorism.

ACTORS: This is terrorism!

ACTOR 6: The school lunch[1] that was turned away in the middle of the road on its way there.

ACTORS: This is terrorism!

ACTOR 4: The abusive increase of public transportation fares, overcrowding, and overpopulation.

ACTORS: This is terrorism!

MC: The people without health care, without education, without recreation, and earning an itty-bitty salary . . .

ACTORS: . . . is a *victim* of terrorism.

ACTORS: Stop to think! Stop to think! Stop to think how it's going to be!

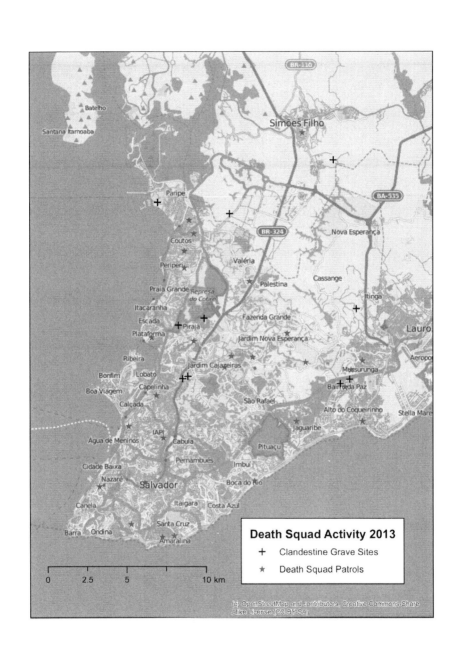

Death Squad Activity 2013

+   Clandestine Grave Sites

★   Death Squad Patrols

0   2.5   5   10 km

3 The White Hand

State Magic and Signs of War

"When fear becomes a way of life . . . a culture of terror has emerged."
—Jeffrey Sluka, *Death Squad*

"For those of us in the Black Movement, the war that is raging in the territory of Brazil in general, and the state of Bahia in particular, is a race war in which the black population is the vulnerable and unarmed victim. Every belligerent and lethal apparatus is aimed at the black population. [The police are] a private security system funded with public money that exist to protect the assets of a specific racial group. A racist culture characterizes the way [the state] conceives of public safety."
—React or Die! dossier on the Nova Brasilia massacre, April 2007

The first few years of the React or Die! campaign were up and down. After the energy of the 2005 vigil faded, the public demonstrations did as well. React or Die! occupied the Office of the Secretary of Public Security five times through 2006, but each time the crowd dwindled. What started off as an initiative, propelled by a series of organizations, became plagued by internal conflicts and tensions. One of the original organizations to participate in the campaign, Culture Shock, was also burdened with its own challenges. Economic hardship hit and participation dropped off precipitously; by 2005, more than half of the actors had to leave the troupe because of unemployment; as a result, the troupe's participation in React or Die! dropped off as well.

As Culture Shock's work began to die down and other organizations distanced themselves from the campaign, Quilombo X—a grassroots community-action campaign against antiblack state violence—emerged as one of the primary organizations driving React or Die! At this time, I was working with both Culture Shock and Quilombo X, albeit separately. Although conceptually and politically connected, the two were and are separate organizationally. It is important to reiterate that the React or Die! campaign is not an organization but a centralized hub of black political efforts to denounce antiblack state genocide. By 2006, Quilombo X had emerged as the driving force behind the campaign.

Coordinated by Hamilton Borges dos Santos and Andreia Beatriz dos Santos, Quilombo X became almost synonymous with React or Die! leadership. In addition to Quilombo X, the Bahian hip-hop movement was one of the primary supporters of the React or Die! campaign during this period between 2005 and 2007. Indeed, this was one of the many bridges that linked React or Die! to Culture Shock and marked the campaign as a black youth political movement. Inspired by the legacy of Afrika Bambaataa, hip-hop has been a vibrant art form in Brazilian urban culture since the 1980s (e.g., Burdick 2013; Pardue 2008; Rocha, Domenich, and Casseano 2001).[1] Black youth living in peripheral neighborhoods often psychologically confront daily problems through this artistic medium. And although hip-hop as a cultural touchstone might be read as an appropriation of U.S. African American culture, it has also emerged as a uniquely Brazilian artistic expression that marks working-class, black youth culture, particularly in Rio de Janeiro and São Paulo (Rocha, Domenich, and Casseano 2001). The northeast region of Brazil also has a strong, unique hip-hop culture and political movement as well.

Many of the actors in Culture Shock from 2003 to 2005, including Sobrevivente and Rafael, were actively involved in the hip-hop movement of Bahia and imagined hip-hop to be the intellectual and political framework for their work in the theater. Several hip-hop groups were also involved in establishing React or Die! in 2005. In fact, MV Bill's inauguration of the campaign in Bahia that year in part symbolically solidified the political connection between hip-hop and React or Die!

I got to know Bahia's hip-hop culture in 2004 when Culture Shock participated in the Hip-Hop Conference of Bahia in Vitória da Conquista. We took a chartered bus all night with other people from the hip-hop movement of Salvador to attend the event. When we arrived, the conference was filled with youth from all over the state—at least three to four hundred attendees, including many hip-hop artists from other regions, the vast majority of them black and between the ages of eighteen and thirty-nine. One of the unique aspects of Bahia's hip-hop culture is its investment in political consciousness—the fifth element of hip-hop. The grassroots conference came together with little financial resources. Attendees slept on the floor in the classrooms at the local public school and in the houses of local militantes. With no showers, few bathrooms, and bitter-cold temperatures for Bahia (it was in the upper forties), the experience was rustic. For breakfast we ate crackers and coffee with powdered milk—the same snack children get for breakfast in public schools.

The challenging conditions did not affect the spirit of the encounter, however. Even feeling cold (the buildings in Bahia are not heated) and a bit tired and worn-out from the hard floors and scarce water, everyone was in good spirits and happy to be in a place where they could interact with one another. I had many similar experiences with Culture Shock while working with them. This same generation became the cultural backbone of React or Die!

One of the early hip-hop groups to get involved with React or Die! was Rap Etnia (Ethnic Rap), a small group from Salvador. The two principal rappers—Clodoaldo de Souza (Negro Blue)[2] and Cléber Álvaro (Bronka)— actively participated in the campaign from 2005 to 2006. Their impact on the campaign, however, would come to far exceed their participation in the rallies and their use of the microphone to denounce police brutality.

It was the first night of March 2007. Negro Blue and Bronka and a group of their friends were walking home along the Old Airport Road (Estrada Velha do Aeroporto) in the Nova Brasilia neighborhood of Salvador. On their way, they stopped at a street corner to freestyle. Laughing and joking, they finished their impromptu rap session and started their separate ways home. Suddenly, an unmarked car filled with armed men pulled up beside them. The men were wearing black ski masks—a death squad. They told Negro Blue and Bronka to get down on their knees. The boys begged for their lives. "React now," the masked men said. Shots rang out. They shot Negro Blue nine times and Bronka three times—twice in the spine and once in the groin. The other boys in the group fled, but one was shot in the leg and wounded. He was never identified.

Negro Blue died of his injuries. Bronka fainted and only escaped death because the masked men mistook him for dead. Hours later, the military police found both lying on the ground. They took Bronka to the State General Hospital (HGE) and Negro Blue to the Quinta dos Lázaros Cemetery.

The day after the shooting, the police and the news media reported that the incident had been drug related. As was the case with the Paripe massacre of 2005, police investigators often blame the victims of death-squad murders by claiming that they are involved in drug trafficking or other crimes in order to shift the focus from the assassins to the targets—a way to distance the police from the crimes and avoid a thorough investigation. However, there are direct ties between death squads and the police. As Edward Herman observes, "In almost all cases the activities of death squads are under the direct supervision of the authorities [in national security states] in their political kidnapping and murder activities" (1982, 117). At times the victims are involved with petty crime, drug use, or drug sales. Yet to reduce these cases of torture and death to drug trafficking or crime control is to ignore the historical and political connection between death squads and the state, not only in Brazil but also around the world. Globally, death squads operate outside the legal parameters of the law while the state sanctions their actions not only by failing to prosecute their crimes (or doing so ineffectively and reluctantly), but also by secretly amalgamating death squads into the very apparatus of the state's security network (Amnesty International 2005; Sluka 2000). This secret sanctioning allows the government to publicly distinguish official state actions from the chain of command in order to "plausibly deny" their reliance on means outside the law (Sluka 2000). "This is terrorism in a form that retail terrorists cannot duplicate" (Herman 1982, 115). *Isso é terrismo.*

In Salvador, black youth make up roughly 99 percent of all homicide victims in the city and are thirty times more likely to be the victims of death squads than their white counterparts (Reis 2008). Importantly, the overall Bahian population is approximately 85 percent black. Yet, these numbers reflect a significant disproportionality. Both React or Die! and Culture Shock characterize Brazil as a nation at war with its own people. In April 2007, in reaction to the death of Negro Blue and others, React or Die! submitted a dossier to the United Nations denouncing the work of death squads in Salvador, calling them offensive and militaristic. They claimed that the war "raging in the territory of Brazil . . . is a race war"—strong, jarring words that drum up uncomfortable imagery of ethnic cleansing, Nazism, and genocide. Yet these intense claims reflect a set of deeper questions about race, state terror, policing, and citizenship in Brazil. Yes, the problem of aggressive policing is also about class, gender, age, and geographic location—important factors to consider in any general discussion of the crisis of state violence. However, because of its controversial and confounding nature, the race factor is arguably one that demands deeper critical reflection at this political moment; namely, what are the subtle codes and secret messages of race embedded in the politics of policing in Bahia and how do they compound and complicate our analyses of this phenomenon?

Veena Das describes the authority of the state as both "literalized and embodied" (2007, 162), "neither a purely rational-bureaucratic organization, nor simply a fetish" (ibid.). Rather, it "oscillates between a rational mode and a magical mode of being" (ibid.). This magical mode of being is theatrical—the magical state. The state is a "distant but overwhelming power that is brought into the framework of everyday life by the representation and performance of its rules in modes of rumor, gossip, mockery, and mimetic representation" (ibid.). The state slips into the life of communities during "spectacular [but] nonetheless grounded" moments of violence (2007, 163). As Talal Asad observes,

> The state, independently of the entire population, embodies sovereignty. Far from being a myth, the state's abstract character is precisely what enables it to

define and sustain the margin as a margin through a range of administrative practices. (2004, 281)

These administrative practices in Brazil include policing black bodies. State magic is wrapped in the mythos of Bahia's public-safety practices. The abstract relationship between death squads and the state is theatrical magic. This chapter considers the subtle, hidden, and magical racial politics of state policing through a reading of Culture Shock's "Terrorism" vignette, the history of policing in Bahia, and cases of police killings. Secret-police raids and assassinations are spectacular performances of authority that embody the magical codes of secrecy of the state. This brings us to the White Hand.

The White Hand

Above each military police (PM) module in the city of Salvador hangs a sign that reads "Community Police, the Protection in Your Neighborhood." The one pictured here sits right above the station on Avenida Sete de Setembro, the busiest thoroughfare downtown, just a short ten-minute walk from Pelourinho. Community-policing efforts are an "organizational strategy" that police departments have implemented around the world, often in conversation with

Figure 3.1. The sign that sits above community police modules in Salvador (photo by Erica Williams).

one another, in order to align policing practices with "citizens' demands" (Brogden and Nijhar 2005; Roberts 1999; Skogan and Hartnett 1997). "Community policing projects emerged in Brazil as a strategy to make the police not only more effective and efficient in crime control and order maintenance but also more accountable to community and more responsive to citizens" (Mesquita Neto and Loche 2003, 179). The sharp increase in homicide and violent-crime rates across the Americas in the 1980s and 1990s led to a series of policing reforms designed to boost the police's ability to curb and prevent crime in urban settings (e.g., Bailey and Dammert 2006; Kahan and Meares 1998; Skogan and Hartnett 1997). Developed in the United States and Europe, the community-policing model has been exported to the global south as part of political efforts to democratize global policing (Marenin 1998). From Rio de Janeiro to Amapá, these projects arose "in most cases as a democratically oriented strategy for crime control and order maintenance or as an alternative to authoritarian responses to the growth of crime and violence" (Mesquita Neto and Loche 2003, 180). Yet, although many urban communities around the world have welcomed—even invited—this approach to policing (as a solution to the increase in crime in cities), a tension between community policing and community repression looms in its shadows both practically and symbolically. Despite being ostensibly about democratizing policing practices, in most cases, community policing includes an increase in discretionary patrolling, including warrantless searches, antiloitering laws, and surveillance of black and brown bodies (Kahan and Meares 1998).

At the center of the community-policing signs in Salvador is an illustration of two hands, one white and one brown. The contrast in color mimics human skin tones, representing two familiar markers of Brazil's racial classification system—white (*branco*) and black (*negro*). The strategic picturing of the two hands in the middle of the phrase "Community Police, the Protection in Your Neighborhood" situates the image directly at the heart of the sign's meaning. In the true spirit of "racial democracy," the sign represents an explicit attempt by the military police to demonstrate a desire to serve and protect Bahia's diverse population equitably, without regard to race. Yet, despite the sign's apparent gesture toward diversity, there is a dissonance between its intended message, its visual effects, and its sociohistorical innuendos. The white hand positioned overtop the black hand, palms facing one another, and the black hand with fingers spread and the white hand clasped, gives the viewer the distinct impression that "Community Police, the Protection in Your Neighborhood" entails the repression and control of black bodies by white bodies. Rather than representing a handshake or cooperative hand gesture, the two hands subtly display an unequal power relationship that looks more like an arrest than community cooperation. Hidden behind the surface of the image, there are more profound questions about the true nature of the politics of race, citizenship, the body, and violence in Salvador.

The sign perched above the PM modules is an overlay—a palimpsestic reality. It is not only about international policing practices and their uneven political spheres of influence, but also Brazil's unique racial history of policing. Although the pelourinho is no longer present, its traces are still visible beneath the practices of authority that the state has erected in its place—specifically, practices of policing.

The mini military police stations sprinkled throughout Salvador sit on street corners and alongside busy thoroughfares. As many as three or more uniformed officers staff these stations daily almost imperceptibly. These officers stay inside a small building, usually consisting of one room with walls made of mostly Plexiglas windows, and monitor the comings and goings of the streets, field questions, and sometimes mediate conflict. At times you will see one officer sitting on a single chair in the middle of the tiny structure. Other times, all of the officers at that station will be standing outside watching the crowd as the world passes by, no doubt suffering from a mild case of claustrophobia from being assigned to the ten-by-ten cell-like space all day. The modules are at tourist attractions like Farol da Barra, Pelourinho, and the boardwalk on Avenida Oceanica on the path from Barra to Ondina—the same path of the carnival route. One sees them also at busy intersections, bus depots, alongside malls, and in commercial districts. Both conspicuous and inconspicuous, the mini police stations give us cause to pause because they are almost everywhere. Nevertheless, people rush by them every day, barely noticing them or the sign hanging above.

When I began traveling to Salvador in 2001, I was so concerned about not getting lost or pickpocketed that I rarely looked up to see these signs. Although the words of the sign project a message of cooperation and protection between the state (here represented by the military police) and the general population (the neighborhood), the image scripted this relationship as a hierarchical, racialized, aggressive power dynamic.

I began to query friends and acquaintances about the signs. Invariably, they responded with a chuckle. They too clearly thought the signs were strange. Most of my colleagues, the majority of whom were residents who socially, culturally, and politically identified as black, retorted that the signs had nothing to do with cooperation or brotherhood. Instead, they were a deliberate, symbolic representation of the racist practices of the Bahian military police. In other words, the intended message was that the white hand overpowers the black hand.

The image above the police modules always brought one thing to mind for me—"this doesn't look like a handshake, this looks like an arrest." During one of my class lectures, one student (unprompted by me) convinced me that I was not imagining things. After trying to reenact the hand position with one of her classroom peers, she brought it to my attention that this hand positioning is very similar to the way hands are positioned when the police hold a suspect to a wall. She and her partner then proceeded to demonstrate this for all of us in the classroom. Whether the police-module sign was intended to represent brotherhood and harmony or secretly designed to send a message about the role the police play in maintaining racial hierarchies through racial profiling in arrests, one thing is clear, the image broadcasts a message that is strong, conflicting, and tension-filled. "In many zones of political emergency, the normalization and routinization of violence [is] accompanied by structures of deniability built into the very strategy of violent enactment" (Feldman 2004, 172). The strategy of violent enactment in Brazil is built into secret codes, signs, rumors, and unspoken understandings about the meaning of race in the city.

The experience of racial profiling in Salvador's peripheries demonstrates that the PM sign is not just a metaphor. In January 2008, military police officers killed four young black men between the ages of sixteen and twenty-one in twelve days. This was one of the many cases of police lethality that Quilombo X and React or Die! took up after Paripe and the Nova Brasilia killing. None of these youth were suspected of a crime. The officers justified their actions by either claiming that they were resisting arrest (as in the case of Negro Blue and Bronka), or by making no justification at all. In response, residents from around the city protested in outrage. Mothers set fire to tires and buses openly, challenging the state's lack of concern for the lives of their children. Family members, friends, and neighbors of the dead protested openly in the streets, crying out for justice. The black body in pain was once again the stage for the state's spectacular demonstration of authority.

The state (politicians and state institutions), mainstream media, and the broader populace publicly denounce racism and champion Brazilian society for being racially egalitarian and harmonious. However, state practices display ulterior messages. The signs that sit above police modules encapsulate this dualism, its coded nature, and its double entendre. Disguised behind the rhetoric of racial democracy, violence dictates a moral, racial, heteropatriarchal social order that antiblackness typifies.

I use the term *disguised* purposefully here. It is not that these codes, signs, and rhetoric actually hide the truth of raced/gendered/sexualized antagonisms. Almost everyone knows that these antagonisms exist and govern themselves accordingly, either by perpetuating the violence that maintains this social order, ignoring it, or pretending not to see it. Rather, explicit messages of racial democracy camouflage coded embodied messages of racial tension. What the state explicitly declares appears as a half-hearted attempt at a distraction from the intended meaning.

In 2005, I interviewed Hamilton about the budding React or Die!/React or Be Killed! campaign. In that interview, we discussed the crisis of antiblack policing in Salvador. As we talked, he told me the story of the White Hand, a mythical death squad that allegedly existed in Rio de Janeiro in the 1980s. Then and now I was struck by the uncanny conceptual associations between the image above the police modules and this story. The White Hand was first identified by the Rio de Janeiro newspaper *O Dia* in February 1980 (Rose 2005, 257). It became famous when an anonymous caller began to phone local newspapers announcing future assassinations that would occur in the city. Although it is unclear whether the White Hand actually existed or was a media invention, irrefutable is the fact that a death squad claiming this name was responsible for ninety-one deaths in 1980, particularly in the Baixada Fluminense region of Rio.[3] From that point forward, death squads would be responsible for thousands more assassinations across Brazil. Borges notes,

> The White Hand went and they killed. Who spread this idea of the White Hand was the military dictatorship. The military dictatorship was already specialized in killing us; it's just that in 1979 they didn't have anybody else to kill because there was the *political opening*.[4] So, they started killing the black people, poor black people. . . . Today it's the same thing.

The legend of the White Hand is part of the genealogy of death squads that connects state repression, urban control, Brazil's military dictatorship (1964–85), and the history of Brazilian policing from 1809 forward (Holloway 1993; Pinheiro 1991; Rose 2005). One can trace the genealogy between the practices of torture, violence, policing, and surveillance that the Portuguese developed under slavery; the emergence of death squads under the Vargas regime; and the repressive, militaristic policing practices that we see across Brazil today (Mesquita Neto 2011; Rose 2005). The White Hand casts an eerie shadow on the imagery of the police-module signs, urging us to reconcile myth with rhetoric and reality as we reflect on why "community police" routinely and indiscriminately kill black youth in Salvador.

We can read the military police–module sign as a transtemporal, performative symbol of the nation-state's continued use of the black body in pain to enact authority and define the social contract: a ghost of the pelourinho. This definition of the palimpsest and the ghost extends beyond our discussion from previous chapters. The palimpsestic nature of Afro-paradise is not only a temporal denomination but also a spatial one. The White Hand is the manifestation of genocidal assemblages—bodies entangled across time and space—all the way from Salvador to Iraq. To follow, by returning to the term *ghost* in conjunction with this conversation, we acknowledge ghosts as echoes that come from life. Like the pelourinho, the PM image that sits across the city is a symbol of warning. However, the signs are not the material site of the state's physical punishment, markers that identify the location where the state performs its violence. Instead, they are a reference to what the state has done, is doing, and intends to do to the black body in pain. In other words, the images refer to violence performed elsewhere: sometimes subtly in public squares, like the routine physical police harassment of the homeless in Pity Plaza; sometimes in the shadows of night, like the killing spree of January 2008; and sometimes under the guise of death squads, like the death of Negro Blue and the Matança de Nova Brasilia.

Terrorism

Peggy Phelan writes, "The 'secret' of theatre's power is dependent upon the 'truth' of its illusion. Enfolded within fiction, theatre seeks to display the line between visible and invisible power. Theatre has, then, an intimate relationship with the secret" (1993, 112).[5] The unreliability of the seen and the centrality of the secret push us to reflect. Culture Shock displays the line between the visible and invisible power of the state and its racialized, repressive practices: terrorism. By 2003, when Culture Shock was performing *Stop to Think* around Bahia, the word *terrorism* had taken on new, added meaning. The United States had thrust everyone into its wars. A new line divvied up the world into "terrorists" and "freedom fighters" (us and them) along an axis of good versus evil with no latitude or longitude. The Bush administration's rhetoric of war marked up the world map with bright lines, assigning each nation a "friend" or "foe" color. Symbolically, Iraq and Afghanistan began to spill over and seep from the battle between nations into intranational politics. Travel (international or domestic) became increasingly difficult for those who had never had a problem with it before. Anyone with a Muslim-sounding name was stopped or at least delayed from boarding planes. Speaking Arabic in public became reason for suspicion and possible detention, especially in the air. Racial profiling expanded, thrusting Arab and Muslim immigrants in the United States and Europe into a conversation previously downplayed as a "black thing." The very racial profiling that many called an overexaggeration when Al Sharpton spoke about it suddenly became a stark reality to those who refused to see it before; this was a new world of unprecedented targeting, discrimination, and suspicion. The link between national security and racial discrimination ceased to be abstract for many who had not previously been able to comprehend it. In 2005, Brazilian immigrant John Charles de Menezes was killed by the London police because something about the "beautiful mixture of races" that caramelized his light Brazilian skin and darkened his curly hair made him look just a little too similar to "Arab terrorists."[6] Suddenly, driving (walking, standing, breathing) while black became inextricably linked to flying (walking, standing, breathing) while Muslim. The global relevance of local racial encounters began to give nonbelievers pause. Somewhere along the line, "terrorist" collapsed with nonwhite/other/foreign. The irony of it all: to "contain" this threat, the very population(s) that became associated with danger would have to be terrorized themselves. The blurry line between terrorist and nonwhite ironically turned the term on its head, and everyone, it seemed, was afraid to move.

The post-9/11 rhetoric of terrorism inspired Culture Shock's "Terrorism" vignette. They observed, like others, that this terrorism rhetoric was, in effect, a recycling of antiblack policing politics that had been devised and perfected globally since slavery (James 2007; Puar 2007). This came into stark relief when U.S. soldiers working as prison guards at Abu Ghraib began torturing the Arab bodies marked as "terrorist" in their custody, photographing that torture, and circulating it. Both Hazel Carby (2004) and Susan Sontag (2004) drew our attention to the historical and cultural resonance between the moment of Abu Ghraib and the abhorrent legacy of white lynch mobs killing and mutilating black bodies in the United States, taking body parts as keepsakes, and taking pictures and making them into postcards (Allen 2000; Goldsby 2006). Abu Ghraib was not an act dissonant from national identity. To the contrary, torturing and disfiguring racially "other" bodies, displaying them spectacularly, and circulating images of these scenes as keepsakes defined the cultural logic of the United States (Goldsby 2006). Yet this was not about American exceptionalism. The intimate link between the war on terror and antiblack violence as a global political project was coming to the fore (James 2007; Jung, Vargas, and Bonilla-Silva 2011). *Stop to Think* inserted Brazil into this conversation. Institutionalized practices of repression adopted by the state in order to discipline and fracture "terrorist" bodies reflect global dialogues between U.S. imperialism, Latin America, the Caribbean, and the Middle East (e.g., Chevigny 1990; Chevigny 1995; Gill 2004; Huggins 1998; Huggins 2005; Menjívar and Rodriguez 2005). It is a transnational politics that leads us back to the White Hand.

In 2013, the *Guardian* and *BBC Arabic* produced an exposé video on the military life of retired U.S. colonel James Steele: "*James Steele: America's Mystery Man in Iraq.*"[7] A veteran of "American proxy wars in El Salvador and Nicaragua," Steele was instrumental in training death squads in both Latin America and Iraq. The genealogy of his work charts connections between the methods of death squads in Nicaragua and El Salvador and death squads run by the Iraqi police after the U.S. invasion. Shortly after the documentary was released, the news program *Democracy Now!* conducted an interview with the documentary's producers and some of the people interviewed in the film. In the second piece, interviewee Aaron Nairan talks about his journalistic work with torture survivors in El Salvador and the patterns that exist between death-squad methods there and in Iraq. During his comments, he mentions El Mano Blanco, "the White Hand," a mysterious death squad whose modus operandi closely resembled the kinds of clandestine actions taken by death squads in the Middle East today. Nairan's invocation of El Mano Blanco apropos of Steele's role in defining repressive police practices in the U.S.–sponsored wars manifests the connections that Carby asserts. "The combination of brutal violence and desire that characterised lynching was developed and refined on the landscape of colonialism, has been taught by the U.S. military to death squads in Latin America, and is to be found today in the prisons and precinct houses of the homeland" (Carby 2004).

In 2015, the *Guardian* published a series of reports on Chicago's Homan Square—a clandestine detention and torture facility that reporter Spencer Ackerman likens to a U.S. domestic "black site" (Ackerman 2015a). For years, people of color in the city of Chicago, specifically black Chicagoans, have been secretly held and tortured there. The story of Chicago police detective Richard Zuley, who served on the force from 1977 to 2007, makes explicit the invisible line that connects the cultural logic of antiblack violence in the United States to Guantánamo (Ackerman 2015b). As Ackerman finds, Zuley, a U.S. navy reserve lieutenant "led one of the most shocking acts of torture ever conducted at Guantánamo Bay [and] was responsible for implementing a disturbingly similar, years-long regime of brutality to elicit murder confessions from minority Americans" (Ackerman 2015b). Ackerman continues, "Zuley's record suggests a continuum between police abuses in urban America and the wartime detention scandals that continue to do persistent damage to the reputation of the United States" (ibid.). This returns us to the myth of the White Hand in Bahia and pushes us to make a historical and political connection between El Salvador, Iraq, and Brazil across space and time.

Martha Huggins (2005) revisits her research on torture in Brazil to present a commentary on the prisoner-torture scandals in Afghanistan, Iraq, and

Guantánamo. She observes that "prisoner torture in Iraq, Afghanistan and at Guantánamo could be predicted from decades of research on ... Brazil and other Latin American countries" (Huggins 2005, 161). She also outlines ten "conditions in the U.S. 'war against terror' ... that laid a foundation for systemic state sanctioned torture" and draws from her extensive interviews with Brazilian police responsible for torture to make these points (ibid.). This discussion lays bare the consonance of these two moments (police violence in Brazil and US torture in the war on terror). However, it was not only the U.S. government's previous proliferation of torture methods in Latin America that predicted Abu Ghraib and Guantánamo. Antiblack domestic policing practices also predicted this connection (Ackerman 2015a).

When Culture Shock slips from Bahia to Afghanistan and Iraq in *Stop to Think*, their observations are backed concretely by historical evidence. The relationship between the United States and death squads in Latin America confirm that death squads in Bahia are not merely reflections of national politics but also transnational formations: genocidal assemblages. The United States has directly engaged in training foreign police forces since the nineteenth century when expansion, trade, and hemispheric control became solidified in state policies. Specifically, the United States has a long history of training Latin American police and military personnel and the CIA has played a key role in this training over time (Gill 2004; McSherry 2005; United States General Accounting Office 1996). These programs included foreign police and military training schools in various countries, including Brazil.[8] After they were tied explicitly to the proliferation of repression under military dictatorships in Latin America in the 1970s, the official operation of these programs was suspended (United States General Accounting Office 1996). Despite this, the war on drugs and the war on terror have provided loopholes for the continuation of foreign police training under different guises (Gill 2004; Huggins 1998; McSherry 2005). The U.S. military's training of security forces in Afghanistan and Iraq, and the federal government's collaborations with Latin American countries to fight drug trafficking and "terrorism," signal that this phase is far from over.

The conflation of the black body with the criminal body, and the labeling of the black body as an internal enemy of the state, has led to decades of overt and covert state violence against black working-class people globally. The politics of racial profiling and death-squad assassinations are a kind of antiblack terrorism in Bahia. Culture Shock's denunciations indicate that this direct but hidden line not only leads us all the way back to Salvador but is also embedded in the politics of performance.

"*Terrorist attacks happen every day, in Brazil, in Salvador, principally in the Northeast.*" The "Terrorism" vignette intensifies the play's commentary on

Figure 3.2. Culture Shock actors pull a black man out of the crowd during the *Stop to Think* performance in Fazenda Grande do Retiro.

discrimination in Brazil by addressing racial profiling. The physical staging of the scene and words is important. The vignette begins by presenting terrorist attacks—the daily police harassment of the black community. As the actors begin to walk in a circle holding up their hands like imaginary guns, actor 5 walks randomly to one side of the circle and tells the people standing there not to run. Actor 6 walks to the opposite side, pulls a young black man randomly from the crowd, and points his imaginary gun to the man's head. Caught off guard, the man playfully tries to pull away, but the actor tugs even harder. People in the crowd begin to laugh at the skirmish when suddenly another young man from the crowd pushes the chosen audience member into the circle, forcing him into the middle of the scene. Resigned yet apprehensive, the young man who has been "profiled" waits to see what the actors are going to say and do with him next. The MC comes up to the man and asks him a simple question, "You [black] man, what do you want, a death certificate?"

The question is obviously rhetorical. It is also symbolic, for we audience members know that no matter what the young man responds, his words will have no bearing on the outcome of his life in this virtual scenario. And the audience knows that although the state does not effectively afford black residents full citizenship rights, like the right to a fair trial, its relationship to black people is still highly bureaucratic and formulaic: you can get a death certificate much easier than you can obtain a college degree. The distribution of state resources is uneven and biased. The question of whether he lives or dies will be as random as the man's having been selected to participate in this scene.

Once again, the relationship between the actors and the audience draws spectators into the politics of the performance. The words and the mannerisms of the actors all indicate that this is a reenactment of the random targeting of black men by the police in the community. And although the play grounds its commentary in the experience of Salvador, transtemporal and transspatial resonances also drum up images of Baltimore, Cleveland, Ferguson, New York, or any of the countless other cities across the Americas that we now associate with deadly police racial profiling. When I first saw this play, it was the tone of voice the actors used and their word choice that made me understand immediately what was going on. "Don't run" and "What do you want, a death certificate?" are phrases we associate with the police transnationally, and particularly with police harassment. Moreover, the actors' gruff and aggressive demeanor and the anxiousness with which they pull their "guns" out of their pockets also signal to us that they are the police because they mirror police action (belligerence, hair-trigger practices).

Two things in this vignette associate terrorism and racial profiling. The first is the seeming randomness with which the actors engage with the black audience—anyone can be a victim. As each actor walks around the circle looking at the audience, onlookers look unsure. Do they fit the profile that the characters are looking for? The audience wonders if the imaginary guns in the actors' hands are intended for them. When actor 6 chooses a black man from the crowd, the tension surrounding this sense of randomness eases. We then realize that this man has been chosen to be the "victim" because he is black and male. The rest of us now have a (temporary) reprieve. Discourses of race/gender/sexuality/class all contribute to the unspoken codes here. This is clear by the way the actors address him: "You [black] man, what do you want, a death certificate?" When the actors recite this line in Portuguese, they again use the term *negão,* revisiting the multilayered social and cultural significance of this reference discussed in chapter 2. Indeed, Culture Shock's commentary is quintessentially *gendered* and racial. This moment of identification implicates his blackness, his maleness, and his youth.

Women are painfully absent from the images we see in the news media of police violence. In fact, women are often written out of the narrative completely, even though women are also victims, and their deaths no less political or consequential. We need only remember Daniela, who died in the Paripe massacre. The absence of women's stories (both the relative absence of women's bodies and the absence of a discussion of gender and sexuality in the analysis of this phenomenon), however, simply reinforces the heteropatriarchal narrative that defines the state's relationship to the black body. The state not only projects itself as the masculine/authority/phallus of the social contract, but also depends upon the emasculation of *black men* in order to maintain itself. To put it another way, the construction of the colonial phallus requires the castration of the colonized, and this process puts the spectacular focus of violent repression onto the male body *despite* the fact that the female body is also equally affected by the state's violent performances.

The young black man who is singled out is tall and thin, with dark-brown skin. His head is shaved and he is wearing Bermuda shorts with no shirt. He looks young, between the ages of eighteen and twenty-five. His profile is that of most of the people who are disproportionately the victims of police violence in the periphery. The police have a preconceived notion of social deviance, Dyane Brito Reis Santos (2002) shows; both skin color and class determine the police profile of a criminal suspect in Salvador. Thus, the police automatically assume that a black man who does not look "respectable" (which the police identify as well dressed with a proper haircut) is a criminal (Santos 2002; Santos 2003). Although Brazilians typically define blackness by skin color, what poverty looks like is unstable. Nevertheless, the police associate young black men with criminality almost exclusively, and blackness in general is a strong correlating factor (Ramos and Musumeci 2005). "[A] black [man], living in the periphery, unemployed, with an elementary school education, between the ages of 15–29, who easily speaks in slang, and generally has a tattoo on [his] body . . . [is] marked to die" (Reis 2008).

Ironically, Bahian residents who fit this stereotype describe themselves when asked to define the criminal suspect type. In an interview, sociologists asked a group of young people from Salvador's suburbs the questions: "Who are the *marginals*?[9] How would you describe them?" (Espinheira 2004, 30). The young people immediately associated their own image with social anomie. They identified themselves as being outside the moral racial social order.

The same logics that lead the police to "offer" black youth death certificates also lead black youth in the periphery to identify themselves as *marginais*. Many of the actors of Culture Shock had personal experiences with police aggression that informed their performances and resonated particularly with the "Terrorism" vignette. William and Douglas spoke with me about the constant terror of policing in their peripheral community, Sussuarana:

WILLIAM: Sussuarana is like that, a peripheral neighborhood . . .

DOUGLAS: Very discriminated against . . .

WILLIAM: Yep, very discriminated against because of the reputation others give
it, like, as a violent neighborhood, and it does not exist, all this violence, [at
least not by] the people themselves, but by the police who invade the places
where they encounter black people . . . they go there and approach them
[frisk and question]. Everyone that doesn't have their document[s], even
being close to their home/business, they arrive [and say], "Up against the
wall!" Attacking, hitting the person, kicking the person violently . . . it's like
that, the neighborhood, the violence there . . . is constant.

William and Douglas's observations help us to understand why the audience
had such a visceral reaction to the performance of the "Terrorism" vignette at
Fazenda Grande do Retiro. Revisiting the video of the performance, we hear
a mixture of laughter and nervousness as the actors begin to walk toward the
crowd telling people not to move. I too felt slightly anxious in that moment,
even thought I knew I would not be picked out because I was filming. The
actors effectively employed audience apprehension about participation in
order to evoke the constant unease of not knowing when you or someone
you know will be targeted by the police. Recognizing this performance as a
critique of police racial profiling hinges on our own embodied memory of
police aggression. The dialogue alone does not signal racial profiling. Rather,
the dialogue, in conversation with enactment, conjures somatic memory,
pushing the audience to automatically respond consciously or unconsciously.

Despite its informality, the play draws a line between audience and stage.
Most people in the audience stand with their arms crossed or eyes wide, watching to see what will come next. From time to time someone calls out to comment on the play and/or recite the lines along with the actors (particularly
the refrain "Stop to Think!"). There is a buzz of continuous side conversation
while the performance is going on, but no one walks into the performance
space—that is, through the circle—"disrupting" the performance. When an
audience member is physically dragged from the space of the spectator to the
inner circle of the stage, this barrier is broken. This gesture is physical and
symbolic. He is no longer a spectator watching this artistic reenactment occur. Not only is he the example here in the play, but he immediately becomes
the social referent as well. Culture Shock attempts to force us to confront the
reality of our experiences with racism. The spectator cannot sit by and watch,
hoping that she or he will not be a target. Culture Shock literally ensnares us
into the social narrative.

After the exchange between actor 6, the MC, and the young black man
in the crowd, the relevance of the terrorism metaphor becomes even more

explicit. The MC recites, "Many people think, many people assume, that terrorist attacks only happen in Iraq. Many people think, many people assume, that terrorist attacks only happen in Afghanistan. But terrorist attacks are much more than this." Once again the vignette ties structural violence against black people to physical violence. Terrorist attacks are not just an "'exotic'" kind of violence that happens a world away. State terrorism is also inadequate school lunches; the underrepresentation of blacks in the university system; poor public transportation; poor health care, education, and recreation access; and ultimately un- and underemployment.

Terrorism is a scenario of racial contact, and racial profiling is a performance. Performance in this sense is anything but a depolitical affair. Again, Culture Shock demonstrates the continuing ways that antagonistic, colonialistic racial politics shape the city and the performative, disciplining acts that produce racial subjectivities and demarcate the boundaries of the social order. These disciplining acts once again, publicly and repeatedly, put black people in their "proper place." The very enactment of state violence not only performs and instantiates the boundaries of the racial contract, but also defines the space of Bahia as a transtemporal colonial war zone where only one side does the killing. Police violence is a militaristic strategy of disciplining blackness. Yet, this message of war is hidden. Just like the cover of night that hides death-squad actions, the relationship between the state, policing, and the discourse of war is hidden beneath the palimpsestic layers of the city—the White Hand.

Shock: Policing Blackness

> It's like this, the name Culture Shock was created by two actors, Giovane Sobrevivente and Jorge Arte. At the time when Culture Shock was created in San Martins, the shock police were coming beating on everyone . . . violence . . . shooting. Whoever was on the corner sitting down was taking a beating, so these actors, Sobrevivente and Arte, revolutionaries, they decided to dub the name of the theater group "shock," but not out of violence . . . like a "culture shock" where, let's say, violence is combated. A shock of culture and not of violence because San Martins already couldn't take any more. And from San Martins we resolved to go out to various locations and that was that.
> —Rafael, Culture Shock, May 13, 2005

There is a complex relationship between the genealogy of policing, death squads, and antiblack violence in Salvador that also intersects with the history of Culture Shock. The name *Culture Shock* is indeed itself a reflection of this tricky relationship. The political impetus of Culture Shock began with its name. The word for *shock* in Portuguese also refers to the military police "shock" forces of Bahia—the *Batalhão de Polícia de Choque* (Shock Police Battalion). The shock police are a manifestation of the militarization of the Brazilian police forces. They are a special-operations force that the state of Bahia organized during the military dictatorship to fight "urban guerillas"— "threats" to the state who opposed the authoritarian regime (Polícia Militar da Bahia 2006).[10] After the end of the military dictatorship and the subsequent reorganization of state police forces across the nation in 1985, these battalions remained in place, seemingly gaining more force and visibility with time (Caldeira 2000; Pinheiro 1991).[11] The Brazilian constitution continues to require the militarization of all police forces in all states in Brazil (Mesquita Neto 2011). This prerequisite, in effect, constitutes the police as an offensive as well as defensive operations force and extends the strategies of social control that were honed during the military dictatorship into the democratic era.

The tremendous problem of police aggression, torture, and killing in Brazil is connected to the militaristic structure of the police force.[12] Paulo de Mesquita Neto (2011) argues Brazil's transition to democracy (signaled by the 1988 constitution) ironically brought about little to no effective change in the militaristic structure of policing and public security. Instead, the police forces remained militarized, exemplified by the military police, who continue to be the explicit connection between the military and quotidian public safety. The military police are responsible for foot patrol and the everyday tasks of curbing crime and violence. Thus, the transition from the urban war on "internal enemies" to serving "public security" was vague and ambiguous. Although the 1988 constitution took pains to outline extensive new civil rights for all citizens, it remained ambiguous about the parameters of democratic "citizen security" (*segurança cidadã*) versus the protection of the state and the government. Once the dictatorship ended, special-operations forces like the *Choque* shifted their attention to urban "criminals," mostly poor, black residents (Pinheiro 1991).[13] Stories of militaristic police raids throughout Brazil evidence this fact.

In 2007 in Rio de Janeiro, 1,350 *Batalhão de Operações Policiais Especiais* (BOPE) police officers (Rio's shock battalion) invaded Complexo Alemão, a region of five peripheral neighborhoods in Rio de Janeiro and killed nineteen people, some as young as fourteen years of age. The stated mission was to assassinate alleged criminals and drug traffickers (Costa et al. 2007). Snipers perched on rooftops in order to pick off suspects. Of those killed, only eight had explicit associations with drug trafficking (*O Globo* 2007). In 2009, the state of Rio de Janeiro created the *Unidade de Polícia Pacificadora*

(UPP) (Pacifying Police Unit), a police forced designed to "clean up" crime and "pacify" violence in Rio's favelas in anticipation of the 2014 World Cup and 2016 Olympics. These UPP units are also in practice in Salvador today. The presence of drug traffickers in peripheries has been used as an excuse to militaristically occupy and criminalize entire neighborhoods across Brazil. These strategies stigmatize the periphery and their residents as internal enemies to be eliminated by the state, and therefore justify the use of deadly force in the minds of the government and many citizens (Caldeira 2000; Lemgruber et al. 2003; Ramos and Musumeci 2005).

Colloquially, soteropolitanos associate the shock police with death and violence. My first introduction to the Choque police came through my experiences living on Rua Democrata in Dois de Julho, the same neighborhood where I lived during carnival 2004. One of the oldest neighborhoods in the city, located in the heart of downtown, Dois de Julho is situated just above the Avenida Contorno (the main highway-like avenue linking the lower city to the upper city),[14] one block from Praça da Piedade, and just behind Carlos Gomes Avenue. Rua Democrata was on one of the quietest and least-trafficked streets in Dois de Julho because it leads directly to the Contorno and is more like a dead-end than a through street for pedestrians and vehicles. Rua Democrata is in many ways a liminal space between two worlds—the world of the bustling commercial neighborhood of the city center above and the world of the Contorno below. When I would visit my neighbors during the day, we would see street kids (primarily boys) in groups of five or ten, probably ranging in age from eight to fourteen, heading down to that little pathway to sniff glue. Sitting in my neighbor's house, we would watch the boys stride down the hill and come back fifteen or thirty minutes later, extremely thirsty, with glazed eyes. We knew they were thirsty because they would stop by the window on their way up from the hill and ask for water—the entire group of them. Periodically, PMs would stop the street boys ascending from the cliff and hold them on the wall, frisk them, and question them. This was relatively commonplace (Hecht 1998). However, the presence of the Choque police meant something more.[15]

My most vivid memories of the Choque police are from watching their black SUVs with the word *Choque* written on the side whiz down Rua Democrata toward the Contorno, dressed in all black, shotguns cocked outside their windows, and lights flashing. I never saw them actually apprehend a "suspect," but I did see them go down that street with frequency. Admittedly, my personal interpretation of the Choque police has nothing to do with anything but gossip and observation. However, as Veena Das (2007) notes, rumors and myths are often where silenced discourses of violence emerge in the wake of extreme repression.[16] The whispers, myths, and stories that accompany extreme moments of violence in Salvador reveal silenced discourses of violence that have emerged out of generations of extreme repression at the hands of the state. Although thankfully I never witnessed any Choque raids on communities or the alleged terror they inflict, I have heard plenty of stories. Keisha-Khan Perry's (2011) experiences with police raids (often perpetuated by the Choque) in the Gamboa de Baixo neighborhood just under the Avenida Contorno provide a glimpse into what this real-life experience looks and feels like. They also let us know where those Choque police cars were going when they whizzed down my street to the Contorno. The saying that sticks with me is that the military police come to beat you but the Choque come to kill you.[17]

The military organization of Brazil's early police forces defined policing practices according to a discourse of offense and war that effectively marked black bodies as enemies of the state. Indeed, the genealogy of policing in Brazil reveals much about how discourses of antiblackness came to frame policing. There are competing histories of policing in Brazil, but for the most part historians agree that the origins of state-organized police forces can be traced to the establishment of the Royal Police Guard (*Guarda Real de Polícia*) in Rio de Janeiro in May 1808. Thomas Holloway (1993) argues that the Portuguese Crown established the royal guard as part of a plan to transition its government from Europe to Brazil (colony to empire).[18] The idea was to construct conditions in Brazil that would be parallel to those in Portugal. The French helped Portugal establish its first policing services in Lisbon (Holloway 1993, 32).[19] The first iteration of this effort was the General Intendent of Police of the Court and the State of Brazil, which was founded on May 10, 1808, under the leadership of the first Intendent of Police, Paulo Fernandes Viana (Holloway 1993, 32). One year later, the royal guard became the repressive arm of Viana's leadership, quickly defining policing as violent repression in the new capital of Rio de Janeiro. Even at that early moment, policing and brutality went hand in hand, and the black body was the target of this brutality. Miguel Nunes Vidigal was the person most associated with the royal guard's repression. As Holloway observes,

> Vidigal became the terror of the vagrants and idlers [racialized terms] who might meet him coming around a corner at night or see him suddenly appear at the *batuques*. . . . Without even pro forma deference to legal procedures, Vidigal and his soldiers . . . proceeded to beat any participant, miscreant, or vagrant they could capture" (1993, 35).

The primary targets of Vidigal's brutality were black people, free and enslaved. He was known for attacking the quilombos (maroon communities) surrounding the city of Rio de Janeiro and was famous for his raids on batuques (African drumming and dancing sessions). His weapon of choice was "a whip with a long heavy shaft tipped by rawhide strips, used as both club and lash" (Holloway 1993, 35). Vidigal's methods and tools extended those of slavery. His notorious raids and beatings were known as "shrimp dinners," "recalling the flaying necessary to get at the pink flesh of those crustaceans" (ibid.). Returning briefly to our discussion in chapter 1 about Elaine Scarry's work on war and the body in pain, we can say that Vidigal solidified Brazilian policing by translating the black body into the language of public security for the new nation, breaking the black body away from the nation and, in effect, disowning it. In other words, the process by which Brazilian policing became defined in contraposition to the black body in pain gelled the impossibility of black ownership of the nation (citizenship) (Scarry 1985, 124).

Early police soldiers were recruited from the lower classes, and, just like the case of slave catchers (*capitães do mato*) then, and the military police officers now, many of these soldiers were black. The state's intent was to create a strict hierarchical system of discipline that would be able to root out the enemy: all of those people who threatened the social contract. As Holloway suggests, "the police were like a standing army fighting a social war against adversaries all around them" (1993, 37).

From its very beginnings the Brazilian police were a brutal state force that operated according to racialized logics. The militaristic structure translated into the use of police forces to control and contain internal factions of the national population that the state interpreted as a threat, and from the imperial period forward, the black body was this threat. Consequently, the spectacular practice of producing the black body in pain (those people beaten and whipped by Vidigal for participating in batuques, capoeira, or quilombo, for example) became a symbolic site for articulating the state's authority.

Early policing entailed the relentless torture and killing of black people and used similar tools (the whip) and logics (criminalization of rebellious black bodies) as those used at the pelourinho. As policing developed throughout the nation, these ghosts remained. The province of Bahia established its military police force, *Corpo de Polícia*, on February 17, 1825, by imperial decree by Dom Pedro II (Araújo 1997, 9). One of the few books that presents a historical account of policing in Bahia was commissioned by the Bahian military police in celebration of their 172nd anniversary, and was written by a military police officer. Consequently, much of the historical information we have about the genealogy of military police in Bahia privileges official state memory. The stories that this text chooses to tell and the memories that it chooses to erase are nonetheless illuminating. The Corpo de Polícia emerged in response to black rebellion, writes author Major Oseas Moreira de Araújo: "In 1813, blacks of the Hausa race staged a revolt. . . . The 1824 revolt of the 3rd Battalion of Hunters, known as the Parakeet Battalion, robbed arms from the Commander's barracks located in Berquo, killing Cel. Felisberto Gomes Caldeira. That same year, on the 16th of October, fugitives from Confederation of Ecuador in Pernambuco landed in Bahia. . . . [As a result] the 3rd Battalion was required to dissolve because of these revolts" (1997, 9; my translation). Araújo's writing is cryptic and filled with silences, passive voice, and awkward halts as if he is taking pains to craft his language carefully to avoid the subject of race, slavery, and blackness and its relationship to Bahian policing. Regardless, the "conflicts and general uprisings" led Emperor Dom Pedro II to travel to Bahia to assess the situation. Subsequently, on February 17, 1825, he decreed that creating a police force (*Corpo de Polícia*) was "necessary for the tranquility and public security of the City of Bahia" (Federico 1999, 17; my translation). The decree goes on to require the immediate organization of the force in order to "conserve the stability" of the city. The province of Bahia designed its police force like the royal guard of Rio de Janeiro: to protect the integrity and social order of the state in a moment when the threat of black revolt permeated the state's thoughts.

The openly declared war against the slave revolts of 1807 to 1835 in Bahia, which led to the black codes of 1822 to 1835, also manifested in the racialized, juridical discourse of criminality that emerged after the legal abolition of slavery in 1888, which associated the black body with social anomie (e.g., Conrad 1983; Fausto 1984; Holloway 1993; Reis 2003).[20] This cognitive association and the state's explicit, organized war on black people would continue over time, reaching well into the twenty-first century. And although the authoritarian regime extended the practice of police abuse and torture far beyond the black body, the return to the disproportionate focus on the black body following the military dictatorship underscores the strength of the correlation between blackness and "enemy of the state" in the discourse of public safety.

As mentioned earlier, the Portuguese strategically built Salvador atop a cliff to ward off militaristic threat (Fausto 1999). Although much of this threat came from Europe (specifically Holland), we cannot forget the transnational conditions of war that produced the colony itself. The territory of Brazil was taken from the indigenous population through war. Scores of enslaved Africans who were brought to Bahia through the mid-1800s to work the sugarcane plantations and sustain the colony's economy were prisoners of war.[21] Although there was a precipitous drop in organized, armed, black insurrection in Bahia after 1835, the racialized discourse of war remained, instilled in state authoritarianism, not just in Bahia but also across the nation. This manifested itself keenly in the militarization of the Brazilian police and led to the emergence of death squads.

Death Squads

As we learned from the history of the shock police (the Bahian special forces that inspired Culture Shock's name), the military created special police shock units in 1969—the predecessors of the contemporary pacifying police units across Brazil—to patrol poor urban neighborhoods, the "internal enemy" (Pinheiro 1991, 168–69). The enemy included the "marginals" (*marginais*) of society—criminals (thieves, vagrants, and prostitutes) and the "*povão*," the poor, majority black masses. Today, the militarization of the police, the police's war strategies to control urban spaces, and the same dicey, surreptitious relationship between the state and death squads remain. And the state continues to illustrate each of these elements, using the black body in pain as its canvas.

R. S. Rose (2005) argues that death squads officially emerged during the presidency of Getúlio Vargas.[22] At this point in time the terms *grupos de extermínio* (extermination groups) and *esquadrão da morte* (death squadron) appear, both of which we now translate as death squads. For Rose, these death squads are born out of Vargas's secret police force. From 1907 to 1983, some version of a secret police force existed in Brazil (Rose 2005, 17, 310 n. 5). These secret police forces changed names over the years, from the "Tomato Heads" of Getúlio Vargas's palace guard to the Special Diligence Group (*Grupo de Diligências Especiais*) (DGE) of the 1950s to 1980s (Rose 2005, 235). However, regardless of name, these forces have been critical to the offensive strategies of authoritarianism and control exercised by the Brazilian state. Bahian death squads are also a part of this chronology. The Vargas administration designed the secret police to function as a state offensive against urban "threats" to national security (Rose 2005). If the secret police were indeed death squads, then Brazil arguably had the first death squad in Latin America; the GDE, founded in 1957 (Rose 2005, 12, 233). This secretive, special task force, led by civil police officer Cecil de Macedo (a former officer for Vargas's Tomato Heads), was, according to Rose, a "novel police unit [that] had the green light to eliminate each and every delinquent circulating in the city. There were to be no questions, no paperwork, and no prisoners taken alive. When it was decided to go after a specific suspect, the individual's death was already agreed upon" (2005, 233). The similarities between then and now are striking.

"Bodies were often unceremoniously dumped in an outlying working-class district north of the city [of Rio de Janeiro] called the Baixada Fluminense. . . . The next day, Rio's newspapers would announce that another bandit was out of circulation" (2005, 234).

The GDE later morphed into the Death Squadron of São Paulo, which was the precursor to the proliferation of similar specialized operations forces during the military dictatorship across the nation.[23] On July 2, 1969, the acting federal government passed Decree-Law No. 667, which centralized the state police under the national army, in essence consolidating what Sérgio Pinheiro calls the "implicit political intent" of the state police to "defend and protect the ruling classes from protest by the lower classes" (1991, 168). This was one of the early repressive actions taken during the military dictatorship (1964–85) to quell the threat of protest and what it termed "urban guerilla threat," which included antigovernment terrorism (ibid.). The associations that we currently make between the state police and public security are, in fact, rooted in the state's desire to quell protest from the masses.

Death squads "came under the supervision of Brazilian intelligence agencies through an organization called Operation Bandeirantes (OBAN) . . . [which] was supported by national and multinational business funds" (Pinheiro 1991, 175). OBAN organized and "refined the traditional death squad practices of kidnapping, torture, and murder," and over time increasingly shifted its focus from urban guerillas to members of society that did not fit within the moral boundaries of the social contract, such as thieves, criminals, and prostitutes. However, these stigmatized members of society were always also racialized, gendered, and sexualized (Ramos and Musumeci 2005).[24]

After the military dictatorship (1964–84), as part of the process of democratization, the police were reorganized by the state into three departments instead of just two: the military police, the civil police, and the federal police.[25] The military and the civil police would fall under the secretary of public security at the state level and the federal police would fall under national jurisdiction (Caldeira 2000). In addition to these basic units, states also formalized the special-operations forces charged with handling urban unrest and threats of extreme violence throughout the 1970s. These included the *Primeiro Batalhão de Choque* (shock police) of Salvador; Comando de Policiamento de Choque in São Paulo (includes shock battalions and the Rota); *Batalhão de Operações Policiais Especiais* (BOPE) in Rio de Janeiro; and the *Rondas Especiais* (RONDESP), a subunit of the Capital Police Command (CPC) in Salvador (Brisolla 2007; Polícia Militar da Bahia 2015; Secretaria da Segurança Pública [Governo do Estado de São Paulo] 2015). Both the military and civil police forces maintained genealogical ties to death squads.

Connections between formal policing and death squads are messy, vexed, and fraught with silences, erasures, and omissions that make it difficult to map where the line between on-duty and off-duty policing begins and ends. Some scholars read death squads as vigilante groups (e.g., Pinheiro 1991; Scheper-Hughes 2006).[27] Yet this line of reasoning is in many ways too simplistic. Is corruption really the only reason that police officers join clandestine killing teams? The vigilantism thesis reads targets of death squads as passive, illiterate, poor, apolitical victims whose deaths were "cruel but usual." But this is no more the case than the notion that perpetrators of this violence should be read as rogue entities acting outside of the law.[26] Reframing the narratives of the dead and survivors (parents, family members, community, witnesses) as protagonists with agency who have been *purposefully* stigmatized by the state and society to mask the political nature of their deaths pushes us beyond this binary framework and into the more complicated identification of death-squad murders as acts of war.

There is a slippage between death squads and the offensive militarized structure of policing formalized by Brazil's state-run police forces that plays itself out in legal, above-board modes of policing. However, beyond the implicit connections between militarized policing and death squads, at times this connection becomes explicit.

The inextricable link between death squads and policing, buried by layers of history, is increasingly becoming visible. The rampant death-squad killings in Bahia won international attention in 2005 because of React or Die!'s political efforts, forcing the state of Bahia to (briefly) address the crisis of death-squad murders with seriousness. On October 19, 2005, a representative from the United Nations visited Salvador to meet with black movement and state representatives about race and the problem of police violence in Bahia (Ferreira 2005). The state also sponsored a forum in the auditorium of the Brazilian Bar Association headquarters in downtown Salvador, a second meeting with UN representatives regarding the problem of death squads in Bahia, and it recognized the existence of death squads for the first time in 2005 (Ramos 2005). As a result, the state founded *Grupo Especial de Repressão a Crimes de Extermínio* (Special Group for the Repression of the Extermination Crimes) (GERCE), a task force to investigate murders possibly linked to death squads in Bahia (Roso 2005). In April 2008, the secretary of public security—SSP, BA—abruptly suspended GERCE; one day later (D'Eça 2008), the State Ministry of the Public (MPE, *Ministério Público do Estado*) created NUGE, *Núcleo de Combate a Grupos de Extermínio*.[28] Why has it been so difficult to create a sustainable agency for addressing this extralegal, extrajudicial practice? These mercurial politics stress the seemingly uncertain relationship between death squads and the state itself.

The state's conflicted reluctance to investigate and prosecute death squads lingers behind this question (Lemgruber et al. 2003). In 2013, investigative journalist Lena Azevedo published a series of damning reports uncovering state corruption and complicity with death squads in Bahia (Azevedo 2013a; 2013b). According to Bahia's State Public Ministry, approximately 80 percent of all homicides in Bahia are never investigated. In Azevedo's interview with prosecutor Ariomar Figuereido of the Special Action Group to Combat Criminal Organization (GAECO),[29] Figuereido states that, of the 1,659 homicides in Bahia in 2012, no cases were opened for 1,340 (Azevedo 2013b). He goes on to note that "the police say that they investigate the cases, but their notes are never annexed" (2013b). It takes approximately three to four months for the state medical morgue (IML) to issue autopsy reports, further complicating the investigation process. In the same interview, prosecutor Ana Rita Cerqueira of GAECO, responsible for complaints that led to the conviction of five policemen and a civilian who were part of a death squad in Santo António, 150 kilometers from Salvador, explains:

> These groups have emerged as "aseptic" vigilantes that "clean up" areas that local business, usually in the vicinity, deem to be a threat. These groups act within their own logic. Bandits are those they identify as bandits. The victims' profile is invariably young and black, whether or not they have a prior criminal record. Slow justice furnishes a sense of impunity and is a rubber stamp from society for these actions. This rubber stamp contributes to the increase in homicides (Azevedo 2013b; my translation).

Although Cerqueira reproduces the idea of death squads as vigilantes, her comments are revealing. The state and society make important, conscious as well as unconscious decisions that, in effect, allow death squads to perpetuate.

During a death-squad murder in Salvador on July 6, 2001, Daniel Santos Souza, nineteen, was abducted from his home in Nordeste de Amaralina by "men using Civil Police jackets" and shot to death (*A Tarde* 2001, 20). Either someone killed Mr. Souza and put on a civil police jacket to frame the civil police, or this murder is an example of the civil police acting as death squads openly and with little recourse. In many cases, police-issued ammunition is found at the site of death-squad murders, like one that occurred in Bairro da Paz in 2007 (discussed in chapter 4). In 2005, the Parliamentary Commission to Survey Extermination in the Northeast (CPI),[30] organized by Brazil's House of Representatives, launched an investigation into death squads in the northeastern region (CPI 2005). In a 596-page report, this commission outlined the death-squad crisis, noting the direct role that local state governments play in perpetuating and supporting death squads by guaranteeing their impunity (CPI 2005, 296). In Bahia, the report explains, the victims of death squads are mostly black males between the ages of fourteen and twenty-nine, mostly poor and mostly without any prior record with the police (296). It also notes that most death squads are comprised of active military and ex-military members and civil police officers (ibid.). Although the report also falls back into the rhetoric of associating death squads with impunity and vigilantism, its findings underscore the very intimate relationship between the state and these killing teams. For example, CPI states that at the time of their investigation, Bahian governor Paulo Souto's refusal to admit the existence of death squads, name state representatives to the federal government's inquiry, and his active "omission and manipulation of data" contributed substantively to the impunity of death squads in the state (297). The report also named active police officers known to be involved in death squads, including Agent Adailton Souza Adan, who in 2012 was appointed by the Bahian government to *investigate* death squads in Bahia (Azevedo 2013b). Despite having been accused and found guilty of extrajudicial torture, killing, and participation in death squads for years prior to this appointment, Bahia still saw fit to name him to lead internal state investigations.[31]

The federal government's active role in investigating death squads across the nation complicates our discussions of terrorism. As it manifests as a regional division of power within a federation, states are the driving force behind death squads and are the entities most actively involved in investigation. Yet this does not mean that the nation-state is not also complicit in this violence. As Edward Herman (1982) reminds us, the state's denial of its involvement in death squads is the very cloak that it uses to dissociate itself from its "illegitimate" practices. In a 2014 public lecture entitled "Hatched from the Egg of Impunity: A Fowl Called Boko Haram," novelist and playright Wole Soyinka stated that in Nigeria, ongoing impunity is what has allowed the extremist group Boko Haram to become so violent and out of control (Holley 2014). The case of Brazilian death squads is similar. The fact that the federal government turns a blind eye to the killing of black youth is what, in part, allows state police to be so violent and out of control.

In Salvador, repeatedly, black residents are being threatened and killed because of their social-movement work and militancy. And although this does not lead us to the definitive conclusion that all death-squad murders are politically motivated, or the reductionist assessment that all death squads are state sponsored and state run, the dubious details of many cases require that we question the extent to which the state is not only complicit in extermination squads but also sanctioning them and why. What is the meaning of this violence, what are its racial implications, and why are black people the preferred victims?

Fourteen years after she conducted her initial research on death and violence in the northeastern state of Pernambuco, Nancy Scheper-Hughes revisited her previous work to talk about the operation of death squads in Timbaúba, the community where she lived. In this assessment she writes that

> a strong popular backlash against the dangerous classes of subcitizens fueled "street-cleaning" campaigns, the Brazilian version of ethnic cleansing (with the support of police, political leaders, commercial firms, and armed response groups), in the *favelas, morros* (hillside shantytowns), and public-housing projects of Brazil's own inner cities. . . . Democratic Brazil had the demographic profile of a nation at war, which in a sense it was. (2006, 154)

Although Scheper-Hughes does not say so explicitly, she implies that the action of death squads in the northeast is genocide and a sign of war.[32] However, in making this claim she falls short of identifying death squads as political manifestations and recognizing that the "ethnic cleansing" that death squads have been engaging in is antiblack. Instead, she assesses death squads as the legacy of the authoritarianism of the military dictatorship, corruption, and the "national sociology of 'racial democracy'" (153). Yet we have seen, from the 1800s onward, Portuguese colonial authorities and eventually the Brazilian nation have used a discourse of war to criminalize blackness and define the black body as the internal enemy of the state for generations.

If death squads are, to follow Edward Herman (1982), a manifestation of the national security state, and death squads in Bahia target black people specifically, what does this configuration tell us about the logic of the Brazilian racial state itself? Returning briefly to the discussion in chapter 1, it would appear that instead of anchoring the performance of state authority in one iconic site, after removing the pelourinho from the center of Salvador, it diffused its violence and varied it. The pelourinho became a ghost and, like an apparition, it continued to appear and reappear through time as a slightly distorted image of its former self. Like the effaced writing of the palimpsest, at times it is barely visible, and at other times clear and apparent but in a new configuration. Quintessentially a performance, it is always recognizable by the spectacular display of violence upon the black body in pain. Policing and death squads are symbiotic state apparatuses and their impact extends far beyond physical death.

Bronka

The family and friends of Bronka and Negro Blue, and militantes from across the city, staunchly rejected the claim that the victims and survivors of Nova

Brasilia were involved with drugs or crime. Negro Blue was a respected artist who participated in the hip-hop movement of Bahia. He was a member
of the group Rap Etnia and a member of React or Die! Just a month before
Blue's death, he was in the streets protesting the racism of state violence and
police brutality.[33] Negro Blue's political weapon in life was rap. He used his
rhymes to speak out against police violence as state genocide against black
people in the periphery. Blue's death hit particularly close to home for the
members of the campaign. It also underscored the need for the movement
to prove, definitively, that death squads were state sanctioned and state run.
And although the news media and the police were criminalizing Negro Blue
and Bronka, witnesses said they heard one of the masked shooters say "react
now" (*reaja agora*) before the two were shot—a message for React or Die!
Militantes suspected that this was not a random act of violence. The two
had been targeted for their political action. Bronka would later testify that
civil police invaded his house months before the shooting claiming to look
for stolen goods. They assaulted him and threatened to kill him, saying they
would throw his body in death's curve—*curva de morte*. Coincidentally, this
was where he was later shot—a location known as a "spawning ground"—
ponto de desova—for death squads in Nova Brasilia. "Spawning grounds" are
scattered throughout Salvador and are best described as "hidden" execution
sites where death squads kill and then "bury" or toss the bodies of their victims (see the map on p. 115). These clandestine cemeteries are usually located
in the periphery. I place the word "hidden" in quotes here because, despite
the fact that they are often in out-of-the-way places, the locations of these
clandestine cemeteries are well-known to the residents who live near them
and the police themselves, as is evidenced by Bronka's testimony. Despite
the fact that local police never launched a thorough investigation into the
Nova Brasilia killing, militantes are convinced that the police were behind
the Nova Brasilia killing to this day.

The Nova Brasilia killing became a new catalyst for React or Die! Four days
after Negro Blue's death, on March 5, a coalition of twelve black movement
organizations, led by React or Die!, turned a scheduled protest titled "Confronting Genocide, No Step Backward" into a protest for answers surrounding the Nova Brasilia case. The demonstrators marched again to the Office
of the Secretary of Public Security in Piedade where the inaugural React or
Die! vigil was held in 2005. When the militantes arrived, they demanded
to speak with the chief of the civil police in order to denounce the death of
Negro Blue and the near-fatal wounding of Bronka. Instead, the office offered to have three representatives from the group meet with a lower-level
official. Indignant, the demonstrators refused and demanded to meet with

the police chief en masse, along with the family members and friends of the victims. Officials refused. After being rejected, the black movement collective attempted to schedule a meeting with the governor regarding the crisis of racism and state violence. Once again, the state refused to meet. Frustrated, the collective approached Congressman Luiz Alberto of the Workers' Party (PT), then secretary for the promotion of equity in Bahia (SEPROMI) and a member of the Unified Black Movement (MNU), for help.[34] Congressman Alberto set up a meeting between the militantes, secretary of public security Paulo Bezerra, and the civil police chief on March 9.

On the appointed day, militantes from twelve black organizations attempted to enter the meeting space with a "Confronting Genocide, No Step Backward" banner, but public-safety officials refused to let the banner come inside. For the protestors, this symbolized the state's broader refusal to acknowledge the political legitimacy of their claims. Officials also refused to allow journalists at the meeting, another point that irritated the movement. How could they be sure that their demands would be registered and promises would be kept if there was no media coverage to record the meetings, publicize them, and hold officials accountable? Nevertheless, one journalist from the black newspaper *Irohin* was (clandestinely) present at the meeting and took notes.[35] After a general discussion on the crisis of racism and public safety in Salvador and the submission of a list of demands and recommendations, the gatherers directly broached the Nova Brasilia killing. They were particularly concerned with Bronka and his physical and psychological state since the shooting because he had been unable to get the medical treatment and the social services he needed to fully recover—both because of the wait times with the public-health system and because he could not afford the alternative private care.

Bronka remained at the state hospital for five days after the shooting while he was treated for his injuries. After that, the hospital discharged him. However, his return home was not the joyous occasion it should have been. He did not have adequate conditions at home for his care. He still had two bullets lodged in his spine, and was now confined to a wheelchair with the looming threat of being a paraplegic for the rest of his life if he did not get urgent, specialized medical attention. The fact that Bronka was paralyzed made it difficult for his family to provide for even his most basic needs. Like many people who live in the periphery, Bronka's family lived in a house situated on top of a steep hill, so he suffered enormous difficulty coming home and was only able to leave his house for urgent matters. He could no longer work and needed family members to take care of him twenty-four hours a day. This task fell almost exclusively to his mother, Dona Simone. Each time Bronka had to return to the hospital for doctor's appointments, neighbors would carry him out of the house and down the steep hill into a taxi so that he could go to the doctor. Bronka survived the attack, but his life and the lives of his family and community were permanently altered by the devastating physical and psychological wounds that he suffered.

One of the outcomes of the March 9 meeting was SEPROMI's promise to React or Die! that Bronka would receive adequate health care at the Sarah Kubitschek Hospital, renowned for its trauma care and physical therapy. Right after the March 9 meeting, SEPROMI representatives got in touch with Hamilton and Andreia, but it took hours to sort out the details for Bronka's care.[36] Finally, the parties agreed that Bronka's treatment would begin on March 12. However, it was not until March 22 that an ambulance came to Bronka's house to take him to the hospital. Instead of going to Sarah Kubitschek, he was taken to another private hospital, Hospital das Clínicas.

On March 23, representatives of React or Die! and the MNU accompanied Bronka to Hospital das Clínicas for his treatment. Yet they soon found that Bronka was not being attended at all. He was seated in a wheelchair waiting for someone to come and get him, but no one ever came. There was no representative from SEPROMI present and no one at the hospital seemed to know who Bronka was or who had sent him. Finally, one doctor offered to help him after Hamilton and Andreia told him Bronka's story. They explained that he was the only survivor of a shooting incident and that he needed special treatment. The doctor on site explained that Bronka would have to submit to a series of examinations in order to evaluate his case and be admitted. The militantes present, including Hamilton and Andreia, requested the presence of an independent doctor and also requested that Andreia, a medical doctor, be allowed to accompany the examinations and discussions as well. However, when Andreia approached the hospital staff as a medical professional, a medical student and a nurse separately dismissed her and refused to acknowledge her credentials. Infuriated and humiliated, both Hamilton and Andreia challenged the staff, claiming that their actions toward them had been racist. The hospital staff called security and approximately fifteen security guards came to "address" the situation. After the incident was over, Andreia filed a formal complaint charging racism against the hospital. But the damage had been done, for now Bronka was stigmatized as a "troublemaker." A police officer, who was called to the scene because of the brouhaha, interrogated Bronka, asking him if he used drugs and knew the leader of a well-known criminal faction in the city. The hospital staff then took away Bronka's wheelchair, alleging that they needed it for other patients. After several long hours of waiting and humiliation with no treatment, Bronka and his mother Dona Simone decided that he would be more comfortable returning home than sitting in the hospital in pain waiting for treatment.

The trauma of death-squad violence reverberates through the survivors and their communities and is compounded by the racial microaggressions that characterize the lived experience of racism for black soteropolitanos. This is where "The Berlin Wall" meets "Terrorism." Bronka's injuries were compounded by the subtle and not-so-subtle injustices he experienced in his journey to get treatment. His harrowing trials as the survivor of a death-squad attempt on his life effectively positioned him to be the further target of racism, forcing him to enter into spaces where he "did not belong," like the private Hospital das Clínicas. Demanding the right to life meant that Bronka, his family, and militantes had to try to push their way through the Berlin Wall of racial apartheid in Bahia, the only result of which could be violence. The effects of the Nova Brasilia killing were not just physical but also psychological and social. In my interview with Andreia in 2012, she stated:

> There is something really important that we have to address when we speak of police brutality and death squads. . . . It is something that the state and the society somehow render invisible . . . the sequelae of this violence. We work most of the time with numbers concerning death or imprisonment, but beyond that there are sequelae that we can't quantify or qualify . . . exercised daily against the [black] communities. . . . When we have a boy that is dead, [a] victim of the state, [a] victim of these groups of violence, it has a devastating effect on the families and on the communities, and we can't quantify, we can't qualify what it means.

Andreia goes on to define these lingering injuries as daily fears that emerge from living with terrorism and the sum of its health effects. She uses the term *sequelae* (plural of *sequela*) to define these aftereffects. A sequela is the "the consequence of a disease; a morbid affection which results from and follows another. Something that follows; a consequence or result" (Kellerman 1981, 879). As a medical doctor, she understands the impact of state violence in terms of illness. She notes that her job when working with these families is to treat not only the physical wounds of those bodies the police violate but also the psychological and physical wounds this violence exacts on those bodies emotionally tied to the immediate, primary victims. In other words, the experience of state violence has a ripple effect on entire communities. And the racial microaggressions that families and advocates experience in their pursuit of justice map onto that experiential continuum.

The subsequent days were excruciating for Bronka. His mother, Dona Simone, who now represented him in all of his affairs because of the lasting effects of the trauma, had to wait days before the hospital returned Bronka's medical records so that he could be seen by another physician. And he still did not have the specialized care that he needed. By June 2007, Bronka and his family were forced to move out of their house because of continuing death threats, and he still had not been able to get treatment at the Sarah Kubitschek Hospital.

When I traveled to Salvador in July 2007, Bronka was still living with two bullets lodged in his spine and was having difficulty walking. Blue's death and Bronka's injuries weighed heavily on the campaign. Almost as soon as I landed, I got a call saying that there would be another demonstration. Again, React or Die! would protest in front of the Office of the Secretary of Public Security. Having worked with the campaign for two years by this point, they asked me to film the demonstration as a way to archive their protest and as a form of protection. With the death of Negro Blue still fresh, it was clear that the state, principally the civil police, were beginning to look closely at the movement. Harassment was imminent.

When I arrived in Piedade, the crowd was much smaller than it had been the night of the vigil in 2005, but the energy was still strong, albeit tense. Zumbi came up to me and greeted me warmly but quietly. With reserve, he slightly smiled, holding back the desire to express any visible emotion of happiness. Like many black organizers, Zumbi followed the code that open excitement, smiling, and joking are inappropriate public displays of emotion at political events. With a whisper he leaned over to me and said, "They killed Blue, did you hear?" I nodded. I had found out shortly after he died. Plainclothes police officers watched us as we rallied and conversed in front of the Office of the Secretary of Public Security. I was immediately aware of the shift in tone during this demonstration, and I felt uneasy. I knew that we were being watched, and as a foreigner, I was exceedingly aware of my precarious position at this demonstration. As Keisha-Khan Perry (2013) notes, the threat of deportation is always looming over foreign researchers who work in solidarity with local social movements. Some of the militantes whispered carefully, talking of rumors that the police were following organizers at the forefront of the campaign. The threat of death was in the air. We did not meet open hostility that day as student protestors had during the military dictatorship. Indeed, since the military dictatorship, "the police generally respect the citizen's freedom of thought, freedom of opinion and expression, and freedom of peaceful assembly and association, even though there are frequent cases of excessive force against social movements" (Mesquita Neto and Loche 2003, 187). Yet the death of Blue signaled that, although the state was not exacting overt repression, it was acting out its repression at night and in secrecy.

I began to film the march. Worried for my safety, one of the demonstrators came up and took the camera out of my hands and began to film. Frightened myself, I did not protest, for clearly I had also been interested in filming the civil police officers who were, themselves, filming us—surveillance as self-defense. Hamilton pulled me to the side and told me that the police had been secretly threatening him and his family. He had no proof, but he knew in his gut that the calls had come from a police officer and the police officer he suspected was there in the crowd watching the protest at that moment. Hamilton and Andreia had also been followed by an unidentified black car. The state had publicly, although reluctantly, been willing to meet with the campaign and address its concerns (exemplified by the March 9 meeting), but privately, and secretly, representatives of the state (at least according to the *militantes*) were harassing campaign members—first Negro Blue, now Hamilton. This was war.

Despite the fact that we stereotypically associate death squads with "uncivilized" (read subaltern, postcolonial, Third World) cultures of violence, liberal democracy and violent autocracy have historically courted one another, and the crisis of state violence in places like Brazil is neither exceptional nor peculiar to the region. As Jean Comaroff and John Comaroff note, "Indeed, the relative ease with which autocracies *have* made the transition to constitutional democracy points toward the possibility that they—autocracy and liberal democracy, that is—share more mechanisms of governance than has conventionally been recognized, not least their grounding in a rule of law, an Iron Cage of Legality itself predicated, more or less visibly, on sovereign violence" (2006, 2). Death squads are an example of these shared mechanisms of governance. They are also manifestations of genocide: political, deliberate, and calculated. Genocidal assemblages necessarily incorporate lines of articulation, strata, lines of flight, and movements of deterritorialization and destratification.

War

Frustrated with the lack of state response in Bronka's case, in June 2007, Hamilton, Sandra Carvalho and Carlos Dias of Global Justice submitted a report to the United Nations regarding the *Matança de Nova Brasilia*. The coalition sent the dossier on the Nova Brasilia killing to special rapporteur Phillip Alston. With appeals to the state moving slowly, the next step was to reach out to the international human-rights community. This, in and of itself, was a conflicted political move. Many militantes had a deep mistrust for international human-rights politics and infrastructure at this time. For them, human-rights institutions maintained a scaffolding of white supremacy despite their gestures toward giving assistance. The politics of "saving" poor black people played into white savior tropes of charity and often failed to engage in the harsh racial critiques that movements like React or Die! were championing. Instead, this collaboration with Global Justice was a politics of "survival pending revolution."[37] That would soon change, however, as Global Justice developed into a strong ally.

In their collaborative letter, the parties outlined the details of the case, the ordeal at Hospital das Clínicas, and the gravity of Bronka's situation. After another series of death-squad killings, another coalition including React or Die!, the Hip Hop Movement, the Homeless Movement, and Global Justice sent yet another letter to Phillip Alston, denouncing the actions of death squads in Salvador, including the Calabetão massacre (to be discussed in chapter 5). In November 2007, Alston visited Brazil to address the problem of extrajudicial killing, arbitrary murders, and death squads there. In the report, he stated that members of the police forces are often behind extrajudicial executions (Alston 2007, 5). The blurred line between state policing and death squads is a manifestation of the magic of the state and a sign of war. Although black communities turn to the law as a resource for seeking justice, this process is "fraught with uncertainty and danger" (Das 2007, 163). The state's duplicity is proof of its war with its own people. It is the representation of rationality, law, and order on the one hand, and the regisseur of magical state terror that embody a combination of "obscurity and power" on the other (ibid.). In his reflections on the situation of state violence in Brazil following his trip, Alston writes, "Extrajudicial executions are committed by police who murder rather than arrest criminal suspects, and also during large-scale confrontational 'war'-style policing, in which excessive use of force results in the deaths of suspected criminals and bystanders" (Alston 2007, 9–10). The black body in pain is also the nodal point for defining the magical state.

Bahia is a war zone caught up in entangled time (Mbembe 2001).[38] The production of the space of Bahia through the repetition of state violence against the black body, from the slavery period to the present, is evidence of this fact.[39] And if Bahia is a palimpsestic space, entangled by war and colonialism, then haunting state practices of engagement with the black body are its layers of meaning, etched over and frequently effaced.

Bronka made a partial recovery and was able to walk again by 2009. But in 2013, a death squad severely beat and killed him, apparently because they suspected that the Nova Brasilia killing case might be investigated at the federal level. As Culture Shock reminds us, "*This* is terrorism."

"The Police Raid"

"Get on the ground and stay quiet! . . ."
The MC and the three actors who just finished the previous vignette "Terrorism" stand to one side of the circle casually talking. All of a sudden, as if he sees what is coming, one of the three actors runs out of the circle very quickly. Almost instantaneously, three actors wearing white cloth masks storm into the circle with their hands extended in front of them, screaming, "Stop!" "Don't move!" "Get on the ground and stay quiet!" "Shut up!" The hooded actors occasionally curse and ad lib as well. The actors wearing white masks point fingers and shape their hands to look like guns. They point these "guns" at the heads and bodies of the two actors who were previously chatting calmly. The actors who are taken by surprise are not wearing masks; therefore, their "blackness"—the darkness of their skin—stands in deep contrast to the bright-white hoods the invading actors wear. The actor who ran out just before the invaders came runs back into the circle, hopping as if being chased. A whirlwind of booming shouts and sharp movements by the hooded figures startle the audience. The context of the actions implies that the circle at this point represents a peripheral neighborhood and the actors with hoods represent the police (on duty or off duty?). The actors taken off guard represent neighborhood residents. As they invade the neighborhood, the three "police officers" run swiftly in and out of the circle around audience members, chasing after "residents." The hooded figures' movements are rough, rowdy,

and belligerent. The "residents" scream in horror, put their hands behind their heads, and kneel on the ground as the "police" chase them around the "neighborhood." As the hooded figures point their guns at residents, they also, by extension, terrorize the audience, frightening many in the crowd as they run in and out of the circle. Several children in the audience begin screaming and crying while others laugh nervously. One young woman from the audience shrieks and breaks through the circle to run to the other side when an "officer" runs up behind her, imaginary gun drawn.

The pace of the scene is quick, as if we are all caught up in a tornado. As the "police" begin to subdue the "residents," however, the vignette slows down. All of the actors—residents and police—pant with fatigue from running and yelling. The residents are now lying down on the ground, prostrate. The police officers are standing over them. Almost as quickly as the raid began, albeit much more quietly, the raid ends. All actors freeze pose (although all of the actors are still panting). The MC, playing a neighborhood resident, jumps up from his position lying on the ground to break the frozen pose. He walks around to each of the police officers and removes their white masks to reveal their black faces. They too are neighborhood residents.

MC: They invaded . . . they invaded Iraq. [They] killed men, women, and children, but where is Saddam?
ACTORS: Alive!
MC: They invaded . . . they invaded Afghanistan. [They] killed men, women, and children. Where is bin Laden?
ACTORS: Alive!
MC: They invaded . . . they invaded, but where is Blair?
ACTORS: Alive!
MC: But where is Bush?
ACTORS: Alive!
MC: They invaded . . . they invaded Fazenda Grande, San Martins, Sussuarana, Bom Júa, Liberdade, Alto de Coutos . . .

A woman from the audience calls out "Plataforma."

MC: But where are the people?
ACTORS: They are dying.

4 Palimpsestic Embodiment

In 1982, photographer Luiz Morier captured a moment that would forever leave a profound impression on Brazil (figure 4.1). He published the photograph, pictured here, titled "Todos Negros," in the Rio de Janeiro newspaper *Jornal do Brasil* and won the Esso Prize for Photography in 1983.[1] The image captures a PM blitz alongside a highway in the Grajaú-Jacarepaguá zone of the city. Intrigued by the sight while passing by, Morier discreetly

Figure 4.1. "Todos Negros," *Jornal do Brasil,* September 30, 1982 (photo by Luiz Morier).

photographed a sequence of shots of the scene, the most famous of which is the one pictured here. The title "Todos Negros" means "All Black(s)," or alternatively "All Black Men," and is a descriptive and social analysis of the obvious politics of race, gender, and power at play in this moment: five black men with similar skin tones, haircuts, builds, and ages being led by a rope tied around their necks by a considerably lighter-skinned police officer who would most likely be classified white-mestizo in Brazil. Although we can only see five men in this shot, we know from the other photographs taken that day that there were seven men in all, tied together. In the picture (figure 4.1) there is at least one person cut off on the right-hand side, on a rope that trails off beyond the frame. In one of the subsequent shots, all seven men are sitting on a curb looking down and off to the side. Denotatively, we do not know why the men are tied together. We can only infer (from their downward stares) that they are being arrested by the whiter, noticeably fatter police officer in the foreground of the image. The officer holds a bunch of rope (left over?) in his right hand. He has his back to the camera with his head slightly turned to the right, keeping the photographer in view with a sideward glance. As in the image here, the whiteness and blackness of the bodies in the photograph draw our immediate attention. Connotatively, the image associates blackness with criminality, victimhood, and powerlessness, and whiteness with authority, the state, prowess (the rope), and control. The title, "All Black(s)," helps us to read this connotative message further. What we are seeing is not only a descriptive commentary about black bodies and white bodies, but also a layered picture of race, violence, the body, and the state in Brazil—the white hand clasped over the top of the black hand: palimpsestic embodiment.

Violence against the black body is a haunting: a series of performative repetitions that mimic, reflect, and refract memory across time and space. Focusing on the scenarios of death squads and police raids, this chapter explores the meaning of the repetition of state violence and its visual economy. Through a look at a series of photographs of antiblack violence in dialogue with "The Police Raid" vignette, I consider how Afro-paradise is the accumulation of repeated images and actions that are both political and diasporic in nature. As Susan Sontag observes, "photography has kept company with death ever since cameras were invented" (2002, 87). Photography is a tool for documenting war, but it should not be read as an objective perspective. Instead, it gives us insight into the politics of the visual. This is particularly relevant for engaging with the black body. "Black bodies in pain for public consumption have been an American spectacle for centuries" (Alexander 1994, 92). "Black bodies on silver gelatin or digital prints constitute the penultimate other—distant and familiar, ready and replenishing" (Brown 2014,

195). The visual economy of black suffering is an "image world" that "captures the complexity and specificity" (Poole 1997, 7) of conditions of blackness in Afro-paradise. An image world is a space in which "representations flow from place to place, person to person, culture to culture, and class to class" (ibid.). The twentieth-century images that I examine here were published in local newspapers and can be read as part of an image world of black suffering that circulates, producing narratives of the black body in pain across time and space. It is not accidental that these photographs conjure memories of lynching photography in the United States (Goldsby 2006). Spectacular images of the black body in pain reveal the performative, transnational nature of Afro-paradise at the same time that they speak to us about the nature of race and antiblackness in Brazil.

Inscribing Blackness

In the early morning hours of July 17, 2001, soterepolitanos living along the Estrada Velha do Cabrito (the access road for São Bartolomeu Park in the Subúrbio Ferroviário region) stumbled on the corpses of three young black men.[2] Nearby residents claimed they had heard shots around two o'clock in the morning but understandably had not ventured outside to see what was going on. The Fifth Precinct civil police investigators who went to the scene

Figure 4.2. Snapshot of the morning after a death-squad murder, Estrada Velha do Cabrito, July 17, 2001 (photo from *A Tarde*).

were unable to identify the bodies. The first was wearing a white tank top, jeans, a cream belt, and white socks. The second was thin and tall, wearing a green tank top, black belt, white socks, and black leather shoes. The third looked similar to the first two and wore a black shirt, gray jeans, a black swim Speedo, and was barefoot. Only one young man carried a hint of his identity—a key ring with the name "Léo" on it. According to *A Tarde,* experts from the Nucleus of Crimes against Life of the Technical Police Department estimated that the young men were between the ages of eighteen and twenty-two (Rodrigues, Lindsay, and Oliveira 2001). Each of the bodies carried the ritualistic markings of a death-squad killing: Their shirts had been pulled up over their faces, their hands tied behind their backs with a thick rope, and they had each been shot multiple times in the head.

We have seen this scene before, are seeing it now, and will see it again.

On September 19, 2007, a disturbing photo of the murdered bodies of five young black men was displayed on the front page of *A Tarde.* Bloody and unrecognizable, in wooden coffins laid across the green grass, the bodies were depicted in a gruesome snapshot of the morning after a death-squad murder. Residents of Bairro da Paz, a peripheral neighborhood along Avenida Parallela in Salvador, had found the young men the previous day. The five were shot to death in a ravine. Four of the victims had had their necks tied together by a thick rope. Curiously, investigators found shell casings exclusively used by the armed forces (forças armadas) and crack rocks in the victims' pockets (Cirino 2007).

The scenes from Bairro da Paz and Estrada Velha do Cabrito, Nova Brasilia, or any of the other dozen *pontas de desova* of Salvador are repetitions; entangled scenarios caught up in palimpsestic time and space. Their frames spill over into one another. Graphically, bodies sit alongside the road. A crowd gathers around them almost as if they are part of the living scene. The bodies are not neatly ordered in the way one might expect to see bodies in a funeral. They are also not carelessly, arbitrarily strewn. The murderers have placed the bodies on the grass on the side of the road, face up, purposefully in full public view. The images of bloody and often unrecognizable victims of death-squad/police killings on the pages of Bahia's newspapers ignite a series of visual associations. The lynchings of black people thousands of miles away in the United States in the twentieth century, like that of Nease Gillepsie, John Gillespie, "Jack" Dillingham, Henry Lee, and George Irwin, in Salisbury, North Carolina, on August 6, 1906, resonate with these death-squad scenes (Smith 2013b); so do the twentieth-century and twenty-first-century racially charged killings of black youth in the Untied States by police officers, like the death of Michael Brown on August 9, 2014. We need only remember that Michael Brown's body lay in the middle of his neighborhood street for four hours, while a crowd of neighbors, friends, and family, including his mother, looked on in horror, waiting for the coroner to pick up his body. And although the African diaspora experience is not a monolith, and we must take into account temporal, political, social, and cultural specificities, there is something about the somatic resonance between these disparate black bodies across the diaspora that presents ethnographic evidence of a common experience that we must listen to even if we cannot fully articulate what it is or how it happened. Like a refracted mirror reflection, each scene reflects similar other ones of killed, tortured, or mutilated black bodies put on horrific display within communities as a sign of "warning"—evidence of the excess of transnational antiblackness.

In Bahia, death-squad assassins intentionally and spectacularly position the bodies of the dead—death without sepulchre (Espinheira 2004). Scenarios of the black body in pain, killed and often tortured by state agents, project multiple messages; some for the witnesses, some for the victims' communities, and some for the city, the state, the nation, and the world. The public exhibition in peripheral communities is a calling card. At times bodies are openly exposed, but sometimes their graves are shallow. In Bahia, the murderers pull the victims' shirts over their heads so that any survivors cannot identify them. They use thick rope to tie their hands or to tie them to each other. Bairro da Paz and Estrada Velha do Cabrito connect with Nova Brasilia and Paripe. Calculated and staged, these killings follow the haunting script of Afro-paradise.

When we think of Afro-paradise as a paradoxical juncture between the consumption of the black body and its killing, we are not limiting the scope of the definition to spaces renowned for Afro-tourism. The production of black exotic spaces is not exclusively tied to localities. In other words, the problem exists beyond tourist cities like Bahia. As an exotic site of entertainment, the fetishization of the black body is also aligned with the deterritorialized body. Like the connection between U.S. lynching and minstrelsy, Afro-paradise is a conceptual space that can be produced and reproduced across miles of difference, from Salvador all the way to New Orleans (Dunn 2007).

The death-squad murders at Bairro da Paz (2007) and Estrada Velha do Cabrito (2001) were reprises—not exact performances of what has already been, but incomplete mimeses, and as such, inherently theatrical (Diamond 1996).The spectacle of policing the black body, like the script of a play, is performed individually by casts of characters in different places according to the creative interpretation of the authors of the moment. They are etchings over that still show the traces of earlier impressions.

As discussed in chapter 1, during the epoch of colonialism and slavery, the Portuguese defined state authority and the social contract publicly and repeatedly in the heart of Salvador. The actions of the early police forces in colonial Bahia echoed those of Vidigal in Rio de Janeiro. These embodied performances evolved over time, changing shape and form but neverthe-less maintaining their essence. And yet beyond being inheritors of the past, death-squad/police actions are transtemporal and transspatial performances: scenarios. The characters of these performances are the police officers and their victims. The plot is the torture of the black body to maintain the hege-monic white, patriarchal social order. The narrative is the story of colonial war. The audience is the family members, neighbors, and loved ones of the dead.

Returning to Estrada Velha do Cabrito in 2001, it is safe to estimate that the three bodies lay in the middle of this neighborhood, alongside the road, in plain view, for at least six hours. It is broad daylight in this photo. The murders happened around two o'clock in the morning, and the picture was taken no earlier than eight o'clock (and this is a very generous estimate based on the sunlight). Ideally, no one would disturb the corpses until the police got there. With no further knowledge than what is printed in this article, we are left to assume that the bodies have been undisturbed or at least left in their original places. Normally it is the job of the civil police to investigate and register all crimes, including murder. However, for several weeks in July 2001, the civil and military police of Bahia were taking part in a city-wide police strike. The slow response time could be attributable to the work stoppage, though it would be hasty to suggest that this incredible lag was entirely caused by the walkout. If we associate the civil police, we can suggest that the delay in registering and attending to the scene has to do with the nature of police violence as performance.[3] That is, the civil police were slow to arrive partly because they were on strike, but they could also have been slow to arrive in order to broadcast a message to the community. By leaving these bodies in plain view for hours, it is as if the death squad responsible for this *chacina* continues to speak long after the act of killing is over. This ritualized murder and placement of the bodies was about disciplining space and performing power. Putting the bodies directly in plain sight, and then making sure, through ritualistic markers, that people know who did the killings, allows death squads to continue to define the terms of the spectacle and performance, even in absentia.

Like the signs above police modules in Salvador, these spectacles broadcast messages that exceed the boundaries of momentary revenge, discipline, or punishment; they expand into the realm of the race/gender/sexuality/class politics of state control. They erase the suffering and sentience of the dead, dehumanizing them. Further, they invisibilize the suffering of the family and community members, rendering both the bodies and the community ghosts.

Neither blackness nor state violence are transcendent categories, despite similarities of process and experience in different domains. Consequently, we must pay attention to spatial and temporal specificities.[4] Yet, although the phenomenon of Afro-paradise is salient and readily recognizable in a place like Bahia, what of cities like Ferguson, Missouri? Can Afro-paradise emerge here as well? If so, what would it look like? We know, for example, that St. Louis, like Salvador, is a city that has been defined by its relationship to black culture—including jazz and the blues. We also know that the history of racial tension in Ferguson is long and tied closely with the economic and cultural politics of the region (Vartabedian 2014). The resonance of the transnational black experience with state violence requires us to at least consider this possibility. Understanding state violence against black bodies as performance zones provides one step in unpacking these connections. Guy Debord's observations on the nature of spectacle helps us think about the transtemporal and transspatial meaning of this violence. The spectacle of state violence is "the sector [of society] which concentrates all gazing and all consciousness" ([1970] 1994, 2). Here, the concentration returns to the black body in pain.

Palimpsestic Embodiment

If state violence against the black body in pain is torture, then the black body is also a wandering ghost, and we must think of its life and its afterlife as performances (Phelan 1993). Indeed, Elaine Scarry makes a cognitive association between torture and performance or drama in her discussion of the body in pain and war. For Scarry, torture is built upon "repeated acts of display" that result in the "production of a *fantastic* illusion of power" (1985, 28; my emphasis). Torture is a "grotesque piece of compensatory drama" (ibid.), a performance staged through the spectacular and the fantastical. By extension, methodologically, performance is a useful tool. It allows us to, following Michel de Certeau (1984) and Diana Taylor (2003), move away from an overreliance on language and discourse in our social analyses of race toward a framework that considers the ways that gestures, looks, feeling, seeing, and hearing define the material realities of the nation, and particularly the lived reality of blackness.[5] This conversation returns us to "Todos Negros."

In 2007, twenty-five years after he took his fateful photograph, Luiz Morier reflected on his piece and gave us further context for the scene. He recalls:

The feeling I had was of humiliation. I felt the humiliation of the scene. Those who were humiliated: people with their worker's cards in hand. I could tell they were not criminals because criminals do not use the types of clothes that they were using. It's obvious that they dress better than they were dressed that day. They were simple people, humble, all black. I felt it was an act of humiliation. They were really being humiliated there, carried along by the neck like slaves (Ramos 2007).

Morier's thoughts leave us with multiple impressions. Not only are all of the prisoners black and the police officer white, but *blackness* and *whiteness* are, in part, being defined by this moment as well. The scene presents historicity/ repetition (like slaves) and affect (humiliation), and an absence of democracy paralleled by the presence of injustice (they were not criminals).[6] Morier articulates something that we already know intuitively when we see this photograph: that this has happened before. What is often simply thought of as anecdotal knowledge—black people in Brazil are always already read as suspects by the police, and contemporary practices of policing are parallel to those enacted during slavery—suddenly becomes material in this image. A temporal accumulation, "Todos Negros" conjures the long history of polic- ing the black body and the ratification of that violence and its implications.

The photo is overdetermined by the masculinization of state authority and the decidedly gendered ways that the state chooses to execute the spectacular punishment of the black body publicly. It conjures the heteropatriarchy of the social contract. It is the colonial phallus once again (Mbembe 2001). These men are not only being arrested but also being emasculated and humiliated in ways that infantilize and degrade them: this is a performance of racial patriarchy. Although women are glaringly absent (and also absent from most images of spectacular state violence against the black body in the news me- dia), we should not read their absence as an absence of the state's repression of black women's bodies. Instead, the concealment of women's suffering at the hands of state repression illustrates that this is a drama written by men, for men, about men. It is a heteropatriarchal fantasy with homoerotic subtexts and a reflection of the material realities of lived experience.[7]

The power of "Todos Negros" lies in its uncanny familiarity and raw disclo- sure: We know this scene even though it is variation. We see in it the image of African women imprisoned in nineteenth-century Dar es Salaam (figure 4.3), for example.

We do not know their names or how or why they became chained together in this work gang, yet we cannot help but notice the similarities between their chains and the ropes around the necks of the men in "Todos Negros"—a refracted image; incomplete mimesis.

Figure 4.3. "Africa, Tanganyika, Dar es Salaam—Women convicts working on road" (photo by E. M. Santos between 1890 and 1927).

Scenes of the black body bound by the state recall one another in ways that give us an uneasy sensation of familiarity. And this sparks our interest, as onlookers, and creates a profound sense of déjà vu–cum-recognition.

This painting by Debret (figure 4.4) is the same one I analyzed in chapter 1 in the discussion of the pelourinho. In 1994, Clóvis Moura published a reproduction of Morier's "Todos Negros" juxtaposed with a snapshot of the left-hand side of Debret's painting *Espèce de châtiment que s'exécute dans les diverses grandes places des villes*. The images appeared on the cover of his groundbreaking text, *Dialética Radical do Brasil Negro*. In that book, Moura argues, in part, that Brazil has been historically defined by a series of racial-economic antagonisms that extend from the epoch of slavery to the present. Moura focuses on the portion of Debret's painting portraying four black men roped together, waiting to be whipped on the pelourinho. The men are guarded by two white soldiers/police officers who are standing to the left of the frame. The eerie resemblance between the two snapshots of time—"Todos Negros" and *Espèce de châtiment*—one witnessed through the lens and the other through the paintbrush, captures something visually that is difficult to put into simple words.[8] State violence in Brazil is a racialized, gendered, classed, and sexualized embodied practice that defines subjectivity

Figure 4.4. Detail of four men tied together from *Espèce de châtiment qui s´exécute dans les diverses grandes places des villes* by Jean-Baptiste Debret, Rio de Janeiro, 1826.

in conversation with time. This continuing revision leaves traces of the past behind and produces the calcified core of the nation-state.

Scenarios

Diana Taylor defines the scenario in the traditional sense of its use in the theater to describe "a sketch or outline of the plot of a play, giving particulars of the scenes, situations, etc." (2003, 28). She expands this definition to life away from the stage as well, focusing on repetition as its central dynamic. Building on the work of Roland Barthes, Taylor argues, "Like Barthes's mythical speech, [the scenario] consists of 'material which has already been worked on.' . . . Its portable framework bears the weight of accumulative repeats" (ibid.). The scenario is that which "makes visible, yet again, what is already there: the ghosts, the images, the stereotypes" (ibid.). What we see when we look at Bairro da Paz, Estrada Velha do Cabrito, "Todos Negros," and Debret's painting are scenarios; as Taylor elaborates, "scenarios conjure up past situations, at times so profoundly internalized by a society that no one remembers the precedence" (2003, 32). The "scenario" is a cross-temporal, cross-spatial model for understanding social structures and behaviors (Taylor 2003, 29). To analyze scenarios, just as we would theater, we must pay attention to "milieu and corporeal behaviors such as gestures, attitudes, and tones not reducible to language" (2003, 28). Such an analysis integrates behaviors and actions, or repertoire. By employing a theory of scenarios to understand police brutality, I move beyond a unilateral discursive focus on racism and race toward an engagement with the totality of actions, behaviors, space, and narrative, active in the social structure at a given moment, an engagement that also takes into account the past that still haunts the present. In short, contemporary society re-performs the familiar dramatic plot of conquest/ colonialism/slavery.

Moreover, the lens of performance extends the milieu of corporeal action beyond the analytical frameworks of discourse and language. In part because of the dynamic of repetition, scenarios of antiblack state violence are entangled (Mbembe 2001). The parchment of the palimpsest—the body—is overlain by layers of violent reenactment, and the faint shadows of the text (discourses of race, violence, and the social contract) are the temporal accumulation of knowledge (sometimes conscious, sometimes subconscious) that remain embedded in the body and retained in our corporeal memory. Therefore, in palimpsestic embodiment, violent encounters iterated in the present are troubled; recited sketches, plots, scenes, and narratives that emerge and reemerge. Ephemeral, nonreproducible knowledge nevertheless holds memory in its repetition (Taylor 2003, 20). The body is a repository of temporal and spatial information. The political conditions of racial antagonism, the violence and uneven resource distribution that the state has enacted over time, and the scenarios that (re)stage the inscription of these politics onto the body all replay gestures of colonial encounter. Scenes of the black body in pain link police violence to the state, the social contract, and global racial antagonisms.

As we have seen, colonial memory fundamentally structures the space of Salvador. As discussed in chapter 1, the black body in pain is a transfer point for defining the Bahian social contract on the one hand, and Bahia's identity as an Afro-paradise on the other. Palimpsestic embodiment engenders this process of transference by interlocking present, past, and future.

The idea of a multilayered embodied practice caught in palimpsestic time and space brings us back to a discussion of entanglement. Entanglement is "not a series but an interlocking of presents, pasts, and futures that retain their depths of other presents, pasts, and futures, each age bearing, altering, and maintaining the previous ones" (Mbembe 2001, 15). Familiarity strikes us when we catch a glimpse of state violence against the black body, particularly when visual representations (photographs, paintings, or even the theater) capture these moments. We may not be in the same exact place each time, and we may not be witnessing the same people, but the plot, characters, and mise-en-scène are familiar.

The position of the bodies and their relationships to one another also remind us of the important differences between times. Although Debret and "Todos Negros" refer to the same city (Rio de Janeiro), they obviously depict vastly different points in the nation's history. The first is set during the height of slavery in Brazil. The second is 125 years after legal abolition. The whipping that Debret portrays at the pelourinho is a decidedly public event, evidenced by the cloud of onlookers standing in the back to the right-hand side of the picture. Morier captures a moment intended to be clandestine even though it occurred on the side of the road in broad daylight. The police officer's evident displeasure with Morier for taking photographs of the scene underscores the

Figure 4.5. A military police officer arrests two men, stepping on one man's head in Rio de Janeiro, 1997 (photo by Luiz Morier).

intended secrecy of the raid.[9] Debret's painting clearly shows the fate of the tethered men: torture on the whipping post. We do not know the fate of the men in Morier's photo, although we can infer several possible story lines by reading this scene in conversation with other similar occurrences. Our lack of knowing, however, is what, in part, makes Morier's photo so disturbing.[10]

In 1997, Luiz Morier took another now-famous picture in Rio de Janeiro. In it (figure 4.5), a police officer steps on a young black man's head while he and another black man next to him both lay on the ground. A series of onlookers in the background watches the scene. In analyzing this photograph, I cannot help but return to Debret's rendition of the public whipping and the picture of the scene at Estrada Velha do Cabrito. In both there is an intergenerational, interracial crowd of people standing off in the distance watching, kept at bay. Morier's 1997 photo also recalls the photo of a police officer stepping on a black man's head on the beach in Ondina in Salvador in 2007.

What happened in Rio de Janeiro in 1997 (figure 4.5) and in Salvador in 2007 (figure 4.6) bear strong resemblance. These public scenes were designed to spectacularly put black people in their "proper place" (Caldwell 2007; Gonzalez 1983; Gonzalez and Hasenbalg 1982).

Scenes of black residents being stepped on by military police invoke discipline (both altered and bounded by violence) because the violence not only

Figure 4.6. A military police officer steps on a vendor's head on Ondina Beach, Salvador, in January 2007.

causes harm, but is also what the police enact in order to produce effects (Foucault [1977] 2003).[11] State agents step on these heads because they are black. At the same time, the fact of their being stepped on concretizes the victims' blackness: a "fact-of-blackness" moment (Fanon 1967). The very enactment of spectacular disciplining solidifies the racial contract (Mills 1997). It also marks the body as the site of accumulated political, social, and historical meaning. These are dehumanizing acts that define the boundaries of citizenship. Ervin Staub (1989) argues that dehumanization has been a necessary antecedent to genocide around the world. We see this process begin to unfold here.

When the police identify, detain, torture, kill, or just harass black people, both in public and out of sight, these acts of violence mark bodies and the spaces around them (the people watching, the streets of the neighborhood) as black, expendable, noncitizen, ghosts. These acts also produce blackness as a collective, transnational, affective experience. Police officers and death-squad agents are *identifying* black people when they enact violence on the black body and *producing* blackness through these acts. In turn, these moments also produce whiteness, albeit with a slightly different relationship to subjectivity. Police aggression engenders whiteness by enforcing white supremacy rather than reflecting the white subjectivity of the police officers involved. Like the actors in "The Police Raid" vignette, the police wear white masks; state terror is also layered and can be peeled back.

Reading police violence as a disciplining practice expands upon the concept of palimpsestic embodiment yet again. The performativity of this violence emerges precisely because these moments are not singular but a summation of interlocking effects of actions. The performative exceeds the momentary into the historical (Butler 1997). Understanding these spaces as accumulations helps us to locate this conversation and its repercussions in the framework of performance and the grotesque.

"The Police Raid": White Masks

Performed by Culture Shock, "The Police Raid" reenacts a police invasion on a peripheral community. As a critique of the hidden narratives of race, "The Police Raid" vignette is a parody laced with dry, not-so-funny-when-you-think-about-it humor. Some audience members laugh when the scene is presented, but most of the laughter we hear, in my assessment, is a nervous laughter akin to relief—*this isn't real . . . is it?* The performance is silly in that the white masks and the hands stretched out like guns seem more like a child's game than a theater presentation. However, it is that simplicity, transparency, and tone that make the piece deeply disquieting. Thus the parody makes you cry and laugh. Its affect draws you into the re-memory of past and present terror.

Like the vignettes before it, "The Police Raid" re-presents state violence as a scenario of racial contact, employing restored behavior to make a political intervention. The result is a biting critique that lays bare the repetitions of Afro-paradise. The performance is rich and layered, with many complex, revealing aspects. However, here I would like to focus primarily on the symbolic use of white masks in the vignette. The masks come to represent the complex politics of racial subjectivity in Brazil, white supremacy, and state violence as restored behavior. As a result, the seemingly simple act of masking becomes a packed site of meaning production.

The vignette begins when three actors storm the stage wearing white masks. The "police" enter the circle/stage, engaged in a series of movements, gestures, and words that suggest sequential connections between the local politics of state terror, the transnational politics of imperialism, and the global politics of antiblack violence. Their representation of the police is not meant to be realistic but symbolic. Actors use white masks as symbols of police corruption and white supremacy, and they signal this symbolism

Figure 4.7. Culture Shock performance of "The Police Raid" vignette.

through incomplete mimesis. The masks distinguish them from their fellow actors, marking them as "police" rather than "residents," and also connect them to other symbols of genocide—like the Bahian police's familiar use of masks in the everyday.

Incomplete mimesis is an important theatrical tool. Elin Diamond (1996) suggests that theater cannot rid itself of the impetus to mimic, the search for the real. The theater is infinitely caught up in the politics of representation. But its mimicry is always incomplete, always not quite how things "really are." There are no illusions of reality in "The Police Raid," yet we witness the *negatives* (refracted representations) that the vignette produces by subverting the very thing it fails to re-create—in this case the police (Phelan 1993).

Not only do the (imaginary) guns drawn and the words said ("Get on the ground and stay quiet!") allow the audience to identify the scene quickly (this is a police raid), but also the white cloth masks the actors wear (figure 4.7) are an obvious play on the masks worn by police at times to cover their faces while engaging in either illegal or overtly political acts. For example, picketing police wore ski masks during the statewide police strike in Bahia in July 2001 (figure 4.8). (Those masks were a double entendre, props to hide the identity of the police officers engaging in an illegal strike and also threats, symbolic reminders to the public of what happens when police officers ter-

Figure 4.8. Masked military police officers during a 2001 police strike, Salvador (photo from *A Tarde*).

rorize communities in the middle of the night.) Police officers participating in death squads often use these same masks to hide their identity when they go on assassination missions. In other contexts, the news media depict police accused of corruption wearing masks (usually black ski masks) protecting their identities by hiding their faces. Thus, the masks exemplify the intersection between mystery and illegality that characterizes police terror. They are a widely recognizable representation of the magical state's subversive tendencies.

But the masks that the actors wear in the Culture Shock piece take this familiar image and invert it, shifting iconic black ski masks into *white* cloth masks—a symbolic association between police violence, white supremacy, and global imperialism. As such, the white mask is an allegorical critique of police violence that frames blackness and whiteness, colonized and colonizer, as antagonistic relationships less about individual racial identity than social relationality and political positionality: metonymical whiteness and white supremacy. "The Police Raid" scene recasts the terms of racism outside of individual racial identification and racial subjectivity into a discussion of the relationship between performance, embodiment, racial subjectivity, and positionality. It also suggests that the process of racial formation is part of the palimpsest of Afro-paradise. Race is layered, historical, etched-over enactment that is defined at the site of the body and in turn defines the nation itself.

When the MC from *Stop to Think* breaks the frozen pose and begins to walk around, taking the white masks off of each of the "police officers," he also reveals the black faces underneath the masks, complicating the racial imagery of this moment. The audience always knows that the actors representing the police, under the masks, are phenotypically black because of the familiarity with the actors at this point, and besides, only their faces (not their arms) are covered. Pulling the masks off is a conceptual move to portray the multilayered raciality of this scenario. This action challenges the argument that black officers perpetrating violence against black citizens are not enacting racism and white supremacy. (Indeed, at the time when Culture Shock was performing *Stop to Think,* government officials and academics were making widespread claims that police violence had nothing to do with racism in Bahia; militantes heard such comments at the state's public hearings on police violence following the vigil in 2005 [see chapter 2]. Rather, it says, racism is an enactment of race as much as it is a performance enacted by racialized individuals. Whiteness and blackness are at least partially defined by the encounter between the police and the community. In other words, racial formation is a layered performance. The white masks cast the identity of the invaders as obvious on one hand, and a mystery on the other. Is this a death squad? Is it a legitimate police operation? Are we in Fazenda Grande do Retiro or are we somewhere else?

As the MC pulls off each white mask, he peels back layers of embodied meaning. He allegorically suggests that in the everyday performance of racism, racial violence is palimpsestic embodiment: an etched-over performance. There are many strata layered here. The first is racial. The perpetrators of racial violence wear white masks even if they are not racially classified as white themselves. This is not just a comment on policing but also a broader observation about the social process of race making. Culture Shock encourages us to take a constructivist approach to reading race in this context, returning us to the conversation on internal colonialism that we took up in chapter 2. This deindividualizes racism, positing it instead as a hegemonic regime of truth that orders the world according to essentialist hierarchies and racial epistemologies. The association between blackness and criminality in this logic is partly why the police disproportionately target people of African descent with dark-brown skin in their violent assaults, not necessarily because the police who target the victims are white in appearance. Nevertheless, as Sobrevivente intimates, the command of the police force is white. This can be taken to mean that either those giving the orders are classified as white, or that the police power structure is constructed on the premise of white supremacy. Symbolically we cannot help but remember the "white hand," with all of its necessary historical connotations. In returning to the white hand, another layer becomes readable: the masks are a symbolic reference to the history of antiblack policing in Bahia from colonialism through today. Underneath the masks are traces of the past.

The white masks over the black faces of the actors indicate a complicated relationship between racial identity and structures of power. This returns us to the discussion of the concept of metonymical whiteness. The masks draw our attention to the body as an important site of racial performance. Black police officers wear white masks that are invisible in the everyday but nevertheless always there.

Although we cannot separate police officers' personal histories from their roles as police officers, we can understand their roles as just that—roles that are instilled with histories and meanings that are enacted according to social scripts. These roles have unique historical trajectories. The geographic and historical disjuncture between the police and residents is messy. As mentioned previously, often the same police officers who invade peripheral neighborhoods and kill with impunity are classified within society as black, and many live in neighborhoods similar to those that they invade (Hoffman-French 2013; Ramos and Musumeci 2005; Santos 2002). However, although black police officers who are from peripheral neighborhoods are not necessarily geographically disconnected from the spaces they invade—and, in fact, their personal histories may share a similar trajectory with those they victimize—as agents of state control they embody racial meaning at the moment of the police raid: metonymical whiteness.

Racism in Culture Shock's interpretation is the effect of a hegemonic racial epistemology that situates blackness as criminal, marginal, and desolate, and whiteness as superior, powerful, and upstanding. This is the cognitive logic behind the genocidal assemblage. When police officers engage in repressive violence against people living in peripheral communities, this violence inscribes "whiteness" and "blackness" onto the bodies of the social actors. This is not to say that race is fluid or that it can be removed and put on easily like a mask, but rather to say that the embodiment of race has as much to do with its performative enactment as it does with its descriptive, social, or even historical identity. Whiteness is a mask that can be *limitedly* assumed by nonwhite people, if and only if, they distinguish themselves from blackness in some way to establish distance and authority. In this case, the distancing is through violent acts of rupture (police violence). These acts are fleeting and may or may not have a bearing on how the social actors who play the role of the police themselves experience violence or are affected by racism in their daily lives, but during this fraction of time, race is enacted symbolically. Violently repressing blackness is a key element of structures of power built upon white supremacy.

We can only get a more complete understanding of Afro-paradise by cross-reading the explicit messages of harmonious blackness that the city portrays against the quieter messages it simultaneously broadcasts throughout the city—like the white masks that Culture Shock uses in "The Police Raid." As Taylor suggests, physical location "contribute[s] to the viewer's understanding of what might conceivably transpire there . . . the place allows us to think about the possibilities of action" (2003, 29). In the social imagination, Brazil's peripheral neighborhoods are spaces of poverty and violence. The relationship between the scenario of police violence and the periphery defined not only by the periphery's literal geographic role as backdrop to this scene (remember we are set in Fazenda Grande do Retiro), but also by how *police violence* defines the periphery socially, spatially, and epistemologically.

This daily performance acts out a narrative of race and produces racialized bodies and racialized spaces, defining the tensions between them. Performance and performativity produce the city-space (Lefebvre 1991).

There are political stakes to this claim. By situating performance as a component central to the production of space in Salvador, we both interrogate the role race plays in defining the landscape as well as the role that performance plays in racial formation. This allows us to disrupt hegemonic social structures and affirm the possibility of subversive identities in order to lay the groundwork for recognizing the collective identity struggles of marginalized peoples, particularly black Brazilians. It also shifts the discourse on racism away from essentialist notions typified by easily identifiable, clearly marked racial bodies toward more complex structural processes (Bonilla-Silva 1997). Policing is not, at its base, a matter of controlling criminality or protecting and serving; rather, it is at times spectacular torture and at times a disciplining strategy of control, and oftentimes this control concentrates on the colonial, internally displaced black body. Brazil's racial state and Bahia's colonial war make and unmake black bodies through violence.

Restored Behavior

Restored behavior is what gives "The Police Raid" vignette meaning for the audience. Revisiting the video of the performance, we hear a mixture of apprehension, fear, and murmuring from the crowd as the actors storm onto stage during the raid. It is clear to spectators that the actors wearing white masks represent the police and that this is a reenactment of a police raid. When they storm into the circle, they do so shouting, with imaginary guns drawn. The refracted mimicry of this representation replaces physical guns with imaginary ones, emphasizing the guns in this "real-life" enactment as extensions of the police officers' bodies themselves, a continuum that extends to the police officers and their militaristic, repressive charge. Their interactions with residents are constantly aggressive, from the screaming and cursing to the acts of pointing their "guns" at the backs and heads of the frightened residents.

The "residents" (actors) are also defined by their embodied practices. They scream as well, raising their hands in fear as they run around the stage/circle being chased by the police. This fear becomes their identifying marker. At no point in the vignette are the names of the residents, or even defining descriptions of the context of this raid, mentioned. We do not know explicitly who is raiding, why, or even what time of day it is. What we know about this scene is informed by our memories or prior interpretation of police violence and the cues we gather from the enactment itself. At no time during the raid do the police identify themselves to say, "This is the police." They do not show badges, don uniforms, or even ride in a police car, imaginary or otherwise. They simply rush in wearing the white masks, with an intonation and script that is familiar enough to the crowd that we, the audience, implicitly know what is going on, just like the "Terrorism" vignette. The meaning is always implied, but it is this subtle implication that makes the performance so powerful.

The utterance of the neighborhood name "Plataforma" immediately brings time and space into play in the performance. At this moment, we realize that we are witnessing a scenario that has been replayed across the city of Salvador. In the final chapter I discuss this utterance at length, but for now I emphasize the act of calling out the name of this neighborhood as a signal of identification with the commentary being made, and the audience's desire to insert itself into this piece and symbolically join with those who cry out against this abuse (Elam 1997). The woman in the audience recognized herself in this performance—her memories, her family, her community, her life. With this utterance she becomes the site of palimpsestic embodiment: affective déjà vu.

The Grotesque

Brazil's horizon of death erases the black body, not in the sense that it deletes it completely from existence, because it renders black people and black bodies ghosts (Ferreira da Silva 2009). These ghosts are often the only thing that remains in the political aftermath of colonialism (Mbembe 2001). And yet the spectacular display of black bodies in full public view also ties the black body paradoxically to the earth, marking it as a hyperreal space. Regardless, these scenarios at best ignore and at worst erase black sentience and black suffering, marking black people as dead and invisible. This is not to say that blackness can truly be reduced to this state of death and invisibility, but rather that this is the political project of state terror and its counterpart, Afro-paradise. I use the term *sentience* to refer to human feeling, and emphasize that this violence marks black people as nonhuman by erasing the suffering that the victims and the families experience with these deaths (Scott 2000; Wilderson 2010). The materiality of blackness comes into being through the process of inscribing blackness onto the body and the landscape by marking bodies, communities, and neighborhoods as black and expendable spaces.

If state violence is a spatial project, it is a spectacular, collective experience as well. There is something grotesque about scenarios of black death that returns us once again to the carnivalesque. Afro-paradise is not, as Mikhail Bakhtin argues of the carnivalesque, subversive in nature; it is not "opposed [to] the official and serious tone" of mainstream culture (1984, 4). Afro-paradise is not a liberatory space. But it does manifest Bakhtin's definition of grotesque realism. "Not only parody in its narrow sense but all other forms of grotesque realism degrade, bring down to earth, turn their subject into flesh" (Bakhtin 1984, 20). It is the "indivisible whole" of the body politic, its simultaneously "cosmic, social, and bodily elements" (19).

Yet Afro-paradise underscores the irony of grotesque realism's "all-popular festive and utopian aspect" (19). The festive and the utopic are merely masks that hide a deeper, more cynical reality of violence and spectacle. The images that I have presented here, and the image world of antiblack violence that circulates in Brazil and elsewhere, establishes the paradox of Afro-paradise. These images and their repetition render the black body both hypervisible and invisible simultaneously. The grotesque realism of the spectacle of the black body in pain ironically turns the black body into flesh, translating what was once a ghost back to the material world. This process manifests itself exactly as parody in "The Police Raid." This parody re-performs the everyday parody of black life that occurs in the space of state terror.

While violence is an abstracting process, then, it is also a process that defines social and material identities. Palimpsestic embodiment is the summation of both the erasure of the black body and its etching over. Etching is the proclamation of blackness as the symbolic image of the nation-state: the face of Afro-paradise. State terror erases the black body at the same time that it puts this body on display and attempts to divorce it from community and suffering in the process. Death-squad assassinations, through dismemberment, torture, spectacle, and performance, sever the dead, their families, their friends, and their neighborhoods from the imagined social community. Allen Feldman (1991) contends that the interplay between violence and the body produces meaning in excess of repression and disempowerment during moments of state conflict: bodies that are violated/violenced are not simply fractured by this violence but become, through these violent acts, coded with meaning. Specifically, "political violence is a mode of transcription; it circulates codes from one prescribed historiographic surface or agent to another (1991, 7). Competing transcripts define the black body in Brazil, fracturing it such that subjectivation is accelerated. This is the point where violence produces racial meaning. One of these transcripts is police violence. The black body is both made and unmade by torture, ritual, and the unspoken, coded discourses of blackness that narrate these moments.

Palimpsestic embodiment, an extension of Afro-paradise, is located at the site of the body, and it also defines communities and families as expendable spaces located outside of the nation. As Bakhtin notes, "Manifestations of this life refer not to the isolated biological individual, not to the private, egotistic 'economic man,' but to the collective ancestral body of all the people" (1984, 20). State terror generates neighborhoods, people, families, and communities.

The militaristic strategies that police special shock forces use to subdue "potential suspects" in the periphery are both deadly and intensely racialized. These strategies are also spatially and temporally defined.

INTERLUDE V

Reprise

MC: They invaded . . . they invaded Fazenda Grande, San Martins, Sussuarana, Bom Júa, Liberdade, Alto de Coutos . . .

A woman from the audience calls out "Plataforma."

MC: But where are the people?
ACTORS: They are dying.

5 In and Out of the Ineffable

> ... the entire call and response performance existed in an
> emotionally powerful relation to absence—to the silenced and
> the dead who would never testify. The presence of these women,
> and the shadows they brought into the hearing room, evoked
> the historical depth and recesses of their witness that could not
> be captured in literal speech. Refusing to ground their language
> in individualized knots of the traumatic, these women invoked
> a dialogic of presencing the unreachable, of giving "impossible
> witness."
>
> —Allen Feldman (2004, 176)

For those seeing *Stop to Think* for the first time, "The Police Raid" vignette comes as a surprise. Unlike previous vignettes in the play, no transition marks a break from the previous scene. Actors enter suddenly and abruptly, loudly and physically barging into the circle of onlookers that make up the imaginary dividing line between onstage and offstage. Then the frame of the scene becomes more apparent (this is a police raid) and the audience begins to react. At Fazenda Grande do Retiro, several onlookers responded verbally and physically. Some children in the audience began crying, and at least one spectator screamed, ducked, and ran to the other side of the circle to hide behind other spectators—another crossing of the barrier between offstage and onstage. Apprehension, fear, and laughter all worked together to frame the vignette, bringing the audience to a point of recognition (this is a police raid), fear/apprehension/humor (I do not know what will happen next, but I know I'm safe because this is just a play), and identification (I too am vulnerable to these random moments of violence just as I am taken off guard in this performance).

The actors then freeze, briefly speaking: "They invaded . . . they invaded . . ." The words refer to the experience of neighborhood police raids. The subject of the phrase is purposefully vague. *They* are the police, but they are also the colonizers, the imperialists, the military who perpetrate the war on terror. "They" are oppressors everywhere. We do not know who invades, but we soon learn the locations that are the targets. As audience members, we move with the words from our immediate physical surroundings to Afghanistan and Iraq and then back again. The same "police" who are invading the circle/space of the stage are not only the people who invade the Mideast in the war on terror but are also the very police who invade the periphery every day. A lone actor recites a litany of peripheral neighborhoods frequently targeted by police raids, including Fazenda Grande where the performance is being held. "They invaded, they invaded Fazenda Grande, San Martins, Sussuarana, Bom Júa, Liberdade, Alto de Coutos." These communities are familiar to the audience. Many of the theater troupes that participated in the festival were from these very neighborhoods. Many of the people in the community know these spaces as well. Finally, in a punctuating moment of synergy between the audience, the play, and the actors, a woman from the crowd standing just outside of the circle calls out "Plataforma."

Adding Plataforma to the roll call, the woman here instantly identified that neighborhood as one of the many peripheral spaces that are the targets of the kind of police aggression that took ten-year-old Joel's life in 2010. She was not officially a part of the production; her words were not in the script. She was standing somewhere behind me as I filmed the performance. I neither recognized her voice at the time nor her face when I eventually saw her. Her tone signaled the spontaneity of her participation. Flatly, she simply added the name of this community in an even-toned, husky voice that reminded me of Jussara's—the grandmother who gave the testimony at the public hearing in 2005. Her interjection was a moment of recognition and radical engagement (Elam 1997). I do not know whether the woman was actually from Plataforma. She left before I got the chance to speak with her that day and ask her about her participation in the play. However, I assume that her act of calling out signaled not only her identification with the commentary being made but also her desire to insert herself into this piece and symbolically join with those who cry out against such abuse. Her participation was a symbolic manifestation of mourning, solidarity, and quite possibly healing. She too wanted her experiences with this violence, whatever they might have been, to be recognized. Interestingly, the intensity of this utterance only became tangible for me when I began to watch the video of the performance repeatedly, afterward. Film can allow us to put our work "within the broad geopolitical and neoliberal circuits that envelop us all" (Schuller and Thomas 2013, 153). Perhaps my being involved in filming and the camera created a barrier between the performance and me that allowed me to distance myself, or maybe because the ephemerality of the performance did not permit immediate reflection. Looking at the play after the fact, I consistently flush with emotion and well up with tears. There is something about the woman's steady and soft, yet heavy and raspy interruption that reminds me of the very real and painful realities behind Culture Shock's performance. It is a touching, raw pause that lays claim to our attention and our sympathy, and builds in us a sense of urgency.

When Culture Shock staged "The Police Raid" vignette at Fazenda Grande do Retiro in November 2003, not even they anticipated the resonance of their performance: Nordeste de Amaralina, in 2010; Paripe, in 2005; Nova Brasilia, in 2007; and Bairro da Paz, in 2007, all suffered police raids. Like the list of neighborhoods the MC calls out at the end of the scene, the neighborhoods affected by state violence lend themselves to reiterated interjection—there always seems to be another place we miss. The vignette is not just an abstract critique; it strikes at the heart of the lived experience of war and racial apartheid in Salvador. Moreover, "The Police Raid" elicits a visceral response from the audience that engages us in a discussion of witnessing. The theater is a space of renewal and healing as well as disruption.

The police raid on the stage clearly triggered a collective memory for the audience. I attended dozens of performances of *Stop to Think* during my fieldwork, noting audience responses that ranged from slight squirms to gasps to wide-eyed stares. But the deepest response was the "Plataforma" interjection. It temporarily and symbolically interrupted the silence that engulfs the question of antiblack violence in Salvador, even among the very people it most affects. Although some people like the militantes of React or Die! and Culture Shock choose to protest loudly and boldly against the state and its genocidal practices, others refuse to speak about it or avoid the topic, preferring to remain anonymous and slip into the shadows. We need only remember the young man who was wounded during the Matança de Nova Brasilia who later declined to step forward to tell his story. Instead of framing this silence as a refusal to speak or acknowledge this violence, or as a dismissal of the importance of the topic within the community, or even as an absence of reflection on race itself, we should read silence as trauma induced by war. The scenario of state violence against the black body in pain is a war zone. It is also the state's political and "spiritual terror" (Brown 2003).[1]

If Afro-paradise is the nation's disavowal of blackness—its celebration of black culture coupled with the imperative to kill black people—then both physical and spiritual violence are essential to this project. This state violence in Bahia is a kind of terrorism, as we discussed in chapter 3. This terror is political in nature, but should not be read solely as a performance intended for "the victims" (those killed). Instead, the political targets of this violence are, I argue, the communities and families of those who die. As we saw with the story of ten-year-old Joel, the families of those killed are often the hardest hit. As Joel's mother, Miriam da Conceição noted, the family is destructured by this violence; it is a pain that never heals (Gaggino 2013). The trauma that this war produces is not only physical but also spiritual, and *witnessing* is then a political and spiritual response to this terror. And while one of the effects of Afro-paradise is the social and physical death of black people, blackness is not reducible to these effects. Instead, black Brazilians have fought and continue to fight this violence constantly. Identifying this as a war rather than a massacre is part of that fight. The impact of state terror on families, its uniquely gendered implications, and the ways that families respond and fight back are the political signs of this war.

Witnessing

Culture Shock and React or Die! are witnessing projects. For militantes, the political consequences of state violence against black people are dire: the erasure of the black body as subject, the invisibilization of black suffering, and the reinscription of the black body as the object of state repression. This schema, in effect, depoliticizes blackness by erasing its ontological presence (Wilderson 2010). The theater, however, creates a counterspace to this erasure. By claiming that the theater is a counterspace, I am not suggesting that it is a utopia or liminal space as in Victor Turner's definition (1974). Instead, it is the eye of the storm, where residents in the midst of the situation can gain perspective while acknowledging their central position amid turmoil and danger.

Theater scholars like Soyini Madison and Dwight Conquergood define *witnessing* as "what it means to be radically engaged and committed, body-to-body, in the field . . . a politics of the body deeply in action with Others'" (Madison 2007, 826). Human-rights advocates often frame witnessing as a therapeutic act of healing for the communities of the violated and the redemption of the violators (Feldman 2004).[2] By re-presenting the lived black experience onstage, however, Culture Shock engages in a witnessing project that more closely approximates Frantz Fanon's articulation of the term in the context of colonial war. In reflecting on the impact of French colonialism on Algerians, and Algerians' fight against that colonialism, Frantz Fanon (1965a) argues that witnessing is the pursuit of spiritual community in the face of colonial violence (Mbembe 2012). Fanon sees the project of witnessing colonial violence as walking "step by step along the great wound inflicted on the Algerian soil and the Algerian people" (1965a, 119). He pays particular attention to the effects of the Algerian Revolution on its people. He writes, "The tactic adopted by French colonialism since the beginning of the Revolution has had the result of separating the people from each other, of fragmenting them, with the sole objective of making any cohesion impossible" (1965a, 118). This separation particularly affected the Algerian family, which would have to be radically restructured and rebuilt because of the revolution. Indeed, in Fanon's assessment, the true target of colonial violence was the family, not just the young men who we typically associate with the face of the revolution (1965a, 99, 118). Women, the elderly, and children bear the brunt of all of the different forms of the violence under colonialism. This experience fundamentally alters those it touches, radically eradicating individualism in a way that also shapes the collective. Out of this process, a spiritual community is born (1965a, 120), although it is not a utopic space of cathartic healing but one of pain and suffering. Like Fanon's observations of Algeria, part of the palimpsestic effect of state violence is the impression it leaves on black people as a collective community, not just the individual traces etched onto the layer of the body. Witnessing emerges out of the mourning and lamentation of spiritual community (1965a, 119).

Witnessing is watching, placing oneself in solidarity with the struggle of the people, peeling back the layers of hidden social meaning that are embedded in the practice of racialized, colonial violence, and politically investing oneself in the active pursuit of the demise of the colonial system. Culture Shock and React or Die! do this work. As Achille Mbembe observes, "In such a context, the task of critique was to bear witness to scenes of mourning, in those spaces of loss and destruction where the lamentations of old were replaced by new forms of behaviour. Having experienced the struggle, one does not weep, nor cry out, one does not behave as one used to. . . . Instead, 'one grits one's teeth and, after one more step, the death of a moudjahid who has fallen in the field of honour will be met with cries of joy'" (2012, 23).

Culture Shock and React or Die! create the space for soteropolitanos to take one more step in the face of death. This crucial step is not reducible to political activism or teleological narratives of resistance. It is the exposure of a series of tensions that proscribe the need for revolutionary action. Witnessing reverberates beyond the question of racism or even white supremacy. Antiblack violence actually pushes blackness to the discursive margins of intelligibility, requiring a radical rethinking of social structure in order to exact its redress. Without witnessing, we slip into the belief that racism in Brazil, while real, has no real impact on people's lives. Embodied performances remind us of the affect of racial experiences. Performance in this case extends far beyond the stage.

Calabetão

In July 2007, a sensationalist photo of three black bodies laid across a floor, hands behind their heads, in a pool of blood, was prominently displayed in the pages of *A Tarde*. The three, Aurina Rodrigues Santana (forty-four), an activist in the Homeless Movement (*Movimento Sem Teto*) and mother of eleven; her son, Paulo Rogério Rodrigues Santana Braga (nineteen); and her partner, Rodson da Silva Rodrigues (twenty-nine), had been assassinated by a group of masked men who invaded their home in the community of Calabetão (Cirino 2007). According to Mrs. Santana's two young daughters who witnessed the crime, the men forced the three to lay face down, execution style, in a back room and shot them to death. They then ransacked the house and stole three hundred reais. Oddly, three bags of marijuana and thirty rocks of crack were found by the bodies. The military police (PM) communications spokesperson, Luís Marcelo Pita, from the Forty-Eighth Independent Military State Police Company of Bahia (CIPM), blamed the victims for their own deaths, noting that Mrs. Santana was an ex-con, and claiming her son was involved in drug trafficking. But neighbors were quick to deny that these murders were drug related.

One neighbor said, "They planted the drugs in the house. . . . What rival drug trafficker would invade a house and not take the drugs?" It was clear to Mrs. Santana's friends and family that they had been victims of a death squad, and that the drugs were a hasty attempt to frame them as dealers. Two months prior to her murder, Aurina Santana had reported military police officers Ademir Bispo de Jesus, Antônio Marcos de Jesus, and José Silva Oliveira from the Forty-Eighth CIPM to the Legislative Assembly's Commission on Human Rights (*Comissão de Direitos Humanos da Assembleia Legislativa*) for invading her home and torturing her son and her thirteen-year-old daughter. All evidence indicated that the very police officers that she had denounced also murdered her and her family. Yet to the police, the lives of Mrs. Santana and her family were expendable; if they had been killed by police officers, they deserved to die.

React or Die! organized an international response. On August 24, 2007, the Movimento Negro Unificado, along with the Movimento dos Sem Teto de Salvador (MSTS) (Homeless Movement of Salvador), Justiça Global (Global Justice), and several other organizations formally denounced to the United Nations the Santana murders, which came to be known as the Calabetão massacre. The complaint was sent to the attention of Hina Jilani, special representative of the UN secretary-general on human rights defenders, and Phillip Alston, special rapporteur on extrajudicial, summary, or arbitrary executions, among others.[3] It decried the immediate crimes and the brutal culture of death squads in Bahia, and it once again made the strong claim that racism motivates death squads. It also brought in questions of gender, family, and patriarchy that do not often get mentioned, even among many militantes who speak out against police abuse: black women and black families as targets of the police.

The Calabetão massacre brings us to a deeply disturbing aspect of death-squad murders and police lethality: that families, much more than individuals, are often the intended targets of this violence. As mentioned in the previous chapter, the audience for death-squad murders is the families and community surrounding the dead. However, the death of Aurina Santana deepens this discussion, motivating us to consider the gendered aspects of this violence. We know that most often those who are killed by the police are black men (Waiselfisz 2012). However, homicide statistics neglect to address sequelae—the lingering effects of murder on the family members of the dead—and these effects fall disproportionately upon black women. Luciane Rocha (2012; 2014), in her study of black mothers' experiences with loss in Rio de Janeiro, notes that the psychological effects of violence on black women are devastating and disabling, relegating black women to a "living death" (Rocha 2012, 60). Rocha echoes the earlier work of Keisha-Khan Perry (2011; 2013) and Vilma Reis (2005), who separately argue that, although black men are most often the direct physical victims of violent policing, black women are also the victims of this violence, and their experiences lead to eventual if not immediate death. Indeed, black women's confrontations with state violence require deeper, more serious reflection from scholars who study the impact of policing on black communities globally (Incite! Women of Color Against Violence 2006). Black women and girls experience a unique intersection of violence between the state and the home that situates them in a distinctly vulnerable position (Crenshaw 1991).[4] This chapter contributes to the efforts to rectify the lack of attention to the gendered racialized dimensions of state violence.

The wounds that black women suffer as a result of state terror are multi-layered. When the police come, women do not know whether they will be killed. And when the police do not kill them, they often kill their children or loved ones—irrevocably affecting their physical and emotional health and well-being (Perry 2011). When we assess the damage caused by state violence, we then must calculate it beyond a body count. We must also consider its communal effects, particularly with regard to the black family. This discussion genders our reading of Afro-paradise and the political stakes associated with it. It also marks black women and black families as primary targets.

Most often, black women are the ones who watch the police drag their family members out of the house to be killed—a kind of perverse torture that few studies of violence name as such. And if the families of the dead are not only witnesses of state terror but also its victims, then their survival is also a political act. This violence is best defined as spiritual terror.

Canabrava

On June 16, 2009, more than one hundred civil, military, and special-operations police officers invaded Canabrava, a peripheral neighborhood in the northern part of the city of Salvador. They claimed to be responding to the murder of civil police officer José Carlos Gonçalves Teixeira, who had been investigating drug trafficking in the neighborhood. The officers summarily executed five young men from the community, alleged suspects in the crime. Three of the young men, Edmilson Ferreira dos Anjos (twenty-two), Rogério Ferreira (twenty-four), and Manoel Ferreira (twenty-three) were brothers. According to their sister, the police invaded their house, pulled their mother out, and shot the boys while they were watching television on the couch and sleeping in a bedroom (Rebouças 2009; Lima 2007). Distraught with grief, the mother of the three, who identified herself to journalists as Maria da Conceição, denied that her boys had had any involvement with drug trafficking or homicide. That same week, police took three other suspects in Teixeira's murder into police custody.

The morning after the Canabrava massacre, the Bahian newspaper *A Tarde* featured a color picture of the ex-wife of one of the murdered young men on the back page of the first section of the paper, caught in bright lights, her face distraught, wisps of hair desperately sticking out, hands outstretched in a crying scream toward the camera. Alongside this image was another photo, depicting four police officers carrying a body in a sheet. Three are in black uniforms and bulletproof vests; one is in the familiar black-and-tan camouflage of the choque police, his assault rifle drawn. The juxtaposition of the two images illustrates the intricate relationship between police-related violence, the spectacle of state violence, and black suffering in Salvador. The glare of the flash in the eyes of the bereaved partner represents the mainstream media, and by extension, general society's lack of concern with black suffering.[5] The police, dressed in all black, storming houses and killing young people in front of their mothers, sisters, aunts, uncles, and other family members, show a grotesque disregard for black life that leaves the families of the dead to grieve in unspeakable ways. They are enacting a performance for the immediate audience (killing people in the periphery to terrorize black families and black communities), but that performance is also palimpsestic—repeated violence against black peripheral communities that extends through time and space and settles into the body.

In using the term *performance,* once again, I do not mean to reduce this moment to superficiality. Quite to the contrary; understanding Canabrava and Calabetão as performances deconstructs the component parts of these moments as a narrated script that is played out by intentional state action. The accumulation of these acts is what, in part, makes them political. When police pull young people out of their houses and kill them in front of their mothers as they did in Canabrava, or kill parents in front of their children as they did in Calabetão, they extend the immediate act of killing through time, affecting generations—a strike of an ax at the trunk of the family tree.

We can see the dismemberment, torture, and spectacular display of the black body in pain by death squads, and the spectacular killing of black people by on-duty police officers as strategies of spiritual, political, and social control. The term *spiritual terror* comes from Vincent Brown's (2003) analysis of slavery in his research on the plantocracy's use of spectacular terror as a form of social control over the enslaved in the colonial West Indies. He argues that slavers who feared losing their "stock" to suicide turned to spiritual terror and fear as a strategy for maintaining social control. Enslavers employed "spectacular punishments committed upon the bodies of the dead" in order to "terrorize the spiritual imaginations of the enslaved" (2003, 24). Brown suggests that the plantocracy used the dead to "mark territory with awesome icons of their power" (ibid.). However, he also notes that, although "the intent was to dominate the imagination, the routinization of terrifying spectacles only aided the creation of new knowledges (understandings, interpretations, and ways of engaging with the world)" (ibid.). Like Caribbean slavers, the police and death squads in contemporary Bahia harness the cosmic and uniquely political power of the dead to terrorize the living: to instill fear, quell political protest, and maintain the race/gender/sexuality boundaries of the moral social order.[6] The spectacular killing of black people, either in the shadows of secrecy or in front of their loved ones, and the deliberate display of dead bodies in peripheral communities is a gendered and collective grotesque display of violence that unites rather than individuates the black body.

Canabrava leads us back to black mothers. The intended, primary audience for these performances of state violence is black "social mothers": black women, scripted within the racial, heteropatriarchal social order as enemies of the state, who must be quieted because of their particular political power.[7] Although the intent of the gendered violence of Afro-paradise is to instill fear

and to intimidate, the result has been the creation of new political knowledges, competing discourses, and resilient political tactics, like witnessing.
In this sense, witnessing is a dialogic relationship that invokes the African
tradition of call and response. It is also the politics of survival and performative, collective authentication.

The murder of Aurina Santana, her son, and her partner was, by most
accounts, the result of Mrs. Santana's denunciation of the torture of her son
and daughter by police to the commission on human rights. As a leader in
the Homeless Movement, Mrs. Santana had a long history of grassroots militancy and protest. Her proactive approach to her children's abuse reflected
her sustained political engagement. Black women's grassroots organizing is
one of the most effective responses to racism, antiblack genocide, and state
oppression in Salvador because of its sustained investment in community, ties
to family, and rejection of masculinist politics (in which community leaders
put ego before the collective good) (Perry 2013). Black women affront and
threaten white heteropatriarchal supremacy.

Aurina Santana's death, and the circumstances that motivated a death
squad, were political acts, and not isolated ones. The state, either directly or
indirectly, routinely terrorizes families in the aftermath of their children's
deaths at the hands of the police. We saw this with Joel, Bronka, and Blue. We
need only return briefly to the story of Bronka to recall how the state enacts
microaggressions (refusing to treat him at the hospital, forcing the community to carry him up and down the hill in his wheelchair to seek medical care,
claiming that he was as a drug dealer, and threating him with violence and
eventually killing him) as well as overt and covert macroaggressions (death
threats) that terrorize families after incidents of state violence.

The violence that affected Canabrava in June 2009 did not stop at the five
young men who were killed on June 16. The police continued to sweep the
neighborhood that night after the boys were killed and for days to come,
and this forces us to reinterpret the killings of that night. The swiftness of
the police response (the police raid occurred just hours after officer José
Carlos Gonçalves Teixeira was killed), the execution-style assassinations of
the three brothers on the couch, and the fact that, days after the raid, three
other suspects in the murder of the police officer were apprehended, led
many to wonder whether the one-hundred-man raid was really about cap-
turing murder suspects or was actually revenge against the community and
intimidation. The extrajudicial killing of the alleged suspects punctuated this
suspicion. Why kill first and ask questions later? If the five were innocent,
what message does their death broadcast?

In August, I traveled to Salvador for the First People's Gathering for Life and a Better Model for Public Safety (I ENPOSP), organized by React or Die!, Quilombo X, and the Association of Friends and Family of Prisoners in Bahia (ASFAP). It was an explicit rejection of the Brazilian government's First National Conference on Public Security, organized that year to garner support for PRONASCI (Plano Nacional de Segurança com Cidadania) (National Citizenship and Security Plan)—a government program designed to address the crisis of violence in the nation by engaging with citizens. Yet PRONASCI had little popular local involvement and support. In contrast, I ENPOSP was a grassroots effort to create a national public forum for victims of police violence, their families, and families of prisoners to debate racism, sexism, homophobia, and the genocidal effects of the public-safety system in Brazil. The organizers intended for I ENPOSP to be a people's response to state violence rather than a superficial state gesture, like PRONASCI. I ENPOSP invited victims of state violence from across Brazil to Salvador for a three-day meeting. Three hundred people participated in this unprecedented event, including militantes, scholars, and activists from NGOs from across Brazil. I was invited to serve as an international observer.

I ENPOSP held its opening rally in Praça da Piedade, where the vigil had been held four years prior. The event organizers rented a platform and microphones, and set up a temporary stage in the middle of the tall shading trees, statues, and the fountain of the square. The squeaking feedback of the mic announced the start of the evening. After speeches and singing, representatives from various organizations spoke out passionately against the violence the state metes out regularly with impunity. At some point, protestors from the Movimento Sem Terra (MST) (Landless Movement) joined the rally after finishing another march down Avenida Sete de Setembro, making separate demands of the government. Many in this group were indigenous people who donned traditional dress for the protest, making a strong, symbolic, visual, political statement of Afro-indigenous solidarity against state violence.[8] In all, the plaza was filled with activists and protestors from various sectors.

As the evening progressed, mothers from Rio de Janeiro and São Paulo climbed the large black stage to speak out, one by one, about their experiences with violence and death at the hands of the police. Many of the women who spoke were those whose children had been killed by the police in the Baixada Fluminense region of Rio de Janeiro. Others were from the Mothers of May (*Mães de Maio*), an organization of mothers whose children were killed by the police in São Paulo in 2006 when the military police retaliated against the community and killed 493 people in response to the First Capital

Command's (Primeiro Comando da Capital) (PCC) revolts that year.[9] The women shared their stories of pain, heartache, and anger at the assassinations of their children. Emboldened by their loss, they struck fists in the air and cried out for justice.

The mothers of the young people killed in the Canabrava massacre, just weeks prior, were also invited to speak at I ENPOSP and participate in the weekend's events. I was naively cheery when I met the mothers from Canabrava. At the time, I had no idea who they were. They were introduced to me as mothers, and understanding the very delicate emotions of the event, I did not talk with them about why they were present or what they had experienced. It was enough just to recognize them as mothers. But I immediately noted a stark difference between their demeanor and that of the mothers from out of town. They were quiet and deeply sad, whereas the mothers from Rio and São Paulo (with more distance between their loss and the rally) were upbeat and excited to have a platform on which to speak.

After some time, several international guests began to ask me when the mothers from Bahia would speak. After inquiries with the coordinators, it became clear to me what was happening. Afraid of (further) retaliation by the police whose headquarters was just steps away, the mothers from Canabrava refused to speak as they had been invited to do. Instead, they stayed quietly in the shadows, sitting under the darkness of trees, watching silently but not daring to participate.[10] Their silence was heavy with meaning, punctuating the liminal space between life and death where all families of victims of state violence reside—the space of the ghosts of the dead and the living.

In 2003 I had briefly volunteered with the youth theater project *Jovens do Amanha* (Youth of Tomorrow), founded by Jamília Tavares, a young black woman from Canabrava. Several times a week, I traveled to Canabrava to teach English to children at the Jovens do Amanha school. I was a horrible English teacher, but we had lots of fun playing games, singing the alphabet song, and chatting about life. The school was organized by and established in the community. Its successes had won it a positive reputation as a model program for "at-risk" youth. Although I never pursued my research work with the theater troupe, I did develop a great deal of respect for the project, the community, and the neighborhood residents that coordinated the program. I also made dear friends.

A small, tight-knit community that is somewhat isolated, Canabrava has a rich history defined by struggle and protest. It was founded by people who sorted trash in order to make a living and grew up around the city's landfill. Many of those same people set up permanent residence there, and the community was born. Eventually, after a long fight led by the women of that community, the state recognized Canabrava as a neighborhood, and they obtained municipal resources such as running water, electricity, and a bus route. The legacy of grassroots struggle still frames the neighborhood's identity. However, nonresidents often stigmatize it (like most peripheral neighborhoods) as a black, drug-infested, violent, and expendable space, and associate residents with the trash of the landfill. The story of the massacre and the state's framing of the police raid as a justified operation devised to root out murderers and drug dealers grated against my personal experiences. I was reminded that propaganda is part and parcel of the state's performance of violence, and that the stigmatization of communities in actuality enables state-sponsored terror and murder.

When the state kills black children, the mothers, fathers, aunts, uncles, and neighbors take to the streets, burn tires, and block traffic, demanding justice. Joel's family did this after he was killed in 2010. When the military police went on a killing spree in January 2008, families did the same thing. When black youth die, grandfathers, cousins, and parents go looking for their dead bodies in clandestine cemeteries. Not only does the act of state lethality inscribe blackness onto the body and the landscape, but the aftermath of these performances and their reverberating effects also define family and community, the collectivity of the material body produced by grotesque realism. Worse, if possible, when communities and families unite to speak out against injustice, the entire family becomes an enemy of the state. The story of Ricardo provides another example.

Ricardo

The story of Ricardo, one of the four black youth killed in the police spree of January 2008, deepens a discussion of the family as the target of state violence. A few days before I ENPOSP began, I attended a preconference planning meeting in downtown Salvador with members of React or Die! The room was dimly lit by a single iridescent light bulb hanging from the middle of the ceiling. It bounced golden light around the room as the sounds of the cars from the street below wafted in through the open window with the cool breeze. We were discussing last-minute organizational questions for the gathering and then just sat and chatted for a bit. I was living an hour outside of the city, so I stuck around well after the meeting to hitch a ride home with one of the organizers. As I waited, I met a gentleman named Mr. Lazaro, with caramel-brown skin and salt-and-pepper hair, probably in his late forties. We struck up a conversation easily. He was carrying a black, soft-sided briefcase with an envelope full of papers. He pulled out a picture of a young, brown-skinned adolescent standing up and balancing on someone's shoulders, smiling brightly. He explained to me that this was his son, Ricardo, who worked in a local circus. As Mr. Lazaro began to recount the story of his son to me, our casual banter quickly devolved into a deeply disturbing, winding tale of pain and loss. Ricardo was home visiting from the circus,[11] playing soccer with his friends, when he was shot and killed by police officers. He had gone out to the neighborhood field as he had done every day during the week he was home, and he was there when the police came. The boys ran, but Ricardo was shot in the back and died. After his death, Mr. Lazaro, an experienced environmental activist and respected community member, joined friends, neighbors, and family members to protest in the streets of the neighborhood, holding placards, burning tires to stop traffic, and chanting for justice. And then things got worse. The family began to receive death threats. They were put into a witness-protection program. They were relocated to a motel in Santo Amaro, just outside the city of Salvador, but everyone in the town knew that they were staying there, for it was no secret that this motel was the state's chosen relocation spot for the witness-protection program. The family started to receive threats again—threats they strongly suspected came from the very police officers involved in their son's death. On top of that, the motel was no place for a family with young children, as it was also where couples regularly went to have sex. So the Lazaros left. Not only did they lose a son and brother to the police shooting, they lost their whole lives. As Mr. Lazaro put it, "In hiding, you can't work, it's hard to be enrolled in school, you can't live."

There was a heavy sadness hanging in the air between us as Mr. Lazaro told me the story of Ricardo. As he spoke, my eyes began to fill with tears, overwhelmed by the randomness and sadness of it all. Ricardo's murder was senseless. Despite my academic and activist knowledge of the deep-seated racism of extrajudicial police violence in Brazil, something made me desperately try to rationalize what had happened. Had he been in the wrong place at the wrong time? Could it have been mistaken identity? I wanted to distance myself. I could feel the depth of Mr. Lazaro's pain and it made me uncomfortable, angry, and sad all at the same time, as if simply hearing his story brought its unpredictability dangerously close, and I, or someone I loved, could be next.[12] I knew that there was nothing that Mr. Lazaro could have done to avoid his son's death. He had raised his children well. He was guilty of two things only: being black and living on the edge of poverty. This was no case of mistaken identity or happenstance. A young black man, Ricardo was not *mistaken* by the police to be a criminal, he was *assumed* to be a criminal, scripted as expendable, his humanity[13] dismissed precisely *because* he was a young black man living in a working-class neighborhood. The fact that he was shot and killed in the back (running away, not threatening) along with another young black man who was a known criminal was not a counterpoint. It was Ricardo's expendability, not his guilt or nonguilt, that made him a target. As the former governor of Rio de Janeiro once said in a remark about the use of excessive force in favelas, "You have to break a few eggs to make a cake" (Justiça Global 2013).[14]

As I sat there listening to Mr. Lazaro tell his son's story, I was struck by his cadence. He had told this story so many times before, his words echoed with repetition and desperation. As he recounted the details of his son's death and his family's odyssey, his voice took on the humming rhythm of desperation. *They killed his boy.* This was not only a reiteration, it was the echo of pain that the liminal space between life and death produces for families of police violence victims transnationally.

In 2012, the police killed Ricardo's brother, Enio.

Spiritual Warfare

Returning to the discussion of spiritual terror, death is a powerful cosmic tool of spiritual warfare. As Vincent Brown notes, Caribbean slave owners used spectacular terror to "deter Africans from self-destruction" (2003, 26). Self-destruction in this instance should be read as rebellion. This strategy was grounded in the knowledge that Africans engaged in suicide because of their strong belief that, in death, they would be able to return to their homeland and be free. The mutilation and dismemberment of dead bodies literally truncated this fantasy, marking the terrors of slavery on the body into the afterlife. Putting the mutilated bodies on display as a deterrent message to the rest of the community played a key role in the slavers' performance. Brown notes that "slavers mutilated the body of the first 'Ibo' slave to die in a given shipment: they beheaded it, or sliced off its nose and pried out its eyes to prevent losses among other captives from the Bight of Biafra, who were widely reputed to be suicide-prone" (2003, 27). Slavers practiced mutilation in order to discourage suicide beyond the Caribbean as well, throughout the slavocracy of the Americas. Brown notes, "As with the punishments for suicide, the punishments for rebellion were meant to inspire in the enslaved spiritual terror by visiting extraordinary torments on their bodies before and after death" (ibid.). We can find similar practices in colonial Brazil. When the Portuguese captured Zumbi, the warrior and leader of the quilombo kingdom of Palmares in the sixteenth century, they quartered him and put his head on display in the public square (Gomes 2005). Spiritual terror has been a crucial aspect of controlling black resistance historically throughout the Americas. The story of Nat Turner in the United States, who was not only sentenced to death but also mutilated after plotting a revolution against slavery, is yet another notable example (Styron 2002).

The connection between suicide and rebellion is an important one to note here, as is the intentional invocation of affect intended by these displays. Marking the territory of the plantation with dead, mutilated bodies was intended to inscribe the landscape with memory and social meaning. The intent was not merely to intimidate but, as Brown notes, "to give governing authority a sacred, even supernatural dimension" (2003, 27). He continues, "Spectacular executions attached worldly authority to transcendent concerns and allowed the plantocracy's power to reach into the spiritual imaginations of slaves" (ibid.). Spiritual terror would have no effect without the affectual pain it evoked—a pain that was designed to destroy the loved ones of the dead emotionally, upturning the possibility for community. This is how the magical state came to organize itself in the Americas.

Yet while slavers actively sought to instill a spiritual fear among captives, we should not read this practice as evidence of the passive victimhood of the enslaved. In Brazil as elsewhere, enslaved Africans and people of African descent actively fought against their captivity in organized, sophisticated ways. Spiritual warfare was a two-way street, and Bahia was one of the primary stages for this tension. The story of this warfare during the colonial period is important historical context for understanding the political meaning of the fight against state terror today. As I outline in chapter 3, some of the first police actions in Bahia were strategic military operations against rebellious enslaved Africans. In turn, some of the first organized resistance to this violence united black people—albeit precariously—in a fight to dismantle state terror. The families who fight back against state violence today are inheritors of this spirit of rebellion.

Beginning in the nineteenth century, enslaved and freed black people (*pretos*) revolted in a variety of ways against the social order in Bahia. Although these actions were by no means unified across all people of African descent, the conditions of slavery and white supremacy were beginning to bring Africans of different nations (for example Yoruba/Nagô, Gêge, and Hausa) and crioulos (Brazilian-born people of African descent) into coalitions according to race that had not previously been in existence (Reis 2003, 73). Within this ethnically diverse population, blackness was constantly in negotiation. The people were distinct and often at odds. But the common enemies of slavery and white supremacy also provoked people of African descent (African and crioulo, freed and enslaved) to engage in political negotiations of solidarity with each other around the new fact of blackness they had in common and the shared experience of antiblack violence. Starting in 1807, blackness (being *preto/negro*) became a site of alliance and collective struggle in addition to a site of tension.

One of the signs that marked this period as a time of war was the establishment of quilombos.[15] A word that comes from Kimbundu,[15] *kilombo* literally means *war encampment* (defined in English as runaway slave encampments) (Lopes 1995; Nascimento 1982). Black people engaged in the sustained practice of quilombismo: escaping to seek refuge in quilombos located away from the plantations and city centers (Moura 1987; Nascimento 1980; Nascimento 1982; Reis and Gomes 1996).[16] Those who escaped slavery in Bahia established quilombos in the immediate vicinity of Salvador (the suburbs) and in the Recôncovo region of Bahia (Reis and Gomes 1996). Also called maroonage—escape, resistance, and the establishment of autonomous spaces—this practice occurred throughout the Americas among enslaved Africans (Price 1973). From the cimarrones of Panama and Peru to the palenques of Cuba and the maroons of Jamaica, enslaved Africans established a practice of flight and fight in response to the injustices of slavery throughout the black Atlantic. Quilombos were the manifestation of this tradition in Brazil. The most famous was Palmares; led by Zumbi and once home to approximately twenty thousand people (Gomes 2005),[17] Palmares existed for almost two hundred years.[18] However, most quilombos were much smaller in scale and had a much shorter duration. In fact, the practice of quilombo in Bahia could be as ephemeral as periodic escape for a few days away from the city of Salvador and/or down the road from the plantations in the Recôncovo (Reis 2003, 68). In this interpretation, we can think of quilombos not just as independent societies of resistance, but also as resting places, where black people could retreat in order to seek religious renewal (practicing candomblé), commune with friends and family, or simply pause. By 1807, this practice of quilombo was widespread. Although quilombos were clandestine forms of resistance, their existence was widely known and their presence was obvious.

In 1807, the Bahian government articulated a harsh, repressive response to this "unchecked freedom" (Reis 2003, 70). On March 30, 1807, the Conde da Ponte[19] (Earl of the Point) ordered approximately eighty "well-armed" soldiers to raid the areas of Nossa Senora dos Mares and Cabula, located in the suburbs of Salvador, with the aid of slave catchers (*capitões do mato*) and the police (Britto 1903, 72). They sought to destroy the quilombos located there, and arrested seventy-eight black people (*pretos*), enslaved and freed, living autonomously in this region (ibid.). The black men who were apprehended were consigned to forced labor, and the black women were sentenced to jail

(Reis 2003, 71). This was one of the first police raids on a peripheral community in Bahia.

In turn, free and enslaved black people organized a tactical military response. Enslaved and freed Hausas, in alliance with crioulos and other enslaved and freed Africans, advanced a conspiracy to overthrow the government (represented by the military and government officials, specifically the Earl of the Point) and thus dismantle white supremacy in Bahia. Although the plan never came to fruition, the express goals of the conspiracy are revealing: (1) to take over the city; (2) to install the African leaders of the conspiracy in the positions of "bishop" and governor; (3) to organize a black (African and crioulo) and mulatto movement; (4) to eliminate the white population through poisoning; (5) to destroy the white population's houses; (6) to remove all images from the churches and burn them in a public square (specifically the Nazareth Chapel); and (7) to burn down the Customs House (Casa de Alfândega) (Britto 1903, 73; Reis 2003, 73). Once all of these goals had been met in Bahia, the rebels would then move to Pernambuco and liberate the enslaved Hausa people there, at which time they would create a new kingdom under Hausa rule that would then reenslave the mulattos and crioulos who were once their allies (Reis 2003, 73). The last step, reenslavement, reflects the complex politics of a notion of black solidarity associated with this moment, because, if allied by a common urgent cause, Africans and people of African descent were not unified. Ethnic and national differences were the source of divisions and often prevented groups of black people from sustaining a movement against slavery, colonialism, and white supremacy. However, temporary unions and collaborations against state authority provide a window into the emerging politics of black racial formation and, more important, the definition of black identity in opposition to the state. These politics are the precedent for the black organizing that we see in Salvador today, such as React or Die! Despite complex politics of racial identification, the conditions of Afro-paradise are increasingly inspiring people of African descent to identify and speak out against white supremacy by building coalitions, although they are also fraught with tensions. The explicit existence of an impetus to organize among black people against white supremacy (symbolized by the state, the church, and the elite class) reflects a new politics of black racial formation emerging at this political moment,[20] and a collective sense of black political identity that is an interesting entry point for returning to the topic of Bahia as a transtemporal colonial war zone.

When the Conde da Ponte intercepted the conspiracy of 1807 and ordered its leaders apprehended, officials found spears, arrows, knives, pistols, drums, and other "warlike accoutrements" in the house where the conspirators were gathered (Britto 1903, 74). The conspiracy of 1807 inaugurated the 1807–35 period of rebellion in Bahia. For the next twenty-eight years, black Bahians, led primarily by Hausa Africans, organized a series of conspiracies, realized and stunted, that can best be defined as a war against white supremacy. I use the term *white supremacy* rather than the phrasing *a war against whites* that the Conde da Ponte used in his official assessment of the situation because it was clearly articulated as such by the Africans and people of African descent who organized and sustained resistance to slavery and the established society at this time.[21]

Like the experience of slavery itself, this war was not only racialized but also gendered. Slavery, the state, and white supremacy were distinctly patriarchal institutions. The conspiracies and fighting led by the Hausas were decidedly masculine. At this time, there were very few enslaved women in Bahia (Conrad 1994; Mattoso 1986; Reis 2003). Most enslaved Africans brought to Bahia were men; thus the black population of Bahia was predominantly male. Although this had to do with the economy of slavery and the perception that men were better equipped for hard labor, we should not fail to appreciate women's resistance to slavery or participation in colonial war. During the raid of 1807, the Conde da Ponte arrested men and women. And although women were not in leadership roles in the revolutions led by men (particularly the Hausas), women held leadership in quilombos, particularly when they were closely tied to candomblé.[22] João Reis notes that one of the quilombolas arrested during the 1807 raid was Nicácia, a priestess who was carried to her prison sentence on a litter by her retinue (Reis 2003, 71). Black social mothers have been enemies of the state in Bahia for generations.

Black insurrection in Bahia during the colonial period ran the gamut from small discussions about the possibility of conspiracy between one or two people, to the calculated, long-term planning and execution that led hundreds of enslaved Africans to stage an attack on Salvador's elite white and mulatto population the night of January 24, 1835 (*Revolta dos Malês*). The outskirts of Salvador (where most peripheral neighborhoods are located today), particularly the areas of Cabula and Paripe, were particularly fertile ground for insurrections.[23] Across these areas, insurgents would employ the tactics that the conspirators used in 1807 to organize armed, highly militarized revolts, and although most of these revolts were never realized, the mere planning and elaboration underscores the fact that black resistance to white supremacy was constant, consistent, and unrelenting. The revolts, fulfilled and unfulfilled, are in conversation with one another. Alliances that free and enslaved blacks made with one another, regardless of their ethnic/national origins, reminds us that Bahian blackness has been born out of the tensions of collective political struggle as much as cultural heritage and processes of racialization. Blackness has been made complex not merely out of its tensions with whiteness, racial democracy and the whitening ideology in Brazil, but also its inherent relationship to an oppressive system.

Brazil's identity as a colonial state was intermeshed with the antagonisms of slavery. It was also in tension with anticolonial revolt; namely, slave insurrection. The history and memory of slave revolt in Bahia is a metaphor for the tensions that still lie just under the surface in Salvador. In fact, although we can read state terror against the black body from the colonial period onward as a symbol of elite, white authority, we can also read it as a symbol of the insecurity of that authority—the insecurity of white supremacy—and of the failure to consolidate rule. In this way, violent policing is a symbol of both dominance and frailty. Returning to Scarry's concept of transference and the body in pain, the spectacular torture of the black body is ultimately also a symbol of the weakness of the social contract itself. State terror has been in place precisely because the nation-state has constantly struggled to discipline and contain the black rebellion that has always been threatening its integrity.

The spiritual, religious practices of the enslaved were a direct challenge to the spiritual terror that the enslavers performed throughout the Americas. While the plantocracy burned alive, beheaded, dismembered, and disfigured those who rebelled and/or committed suicide (which we should read in continuum), Africans also tried various methods to reclaim the dead by harnessing spirits, catching shadows, and stealing the ears and personal effects of dead slavers in order to control their ability to haunt after death (Brown 2003). Many of these practices were based in the same religious traditions that influenced candomblé in Brazil. The dead were an active presence on all sides, so harnessing the powers of death meant harnessing the powers of freedom and liberation for the enslaved. The courageous actions of black parents and family members in the face of death, including the theater of Culture Shock and the work of React or Die!, harness the spiritual power of the dead as a tactic of subversive confrontation against the state in the continuation of this war.

Breath and Trauma

The black community's response to state terror marks the weakness of white supremacy, the racial state, and Afro-paradise itself. Some scholars argue that there is no such thing as a black community in Bahia (e.g., Sansone 2003). Indeed, some have even argued that there is no such thing as a black family (Frazier 1942). The lived experience of blackness in Bahia, however, particularly in peripheral communities, goes against these claims. Even when verbal discourses of racial solidarity are absent, the grotesque nature of state violence produces the collective black body (Smith 2014). Many black people self-identify and organize as black; they also construct communities based on neighborhoods, collective memories, and family and have been doing so in an explicitly political way for generations. These expressions of blackness in the face of oppression have been decidedly political and tactical.

The effect of terror inflicted on black families by police raids and death-squad murders goes largely unremarked and is rarely the focus of what little political attention Brazil pays to state violence in Bahia. Yet as we have seen with the efforts of React or Die! and the theater work of Culture Shock, many militantes organizing from the community for the community are acutely aware that the family is at the heart of global antiblack genocide, and articulate this violence as communally felt. Black women and black families continue to speak out against the very horrible nature of spiritual terror.

The haunting story of Mr. Lazaro and his family, the murder of his two sons, and the sequelae his family still experiences underscore the intergenerational, communal consequences of state violence that extend the boundaries of death beyond those killed. Families are the targets of antiblack genocide and die as a result of state terror. What then is the response to this violence and what shape does a resistant politics take?

Fanon's (1965a) assessment of colonial violence extended beyond the parameters of the political to also include the clinical, "the cause of deep psychic damage," whether perpetrated by the settler or the colonized (Mbembe 2012, 21). Fanon framed this deep psychic damage as "the pain and suffering caused in general by the colonial *nomos* [that] undermine the ability of the subject or of the patient to return to the world of human speech" (ibid.). For Fanon, the daily travails of "aggression, racism, contempt, interminable rituals of humiliation, murders" that the colonized undergo within the framework of colonialism (and here I extend that to the conditions of internal colonialism today), would inevitably cause a person, a people, to lose the ability to speak. In this sense, the colonial condition is "phenomenal" in that:

> [i]t touched both the senses, the psychic and affective domains. It was the purveyor of mental disorders, which were difficult to treat and cure. It excluded any dialectic of recognition and was indifferent to any moral argument. Over time it attacked even the most private, innermost areas of subjectivity and ran the risk of depriving the colonized of any mnesic trace that turned such "loss into something more than a haemorrhagic void." (Mbembe 2012, 22)

In this passage, Mbembe revisits Fanon's theories of colonial trauma and the ways that colonizers attempted to erase even the affective memories of the colonized (loved ones, family ties). This was a war strategy. Like colonial violence, the contemporary trauma of antiblack violence in Bahia is a phenomenal trauma that affects the senses, the psyche, and affect. Consequently, it often results in a loss of the language necessary to articulate race as an experiential phenomenon. The rhetoric of racial democracy fills this void, but it is not, I argue, an expression of the inner psyche or the affective domains of black people. Rather, this rhetoric is a colonial one that holds this empty space like a prerecorded message. Silence is the end result of antiblack genocide in Bahia.

If this silence is a symptom of trauma, then the theater is potentially a radical space for the restoration of speech. Speech and the discursive realm do not hold ultimate importance. Rather, restoring speech is a key step toward redressing the erasure of the black body, and it can happen through witnessing. The embodied, refracted representation of violence on the stage, and its interrogation through the theater, can excite a form of call-and-response testimonial within the community that reconnects the black body in pain to communal suffering, bringing the black body out of the realm of the invisible, into the realm of the visible; that is, in the face of unimaginable torture and death.

In addition to being a richly layered critique of police violence in Bahia, US imperialism, the war on terror, the transnational police state, global antiblackness and racism, and the hegemonic narratives of racial democracy in Brazil, "The Police Raid" vignette creates a pause for the audience participants by allowing them a moment (or a stunning fifteen-minute performance) to stop to think about their realities. The audience in this sense is not only the crowd that gathers to watch the play but also the greater "audience" of police violence—the family members and communities of those who fall victim to this terror. Thus, this performance brings us back to the question of the political potential of the theater and the role of that witnessing as political practice.

Returning to the "Plataforma" interjection, this utterance indicates pause and recognition between the audience members and the play. This is not necessarily a utopic political interpretation, although some may read it as such. It is not that the performance, in its intense engagement with the real, elicits an emotional response from the audience, for not all audience members connected in this way. However, this utterance signals the deeper, political dynamic of witnessing.[24]

To be clear, the utterance of "Plataforma" was not the witnessing that human-rights advocates' refer to as the therapeutic, often medicalized process of telling—a process that the victims of state abuse are often called upon to perform for the state and international entities (like the United Nations or Jussara's testimony in 2005). Instead, this human-rights ritual is meant to enact justice in the aftermath of torture, abuse, and killing with impunity, and it embodies the notion of redemptive, restorative healing that accompanies it (Feldman 2004). However, following Nadia Seremetakis (1991), I would like to think of the "Plataforma" interjection as something resembling "antiphonal witnessing." In her work examining women's mourning practices in contemporary Greece, Seremetakis defines *antiphonal witnessing* as evidence of affective communities that emerge out of experiences of suffering and pain. Antiphony is a call-and-response chant organized in a musical round (like the repeated refrain "Stop to Think" that punctuates the vignettes of the play). The word names the activity of the chorus in Greek tragedy, but African communities and people of African descent in the diaspora also use call-and-response witnessing; in particular, it marks African descendant practices in the Protestant Christian tradition (Gates and Anozie 1984). Antiphonal witnessing is a contract that mourners establish between discourse and pain (Seremetakis 1991, 120). It is an affective practice that invokes the dead in order to maintain their cultural memory and political presence. Allen Feldman employs Seremetakis's use of antiphonal witnessing to analyze the practice of call-and-response witnessing among black women in South Africa during the Truth and Reconciliation Commission hearings, tying it to indigenous practices among the Xhosa as well. The Xhosa word *phefumla* refers to the soul, but, as Feldman points out, it also refers to breath (*phefumlo*), and implies that

> [a] person in mourning, a person harboring great suffering and emotional stress, experiences a heavy weight on the chest and shoulders, and cannot breathe easily . . . speech is exhaling the soul, the release of blockage, and an emergence from social death that is incomplete unless it is witnessed and historicized by congregational modes of performance, rather than passive recording (2004, 177).

"Plataforma" is *phefumla,* a released breath that emerges from the soul, and as such is a mode of witnessing that signals the speaker's representation at this moment as an embodiment of the absent dead and suffering. By using the cultural frame of South African mourning practices to read the "Plataforma" utterance, my intention is to again push us beyond discourses of Brazilian exceptionalism to locate this moment not only in the Bahian experience but also as part of a diasporic experience. This lone audience member who uttered "Plataforma" was not an atomized, traumatized victim, but a representative embodied figure for the wounded, tortured, disappeared, and dead who have been the victims and survivors of violence within genocidal assemblages.

Nonetheless, reading *Stop to Think* solely as a space of resistance is limiting and reductive in that it leads us to a simplistic, flattened interpretation of the theater that does not account for its ephemerality. *Stop to Think* literally happens while the state continues its practices of violence, and we cannot tie the play to any measurable change in state practices. Moreover, we cannot even explicitly tie performances of the play to direct acts of subversion or rebellion by the black peripheral communities that are the play's audience. Rather, the best way to think about the effect of Culture Shock is to remember that witnessing is an act of engaging with the performance that incorporates the audience into the act of protest;[25] as Elam argues,

> When most successful, the social protest performance [is] an interactive process. All elements of the exchange between audience and stage [contribute] to make the performance a participatory, collective communion. (Elam 1997, 130)

Audience participation in social-protest theater is a "symbolic act of rebellion" (Elam 1997, 131). The barriers between stage and spectator have been momentarily dismantled, and the observer has become a willing participant in the act of subversiveness (Boal 1979). It is not the actual, tangible subversiveness of these acts, but rather their role as acts of witnessing that give them political weight.

The interruption by the woman in the audience at Fazenda Grande do Retiro, albeit brief, reveals the unspoken and often overlooked narrative of black women in the discourses of police violence in Brazil as well. Black women play key roles not only as survivors of state violence but as denouncers and subversives amid the gendered politics of the state. If we return to the intensification of the black body as hyperreal juxtaposed to the black body in pain and the suffering community, then we realize that one of the primary outcomes of state violence is the muffling of the voices of black women whose lives are disproportionately affected by this terror (Canabrava). Violence, and the violent display of a mutilated and tortured body in peripheral communities, dissociates the black body from community, home, and family. It is an attempt to individuate that which is collective and to decontextualize communal ties.

Theater has political power as a space of undoing.[26] Through the embodied practice of performance, the play publicly undoes the erasure of the black body and discourse of antiblackness in the social imaginary and deconstructs the rhetoric of the Brazilian racial, sexual contract. Culture Shock radically reimagines the black body, redefining the black body in pain beyond its usage as the canvas for the state's performative instantiation of social authority. Instead, the practice of witnessing, inspired by the play, evokes the affective materiality of the black community and declares the weakness of white supremacy as part of a dying colonialism in order to consolidate its authority. Witnessing, as breath and release, is the community's counternarrative to the state's attempts to harness the power of the dead.

To witness state violence in Bahia—and survive it—is to refuse to forget the names of the dead that have been effaced by the myth of Afro-paradise. The utterance "Plataforma" manifested this impossible (a voice emerging from the invisible, the interstices) witness, marking the presence of community survivors and their political voice.

"Plataforma" was an interval that gave temporary voice to the ineffable. The audience member's utterance was a pause in the trauma of Afro-paradise, a flash of memory induced by this theatrical representation (Moten 2003). The theater can be a subversive space where those with few resources can confront systems of oppression head on; its work is creative and ephemeral, shifting with the attitudes of those who produce (and attend) it and reflecting a social moment. This reflection (and refraction) connects it to local and global social processes and creates in it a domain for critique. Culture Shock's use of the theater is a politics of emergence.[27]

The war rages on. But black people are not sitting by idly while being killed. The power of Culture Shock's performance is its potential as a momentary space of healing. Like the momentary practice of quilombo during the epoch of slavery, this healing is restorative, demonstrating the power of black agency and the political stakes of witnessing as a subversive practice. Death does not happen without gut-wrenching emotions and feelings of loss and pain. Nevertheless, people are continuously discovering methods of restoration. Restoring speech is just one example of this and is a marker of the spiritual community that also demonstrates black radical agency in the face of extreme violence.

Theater can undo erasure, making the etchings of the past visible in the palimpsestic overlays of the present. It wrests the black body away from the spiritual domain of the state, where it is a symbol of the heteropatriarchal, antiblack social contract, and recasts it as a part of the whole body of a spiritual black community defined in part by its collective suffering and struggle. These acts are collectively healing—a kind of political mourning that emerges from the spiritual. Witnessing as mourning is also a performative, collective authenticating act that harnesses ghost stories and then reembodies them radically and politically in the present, keeping the memories of the dead alive and forcing the state and society to reconcile with their disturbing presence. As Allen Feldman observes, in South Africa, "[t]he dead may have died as isolated individuals within the structures of the state, but their witnessing by the social mothers was a ritual of a social reincorporation, and due to the dead's potential but unrealized status as ancestors, a rite of reorigination for the surviving kin-groups, from which the dead had been subtracted by violence" (2004, 177). When witnessing is harnessed by the communities that the state targets with its violence, it can also be a radical act of reintegration—making a fragmented community whole again.

The murder of Aurina Rodrigues Santana can be read as the state's successful use of spiritual terror to quell a threatening voice. I am convinced that the recent memory of her death, the death of her partner and son, and the image of her two little girls who lived to witness was actively present with the mothers of Canabrava as they sat in the shadows that day in Praça da Piedade during I ENPOSP. The mixture of the threat of losing one's own life or that of one's family members to torture, and the possibility of death leaving one's young children behind to fend for themselves, is overwhelming. The direct connection between Mrs. Santana's denunciation of the police and her assassination sends a clear message: witnessing is an offense punishable by death.

But this plot also has another possible interpretive reading. Mrs. Santana knew that she was running the risk of being killed when she denounced her children's torture. She knew that this would invite the masked backlash under the cover of night of the very police officers who came to her home in uniform during the day to torture her children in front of their neighbors. Let us honor her choices. The state hopes to prevent social mothers from giving birth (politically, biologically, philosophically) to children (read as biological, communal, or revolutionary) that the state will then have to kill in order to preserve the moral social order. As a result, the state performs its violence to traumatize these social mothers, and the families and communities that they represent, in order to silence them and to eradicate, if only temporarily, the possibility of revolution. Aurina Rodrigues Santana was a mother whose speaking out challenged the life-and-death configuration of this structure, explicitly naming the state as torturer and murderer. Her death at the hands of a death squad was an act of race/gender terrorism performed to ensure maternal, communal silence and tacitly designed to abort a culture of resistance lest it rise up and speak. But she had already risen up to speak, reconfiguring the political choice in the face of spiritual terror. Instead of choosing to remain silent, she chose an act of revolutionary suicide: speaking out, in the face of certain death. In many ways, hers is an analogue of revolutionary suicide (Newton [1973] 2009).

Suicide and rebellion are retaliatory responses to the spiritual terror of slavery; they harness the powers of death. These struggles are far from utopic, romantic visions of social resistance. They are in actuality the residual effects of war. By removing the power to kill from the state, however, and redefining the terms of silence, subversion, and death, black communities reconceptualize resistance outside of the current political framework of spiritual terror. This reconfiguration—at once terrifying and potentially liberating—challenges the life/death power of state-sanctioned murder and shifts the control over life and death back to black people. Those who teach revolution and/or speak out challenge this configuration of life and death by naming the state as murderer and taking away the state's power to kill by harnessing the spiritual power of the dead, both through witnessing and transforming suffering into affective community. Speaking up and speaking out mean controlling how and when you die—even if there is no choice to live.

As Fanon shows us, colonial war is inherently separating. But it can also inadvertently be reintegrating; that is, the political context of state violence in Bahia has produced a unique and powerful response: experiences with suffering have defined black people living at the margins as a community, and this is a political configuration. We can hear Aurina Santana's death, the silence of the mothers of Canabrava, and the suffering of Mr. Lazaro and his family in rhythms of call and response. They are witnesses, survivors of violence that marks the political boundaries of the state and its social contract. The palimpsest of Bahia, like Feldman's antiphonic witnessing, is the "magic writing pad of overlapping and discontinuous, visible and less visible, strata of memory" (Feldman 2004, 177). A palimpsestic embodiment, it incorporates not only the discourses of pain and trauma associated with state violence, but also the afterimages of its echo, not in the dead this time, but rather the living. As Fanon reminds us, witnessing means traveling side by side with the colonized and walking alongside the community in its suffering: "We must not simply fly over it. We must, on the contrary, walk step by step along the great wound inflicted on [colonized] soil and on the [colonized] people. We must question [colonial war] meter by meter, and measure the fragmentation of the . . . family, the degree to which it finds itself scattered" (1965a, 119). The politics of survival and community stand in contraposition to the realities of antiblack genocide, and the fight of the people is embedded in the breath of survival.

This book has been a project of witnessing as well. In saying this, I do not wish to invoke the much-critiqued trope of anthropological witnessing and fall back into well-worn conversations about ethnographic authority and ethical positioning. As Liisa Malkki (1995) notes, anthropological witnessing can often make fieldwork seem more like police work. And Asale Angel-Ajani reminds us that "the act of anthropological witnessing is largely a veiled attempt to (re)establish the authority of the ethnographer" (2008, 135). However, in structuring this book around *Stop to Think* and the stories of those people who have becomes martyrs for the React or Die! campaign, I have asked the reader to engage in a project of witnessing that does not distance us from the fact of antiblack violence currently plaguing Salvador, but instead implicates us in that violence. I ask you to walk step by step with the struggle of black people in Bahia, recognizing that coming to know the stories of the dead incriminate us all.

Appendix

Methodology and Timing

I conducted the bulk of my fieldwork with Culture Shock from 2003 to 2005. After 2005, I returned to the United States but continued to travel to Salvador frequently and to collaborate with Culture Shock until 2007. My work with React or Die! and Quilombo X expands across a broader timeline. The first interview I conducted in Salvador in 2001 was with Hamilton Borges dos Santos, co-organizer of React or Die! and Quilombo X. At that time, Hamilton was an actor and educator living in Belo Horizonte, and I was a graduate student beginning to do research on the use of poetry and theater as a form of black protest in Bahia. I met Hamilton at the Vozabilidades theater troupe performance in downtown Salvador that June. Struck by his use of poetry and theater to reflect on black political identity, I approached him after the performance and asked whether he would allow me to interview him. Sternly, he looked me up and down and began to ask me a series of questions: who I was, what I was doing in Brazil, and why I thought he should take time out to talk with me. Naive, flustered, and speaking Portuguese terribly, I began to talk to him about the black struggle in the United States and its waning after the demise of the Black Panther Party in the 1980s. I felt that the black movement in Brazil had an energy that the United States had lost. (It is interesting to revisit this amid the dawn of a new black social movement in the United States, #BlackLivesMatter). Somehow in all of this, I managed to stumble over the phrase *estamos na mesma luta* (we are in the same fight), and remarkably, he smiled. A few days later I interviewed him. From that moment on, we built a friendship that has grown over the years.

When Hamilton returned to Bahia in 2003 and began grassroots organizing in the poor, outlying majority black neighborhoods of Salvador—*a periferia*—I volunteered to help him from time to time out of friendship and solidarity in the struggle. Sometimes this meant lending my budding filming skills. Sometimes it meant translating into English or just helping out at workshops. All of this happened while I was conducting my formal field research with Culture Shock. In 2005, when Hamilton became one of the key militantes to organize React or Die!, I volunteered to work with the movement as an international liaison. At first this relationship was a bit awkward. No one really knew what to do with the "black American girl." Still, I went to meetings and volunteered my services and filming. As the years went by, I would help as much as I could, remotely, and then jump back into things when I returned to Bahia. As time passed, the campaign shifted due to internal ebbs, flows, and challenges. My role changed as well; I became more involved in community outreach and mission.

I first met Culture Shock on Friday, October 3, 2003, at a women's conference hosted by the Unified Black Movement (MNU) in downtown Salvador. Performance is integrated into many political gatherings of the black movement in Bahia. For this reason, the performance of Culture Shock at the MNU Women's Conference in 2003 was not an anomaly, even if it was a shock.

As part of the opening of the program for the conference that evening, Culture Shock performed *Pare Para Pensar* (*Stop to Think*). Four actors—all young black men in their twenties and thirties—caught the crowd off-guard when they interrupted the opening ceremony, screaming, "Silêncio! Silêncio!" (Silence! Silence!). Even though we knew that a performance was going to happen during the event, they still startled us by interrupting the conference and storming into the aisles from their "hidden" seated positions in the auditorium. After a few minutes, we realized that the impromptu interruption was not impromptu at all but the beginning of a play, and everyone sat in rapt attention.

Culture Shock's presentation was assertive, straightforward, and biting. The actors spoke about racial injustice, teen pregnancy, the moral hegemony of Christianity, and police violence in peripheral communities. I had never seen or heard of this group before, but I was impressed. A few weeks later, I approached them about my dissertation project and subsequently worked/exchanged with the group for the next seventeen months, from November 2003 to August 2005.

Media of Exchange

My relationship with Culture Shock has always been based on a system of exchange. My proposal to collaborate was initially met with skepticism. The troupe had been burned by several foreign researchers before. Two important factors led them to work with me: my video camera and my dedication to African diaspora politics. Like Hamilton, they wanted to know that I was in solidarity with their struggle. Given the troupe's modest financial resources, combined with their desire for public exposure, the opportunity to have their performances recorded and then transferred to VHS was just too good to be true. At that time, hardly anyone had a video camera. Therefore, my free services were a great opportunity (despite my lack of filming expertise). Many of my friends and acquaintances in the black community treated my video camera as a community asset, calling on me to film everything from candomblé ceremonies to community forums. The relationship that developed between Culture Shock and me was one aspect of this broader context.

My real chance to initiate a formal relationship with Culture Shock came from filming their performance at a neighborhood event in Gamboa de Baixo a few weeks after the MNU women's conference. My entrance into communities, whether neighborhoods or organizations, has always been mediated by my social networks.[1] I had been invited to the event in Gamboa de Baixo to film it for the neighborhood association. The invitation was a result not only of the neighborhood association's desire to archive the community's events, but also of my social network and relationships with black organizers in the city. I knew Gamboa de Baixo through the work of Keisha-Khan Perry (2013), a fellow anthropologist and colleague who has worked with that community for almost two decades. I was only welcome because I had preestablished ties in the community; trust was then, and continues to be, an important element of engaged field research. In other words, my political alliances and identifications have shaped this project as much as my research. Many subaltern communities in Bahia are wary of researchers and their prodding presence, a wariness I found warranted.

I asked each group that presented at that neighborhood event whether I could have permission to film. This led me to my first real conversation with Culture Shock. I walked up to them to ask if I could record their performance and they gave me permission to do so on one condition: that I give them a copy of the video. I naturally agreed and we exchanged contact information. I then filmed the entire afternoon.

What happened next would define my relationship with the troupe for years to come. Sobrevivente, Culture Shock's director and founder, immediately began to call me regularly to ask me when the tape would be ready. I told him I was ready to do it, but the only problem was that I did not have a VCR to use to transfer the DV (the media that my camera used) to VHS (how dated this all sounds now). Thus began the great adventure to find a way to transfer the footage that took me around the city and back again. My first attempt at a solution was to go to Gamboa de Baixo to borrow a friend's VCR. This turned out to be a fiasco. At first she did not have the necessary cables (apparently she had never hooked the VCR to the TV before). Then we realized we could not switch to DV input in order to transfer the material. This may seem like something relatively innocuous, but it took days to assess the problems. After a failed first attempt at DV transfer, I packed up the VCR, carried it up the steep hill along the Avenida Contorno (which I talk more about in chapter 3) from Gamboa de Baixo to my neighborhood, Dois de Julho, to see if it would work with my television set. It didn't. So I packed up the VCR and took it back down the hill. I was now at end of my rope. I asked my landlord if he had a VCR, to no avail; he didn't have one with a remote that could change the input to DV so that I could record. Tired and frustrated, I called Sobrevivente and told him I had been unsuccessful and I got the distinct feeling he thought I was giving him the runaround.

The next few weeks were painful. The word *VCR* gave me hives. Sobrevivente, another Culture Shock actor named Rogério (who works in technology), and I were on the phone constantly trying to resolve the problem. I called everyone I knew to see if they had a VCR and remote that I could borrow, and Culture Shock kept throwing out ideas that seemed to me wouldn't work: "What if we hook it up to . . ."; "I seriously doubt that's going to work."

Finally, Rogério came up with a solution. One of his neighbors had just bought a brand-new VCR with remote, and she said that we could use it to transfer the tape. Eureka! I packed up my camera, all of the cords, the manual, and the DV tapes and headed out the door to the Lapa bus terminal located in the heart of downtown to take the bus to Terezinha, one of the outlying peripheral neighborhoods of the Subúrbio Ferroviário region that sits to the north of the city. It took an hour to get to Terezinha by bus. Along the way I watched the landscape change through the slightly whitened Plexiglas window of my public bus seat. Crowded city streets gave way to quieter, smaller roads with elderly people and children playing in plazas. The economic landscape changed as well. The farther we moved toward the edge of the city, the more working class the neighborhoods became—no high-rise apartment buildings, fewer cars, small concrete houses with wooden doors, progressively less pavement on the roads, and government housing projects. The landscape became greener as well. We started to see more trees and patches of forest. This was my first introduction to the peripheral region of Salvador. Far and out of the way, most people in the city, visitors and residents, rarely if ever venture into the Subúrbio unless they go there to visit someone. In one short hour, I quickly came to realize that there was much more to Salvador than I had previously known.

The bus slowed and came to a halt at the end of the line, which also happened to be the end of the paved road. When I got off the bus, a little stiff, Rogério was there waiting for me. We proceeded to a small cluster of tiny barrack-like white houses where his friend lived. Her house was small and simple, with white-washed concrete walls and a tiny "American-style" kitchen (one that has no wall between the cooking space and the living room). A single red silk rose and a colorful tablecloth decorated her kitchen table. The living room's two-seater sofa was similar to those that I had seen at the many furniture/appliance stores across the city. There, in front of the sofa, was her new television and VHS player—of which she was clearly proud. I, for one, was beside myself with elation. The previous weeks had been some of the most stressful I'd spent in Salvador. My word and reputation, as well as my relationship with Culture Shock, hinged on this one seemingly small act.

Rogério knew exactly what he was doing, and soon the material was recorded. The three of us spent the next couple of hours watching that tape and chatting about life while eating Nestlé cookies and cream chocolate. Sobrevivente was very happy to receive the tape and immediately his demeanor changed. I had passed the first test of trust, but there would be many more to go. As annoying and emotionally draining as the VCR incident may have been (it took a month to get the whole thing resolved), that experience formed the foundation of my bond with Culture Shock.

Forming Political Kinship

Soon after I completed my mission, Sobrevivente invited me to discuss the possibility of working with the group for my research project. I arrived in the neighborhood of San Martins, where Culture Shock is based, with little trouble—taking the bus from the *Elevador Lacerda*[2] to Cidade Baixa and then taking another bus to arrive at the pharmacy in San Martins. Culture Shock rehearsed at the *Escola Fonte do Capim* (Grassy Springs School). The director of the school was living in the community and gave the troupe access because of the outreach work they did with children and teens in the neighborhood. Rehearsals involved the older group members, who performed plays in neighborhoods and at functions, and the younger cohort members or the children from the community, who came to learn how to perform (*fazer teatro*). It was getting dark by the time I arrived and the school security guard had to unlock the padlock and chain on the gate to let us in. Given the community's experiences with violence, the school stays under lock and key after hours, and a security guard is constantly on patrol.

That night, I met with core group members, four in all: Sobrevivente, Rogério, Raphael, and Uilton. They asked me about my project and intentions. We swapped stories about our experiences with collaborative research projects, the highs and the lows. They did not want to be exploited, but they were willing to give me a chance.

The conversation then turned more toward the subject of trust and politics. "Tell us about the struggles of black people in the United States," they said. I began to explain the politics of race and racism in the United States, from everyday discrimination to disproportionate mass incarceration and police brutality. The decimation of the Black Panther Party by the U.S. government, the aftermath of COINTELPRO (the covert and at times illegal counterintelligence projects conducted by the FBI involving domestic political organizations), and Reaganomics had devastated the mythical struggle of black power that many of my Brazilian friends admired. I told them of my respect for the history of black politics in Brazil and of my belief in the connections between the condition of black people all over the world, and how this fueled my desire to speak out against racism, inequality, and injustice in my work. The four troupe members then shared with me something I had heard from my black Brazilian colleagues and friends: they too believed in a global black political struggle that put our experiences with suffering and racism into conversation. This did not mean unilateral trust of all black people, ignorance of imperialism, or an insistence that blackness is a monolith; rather, it meant recognizing the commonalities of our struggles and the urgent politics behind them.

I did not record our conversation that day; I reconstruct what happened from memory and my notes. That too was a political decision on my part, since it would have been inappropriate to record our first meeting; as many anthropologists have noted, recording equipment can sometimes hinder the ability to establish trusting relationships. It may seem that I am romanticizing this encounter in San Martins, but I do not believe that I am. Our relationship has been complex over the years, like any relationship with an organization. My racial politics and convictions had everything to do with the affiliation I subsequently built with Culture Shock that day. Their intense interrogation was meant to test my sincerity and commitment.

My point in recounting this story is not to slip into essentialist pan-Africanist arguments, but to highlight the way a shared, imagined, black political community facilitates my relationship with Culture Shock and my relationship to my field research. Culture

Shock's interview of me that day was not the first time I had been interrogated by a militante as a condition of working together. Indeed, this conversation recalled my interview in 2001 with React or Die! cofounder Hamilton. The development of this research project has hinged on my explicitly expressed political convictions.[3]

My ability to work with Culture Shock was facilitated by their perceived belief that we shared political convictions, not simply based on historical ties to the African diaspora or our skin color and shared African features, but because of our shared, expressed political convictions. The history of racial-identity politics in Brazil has conditioned many black Brazilians who self-identify as black, both culturally and politically, to evaluate comradery not first by skin color, as is customary (at least superficially) in the United States, but by political expression: It is not so much appearance as what one says and how she or he communicates that leads to recognition and kinship formation.

For the rest of November 2003, I attended several Culture Shock performances per week. That November was the busiest I've seen Culture Shock. They performed in the neighborhoods of Sofia, Rio Vermelho, and Fazenda Grande do Retiro, and I attended all of their performances. Ultimately, I decided to focus on the performance at Fazenda Grande do Retiro for this book, as I explain in the introduction. In making this decision, I do not want to simplify or limit my perspective of Culture Shock; quite to the contrary, the richness of their work was captured by their presentation that day. Admittedly, focusing on a different presentation at a different time and place might have led to a very different experience of the play . . . but that is the nature of performance.

Notes

Introduction

1. To access the Bahiatursa propaganda video featuring Joel, see http://mais.uol.com.br/view/1575mnadmj5c/veja-propaganda-da-bahiatursa-com-joel-da-conceicao-04021C306AC4C13307?types=A&.

2. I prefer the term *periphery* (which translates directly to *periferia* in Portuguese) rather than *favela*. *Favela* often carries a negative connotation. Within Brazil, the two terms are often used interchangeably, and *periferia,* even with its own shortcomings, does not carry the same kind of negative weight; see Holston (2009).

3. Unlike the United States, Brazil's inner cities have historically been the space of the upper class, whereas the suburbs are marked as geographically, socially, economically, and racially marginal. The urban geographic breakdown from center to periphery reflects class stratification from wealthiest to least wealthy and race distribution from white to black (Telles 2004).

4. This is a quote from Jeanderson Castro, recorded in the 2013 documentary *Menino Joel* by Max Gaggino (Gaggino 2013; available at http://vimeo.com/62610843).

5. Testimony from Míriam da Conceição, Joel's mother, in *Menino Joel.*

6. *Menino Joel,* http://vimeo.com/62610843.

7. Although Bahia is a state, historically the city of Salvador has interchangeably been referred to as the city of Bahia. Thus, I use these two terms interchangeably throughout this book, not because I want to conflate the state with the city, but because within the culture of the region itself, the two are often interchanged. For more on the discussion of the city of Bahia, see, for example, Reis (2003).

8. This is slowly changing; for example, see Romero (2013).

9. The site goes on to note that this image in part comes from the many parties and festivals the city holds each year. The most notorious of these festivals is of course carnival, which I discuss in chapter 1.

10. Here and throughout this book I use the term *police* to refer to the military and civil police in Brazil. The Brazilian police are organized into three different bodies, two

of which fall under the purview of the secretary of public security and operate at the state level: the civil and military police. The third body is under the control of the federal government even at the state level, the federal police. The civil police are plain-clothes officers responsible for criminal investigation. They are the administrative branch of domestic policing and do everything from issue identity cards to investigating murders and registering criminal complaints. The military police are uniformed foot patrol. They are responsible for day-to-day surveillance in neighborhoods, arrests, and pursuit of criminals and criminal activity. The term "military police" should not be confused with the use of the term in the United States (and elsewhere) to refer to those who police military personnel. For a more detailed discussion of this breakdown and its history see Caldeira (2000, 108–109).

11. It is important to note how odd it is that the civil police report killing the exact same number of people for 2011 and 2012.

12. Several states still refused to present their data, and FBSP had to subsequently draw from statistics produced by the *Sistema Nacional de Estatísticas em Segurança Pública* (SINESPJC) (FBSP 2013, 122).

13. Official statistics that address "external death" do not adequately reveal the extent to which state violence factors into violent death. Most reports include all deaths by homicide and accidents, including traffic accidents. As a result, when the numbers of "external deaths" are aggregated by race, they often reflect a warped picture of who dies. For example, although black Brazilians and white Brazilians die of traffic accidents, white Brazilians tend to die because they are *driving* cars and black Brazilians tend to die because they are *hit* by cars. We must aggregate external death figures in order to understand the complex race, class, and gender realities that define them and get a true picture of the landscape of death by nonnatural causes in Brazil.

14. The establishment of SEPPIR has led to an increased focus on issues of race at the federal level. The Statute of Racial Equality (Law 12.288) was decreed by President Dilma Rousseff in 2010. It expands the government's ability to implement programs to redress racial inequality in the nation and prosecute racism; see http://www.planalto.gov.br/ccivil_03/_Ato2007–2010/2010/Lei/L12288.htm.

15. Bolsa Família is a conditional cash-transfer program for the poor that the government of President Luiz Ignacio Lula da Silva established in 2003. It is the most successful such program in the world (Soares, Ribas, and Osório 2010).

16. I build the term Afro-*nationalism* from Jasbir Puar's concept of *homonationalism*, which she defines as "the complexities of how 'acceptance' and 'tolerance' for gay and lesbian subjects have become a barometer by which the right to and capacity for national sovereignty is evaluated" (Puar 2013, 336).

17. Rahier draws on Charles Hale's (2004) notion of the *indio permitido* (permissible Indian). Hale argues that the neoliberal multicultural state includes indigenous identities only when the people who seek rights play within the rules of the dominant power structure.

18. For a rich discussion of global white supremacy, see, for example, Jung, Vargas, and Bonilla-Silva 2011. I borrow the term *white ascendancy* here from Rey Chow (2006).

19. Although death squads are not exclusively tied to the police, there is a strong correlation that is both historical and cultural (Amnesty International 2005). I discuss this further in chapter 3.

20. One of the few comprehensive analyses of racialized experiences with police violence nationwide was conducted by Michael Mitchell and Charles Wood (1999) using a 1988 PNAD survey. Mitchell and Wood found that *pretos*—men of African descent with dark skin—were 2.4 times more likely to be victims of police abuse than any other subset of the population throughout Brazil, even when controlling for socioeconomic factors. Subsequent work by Ignacio Cano, Julita Lemgruber, Leonarda Musumeci, Ana Paula Miranda, and Sonia Travassos takes a more comprehensive look at experiences with police aggression and harassment at the regional level, particularly in Rio de Janeiro and São Paulo (e.g., Cano 2010; Lemgruber et al. 2003). This latter research also finds significant disproportionalities to varying degrees.

21. Aiyana Stanley-Jones was a seven-year-old black girl shot to death by police officer Joseph Weekley on October 4, 2011, while she was sleeping on the couch in her grandmother's home in Detroit, Michigan.

22. I use the term *militante* (militant) in solidarity with the organizers who say that activists are those who "do activities" and militants are those who take on radical political action as a direct call. The distinction is a decidedly controversial one that emerges from long-standing debates about the relationship between activism, neoliberalism, and NGO work in Brazil. See, for example, Alvarez (2009).

23. Genetic racial testing is very controversial and anthropologists frequently note the flaws in this testing (Mullings 2005). The complete online version of the study elaborates on the motives behind the project and the controversies surrounding it: http://www.bbc.co.uk/portuguese/noticias/cluster/2007/05/070427_raizesafrobrasileiras.shtml.

24. For an in-depth discussion on this topic, see Santos (2006).

25. Mary Pratt defines *contact zones* as spaces of colonial encounter "in which peoples geographically and historically separated come into contact with one other and establish ongoing relations, usually involving conditions of coercion, radical inequality, and intractable conflict" (1992, 6).

26. Taylor argues that, "[l]ike Barthes's mythical speech, [the scenario] consists of 'material which has been worked on.' . . . Its portable framework bears the weight of accumulative repeats" (2003, 28).

27. Taylor suggests that we use the idea of the "scenario" as a cross-temporal, cross-spatial model for understanding social structures and behaviors. In order to analyze scenarios, we must pay attention to "milieu and corporeal behaviors such as gestures, attitudes, and tones not reducible to language" (2003, 28).

28. Schechner (1985) defines *restored behavior* as a summation of events that extend into the past, incorporating everything up to and including the final performance.

29. I engage with *performance* as the theatrical, the spectacular, and the everyday embodied practice (gestures, looks, glances, and unspoken codes). For a detailed discussion of the definition of *performance*, see, for example, Carlson (1996).

30. The application of racial formation theory to Brazil is predicated on the idea that race is a global phenomenon that has created similar patterns of racial formation around the world (Winant 2001).

31. Fanon's approach resonates with the theoretical perspective of black Brazilian political scholars such as Abdias do Nascimento (1979) and Lélia Gonzalez (1983), who separately argue that black people have a place in Brazilian society that has been defined by a politics of race that makes the black experience salient, isolatable, and consequential.

32. Frank Wilderson (2010) employs Antonio Gramsci (1992) to outline what he calls "structural antagonisms" that frame race in global society. This approach is helpful for thinking about the ways that positionality rather than identification informs racial politics.

33. The idea of dialogic constructivism comes from Judith Butler's work and is applicable to race, even though Butler does not deal with race explicitly in her early writing (Butler 1990; 1993). Her work on injurious speech, precarious life, violence, and mourning (1997; 2004; 2009) incorporates a more robust discussion of violence and experience.

34. José Munoz defines *racial performativity* as "a doing," following J. L. Austin (1962). Munoz writes, "More precisely, I mean to describe a political doing, the effects that the recognition of racial belonging, coherence, and divergence present in the world" (2006, 678–79).

35. Both Saidiya Hartman (1997) and Frank Wilderson (2010) employ the term *fungibility* to frame blackness as the result of both accumulation and giveness.

36. Vargas (2008) notes that few scholars seriously examine the politics of antiblack genocide in the contemporary African diaspora. His approach to genocide is inspired by the document *We Charge Genocide,* authored by the Civil Rights Congress (CRC) (Patterson [1951] 2007) in the United States in 1951 and Abdias do Nascimento's (1979) writings on antiblack genocide in Brazil.

37. In his essay, "Genocide: The Social Lynching of Africans and Their Descendants in Brazil" (1979), Nascimento deconstructs the myth of racial democracy by demystifying the history of slavery in Brazil and debunking Gilberto Freyre's ([1933] 1973) luso-tropicalism theory. He argues that "Brazil as a nation proclaims herself the only racial democracy in the world, and much of the world views and accepts her as such. But an examination of the historical development of my country reveals the true nature of her social, cultural, political and economic anatomy: it is essentially racist and vitally threatening to Black people" (1979, 59). Nascimento's assessment includes a biting critique of the sexual exploitation of black women, the Catholic Church, and cordial racism. However, his analysis maintains heteronormative patriarchal assumptions about race, gender, sexuality, and nation.

38. Jasbir Puar (2007) pushes us to analyze "sexuality, race, gender, nation, class, and ethnicity in relation to the tactics, strategies, and logistics of war machines," emphasizing the ways that assemblages cluster and overlap across political terrains (2007, xi). Puar's definition of *assemblage* is influenced by the work of Deleuze and Guattari (2007, 193) as well.

39. João Biehl engages directly with Agamben's (1995) concept of bare life as the existence of life with no political meaning in his analysis of Brazil (Biehl 2001; 2005).

40. He writes, "Today, in the democratically and economically readjusting environment of Brazil, sick and impoverished groups are not directly killed by the state (even though police violence is still frequent) or made politically dead (that is, excluded from political life)" (Biehl 2001, 139).

41. Foucault ([1977] 2003) defines *biopolitics* as government technologies of managing life to harness power.

42. Ferreira da Silva disputes applying Agamben's theories of bare life and sovereignty to global questions of race, particularly in Brazil. Instead she employs Kant's concept of *jus necessitatis* (right of necessity) (2009, 231).

43. Ferreira da Silva writes, "Racial violence . . . *does not require stripping off signifiers of humanity* [my emphasis]. On the contrary, this collapsing is already inscribed in ra-

ciality, which produces humanity, the self determined political (ethical-juridical) figure that thrives in ethical life, only because it institutes it in a relationship . . . with another political figure (the affectable I) that stands before the horizon of death" (2009, 234).

44. Frank Wilderson (2010) asserts that there is a global epistemology that associates blackness with slave status/nonhuman. As Sylvia Wynter observes, the Western notion of the human (and by extension humanism) was conceived in relation to the white male subject, necessarily locating nonwhite male people outside of its purview (Wynter 2003; Scott 2000).

45. Roach's work builds on the previous scholarship of Paul Gilroy (1993).

46. I borrow the terms *phenomenology of violence* and *spirit of violence* from Achille Mbembe, who uses these terms to define "the state of depravation or non-actuality called death" and omnipresence of violence in the postcolony (2001, 173, 175).

47. For a detailed explanation of my methodologies for this project and my use of video, see the appendix.

48. As David Theo Goldberg (2002) argues of the racial state, racially oppressed groups within the racial state must assimilate or be eliminated, and both paths are a means to the same end: the eradication of the racialized communities that are not in power.

49. Omi and Winant (1994) define racial projects as "simultaneously an interpretation, representation, or explanation of racial dynamics, and an effort to reorganize and redistribute resources along particular lines" (1994, 56).

50. At the heart of Goffman's theory is the necessarily social nature of performance. One cannot act without an audience. He defines performance as "all the activity of an individual which occurs during a period marked by his continuous presence before a particular set of observers and which has some influence on the observers" (1959, 22).

51. There are, of course, notable exceptions to this trend; see, for example, Hautzinger (2007); Perry (2013); and Williams (2013).

52. http://www.press.illinois.edu/books/smith/afroparadise/.

Interlude I: Culture Shock

1. I am not certain whether these kinds of street performances occur with any regularity in Fazenda Grande do Retiro, but I do know that street performances are not an anomaly in the city. In downtown Salvador, particularly in the Pelourinho tourist district and Praça da Piedade, street performances happen fairly often.

2. A style of theater that shares a genealogy with the agitation propaganda that came out of Bolshevist Russia.

3. Here I am referring to the theatrical approach of Bertolt Brecht (Willett 1964). Indeed, many of the theater groups I worked with while in Bahia follow his teachings, even though some employed them without having formally studied theater. Actors and directors expressed this connection in my personal interviews with theater troupes from the suburban region. At the festival in Fazenda Grande, I was boldly challenged by one of the festival coordinators who asked me how my project engaged with the work of both Brecht and Boal (1979). After having a brief conversation with him about the two, he smiled slyly and told me not to underestimate the intellectual rigor of their popular-theater movement. The message he wanted to convey to me was clear—we are as educated and aware of theory and technique as the more "elite" actors and dramatists of the city.

4. Augusto Boal's (1979) deconstruction of the Western theater and map for a theater of the oppressed that draws the audience directly into performance and use of the stage as a participatory classroom for radical change is clearly present in Culture Shock's work.

5. Despite the convenience of the metaphor comparing Culture Shock's performance to hip-hop, there are obvious differences. Culture Shock does not perform over music tracks or specialized beats (although there is a drum that is often played as a base rhythm for some of the scenes). Each monologue is different; some monologues rhyme, some do not. And at times the play sounds more like poetry than rap, lacking the complex linguistic syntax structure that goes into rhyming in hip-hop.

6. See the appendix.

7. The play uses the term *estantes* here, which literally means shelves, and rhymes with the use of the word *instâncias* in the latter part of the sentence. However, translating the word *estantes* as *structures* presentes a clearer picture of the intended meaning.

8. The one instance of dialogue occurs during "The Berlin Wall" scene (discussed in chapter 2).

Chapter 1: Afro-Paradise

1. It is important to note that "violent" causes, according to public-health records, also include accidents and inebriation.

2. See, for example, Perry (2013).

3. The FASEC (2007) report finds that 2 percent of those reporting physical assault identified the police as the aggressors. However, given the very complex politics of reporting police abuse explored in this book's introduction, this number seems under reported.

4. Not all carnival blocos are predominately white and elite. There are dozens of smaller, neighborhood-based carnival groups that tend to be more informal and affordable. Examples would be the samba blocos and Afro-blocos. Afro-blocos (which I discuss at the end of this chapter) are predominately black carnival groups that often engage in an Afrocentric politics. I have paraded several times with Afro-blocos over the years, including the oldest Afro-bloco, Ilê Aiyê. My experience with Afro-blocos has been quite different from what I have witnessed in the elite blocos. There was no violent pushing, shoving, and "moshing" when I paraded with Afro-blocos—a contrast to what I have seen in more mainstream carnival blocos like Chiclete com Banana. That said, Afro-blocos and nonelite blocos still employ cordeiros. Obviously, this can be read as a controversial counterpoint. However, I maintain that we think of cordeiros as occupying a metonymical space of blackness that is both classed and spatialized regardless of the identity of the blocos they "protect." The matter is a complex one fraught with questions of class.

5. As a counterargument, some people argue that employing cordeiros provides jobs to people who badly need them. For a detailed discussion of the gendered racial economics of cordeiros and vendors, see FASEC (2007).

6. See also, for example, Hoffman-French (2013) and Sansone (2002).

7. Indeed, as John Collins argues, the Bahian police play an integral role in protecting the space of Bahia as a cultural patrimony (2014, 476).

8. See, for example, Hall (1997).

9. These ribbons are an iconic tourist item in Salvador and are found in almost any tourist place; see, for example, Ickes (2005).

10. This discourse of availability far exceeds the boundaries of heteronormativity, complicating the politics of desire (Williams 2013).

11. The first two routes are Campo Grande (popularly thought of as the most traditional) and Barra/Ondina.

12. The Globo communications conglomerate has played a key role in shaping Brazilian popular culture since the 1950s, and has been closely linked to the state and national politics since the military dictatorship. It is the most popular television network in Brazil and the largest in Latin America (Straubhaar 1989; Brittos and Bolaño 2005).

13. There has been a long history of heated debates within Brazilian studies about U.S. African Americans' place in discussions on race in Brazil. See, for example, the February 2000 special issue of *Theory, Culture, and Society* 17 (1). Yet the state's anesthetized disavowal of slavery gestures more toward its own colonial entanglement than its desire to appeal to the imperialist desires of African Americans. African American "heritage" tourists make up a miniscule percentage of Bahia's tourist industry, and although the state has sought to appeal to African American tourists in its advertising efforts, the emphasis on black culture in Bahian tourism is as much a response to Brazilian national tourists' tastes for "exotic" black vacation destinations that recall colonialism and slavery as it is a desire to attract "roots" tourism. Moreover, although we can read my dismay over the "hidden" history of the pelourinho as African American hypersensitivity to race, that interpretation is reductionist at best and ahistorical at worst.

14. As recently as 2015 there was still no historical marker or reference to the history of slavery and the legacy of the pelourinho in the neighborhood.

15. On December 18, 2013, the Secretariat of Tourism for the State of Bahia (SETUR), under the leadership of Secretary Domingus Leonelli, launched a website dedicated to ethno-Afro tourism (http://bahia.com.br/segmentos/etnico-afro/). The state designed the site as way to celebrate black culture in Bahia and capitalize on Bahia's African heritage as a unique element of the tourist industry. This effort is the result of decades of intense discussion and critique surrounding the commodification of black culture. It is also an attempt to reconcile Bahia's black identity with its history of racism and the disenfranchisement of its majority black population.

16. See the photo at http://www.panoramio.com/photo/30776054.

17. The first known location of the pelourinho was the Praça do Palácio, where the Portuguese Crown's palace was located. Silva and Pinheiro write that, "until the second half of the sixteenth century, the pillar was exposed in the core-matrix of the city, in the Praça do Palácio, in front of the thirteen windows of the noble building of Casa da Camara e Cadeia, as a symbol of the 'autonomy' and 'Justice' of the city" (1977, 81).

18. I discuss this ironic relationship in more depth in the fourth interlude.

19. Audre Lorde cautions us against the male misnaming of the erotic in the service of oppression. "In order to perpetuate itself, every oppression must corrupt or distort those various sources of power within the culture of the oppressed that can provide energy for change" ([1984] 2012, 54). In the case of the pelourinho, the distorted power is the power of feeling, caring, and wholeness denied by torture through a forced, violent, public os-

tracization of the criminalized black body from society, and the symbolic separation of this body from other similarly subjugated black bodies through the use of enslaved black people as torturers and as audience.

20. In Debret's notes he also describes how those who were whipped were subject to the ritual of having their open sores washed with vinegar and hot pepper once back at the prison to "prevent infection" (Bandeira and Lago 2007, 187).

21. Enslaved people who rebelled or otherwise offended their owners and the established order were punished by a range of cruel and unusual techniques, from hitting the palms of their hands with rulers to iron masks, chains, branding, whippings, and death. For a detailed discussion of the range of these punishments and their use, see, for example, Goulart (1971) and Lara (1988).

22. In Cascudo's assessment, the pelourinho represented the people's sovereignty by consensus and the metropole (1950, 1–2).

23. The idea of the social contract is attributed to British philosopher John Locke, who in 1689 wrote *The Second Treatise of Government.*

24. Carol Pateman (1988) argues that the social contract is, in fact, a contract based on gender domination. Following Pateman's analysis, Charles Mills (1997) argues that the social contract is also defined by the logics of white supremacy.

25. Although Reis calls this revolt the most serious, we should not discount the Haitian Revolution (1791–1804), which is the only insurrection against slavery in the Americas to result in the establishment of an independent nation.

26. Franklin Knight takes care to note that, although the American Revolution was also successful, it in essence left its social structure intact, preserving slavery and maintaining the status quo (Knight 2000, 103).

27. John Collins (2011) argues that what, in part, came to define blackness and race in Bahia from the 1990s onward were the research projects and conversations the government had about residents of the Pelourinho amid the efforts to gentrify the historic center.

28. Milton Santos's articulation of space is also similar to the work of Henri Lefebvre (1991) and Edward Soja (1980).

29. Santos interprets the Pelourinho as both layered and haunted. Santos importantly distinguishes between understanding the changes of the neighborhood in terms of land-scape, and understanding them in terms of space (1995, 13).

30. Alexander builds her idea of palimpsestic time on the work of Ella Shohat and Robert Stam (1994).

31. Thomas's proposal that we use both historical and aesthetic analysis to think about the politics of violence in a space like Jamaica is inspired by the work of Neil Whitehead (2004a; 2004b) and Joseph Roach (1996).

32. We can read the locales that emerged out of the transatlantic slave trade as dialogic, palimpsestic, *political* spaces that have defined one another since at least the 1500s. This space is uniquely modern and globalized; the projects of colonialism and slavery have given birth to their contemporary state formations.

33. Both Saidiya Hartman (1997) and Frank Wilderson (2010) argue that one of the consequences of the antiblack politics of slavery is the popular dissociation between the black body and sentience in global discourses of blackness.

34. Here I invoke scholars' discussions of the fluidity of blackness in Bahia; see, for example, Pinho (2010) and Romo (2010).

35. See arguments by Frazier (1942) and Degler (1971).

36. Here I am specifically referring to the censure of the play *Anjo Negro* in 1948 (Nascimento 1966).

37. The Afro-bloco movement was inspired by the similar phenomenon of black samba schools in Rio (Dunn 1992; Rodrigues 1999).

38. BTO eventually grew apart from Olodum when BTO took a stance against the revitalization of Pelourinho. The two groups also grew apart over political issues and the question of race (Uzel 2003; Meirelles and Bando de Teatro Olodum 1995).

39. For more on the political project of social protest theater, see, for example, Elam (1997).

40. See, for example, Sterling (2012).

Interlude II: "The Berlin Wall"

1. Indicates actors 1, 2, and 3 acting and speaking in unison as the wall.

2. Brazilian currency.

Chapter 2: The Paradox of Black Citizenship

1. Here, I refer to Roland Barthes's use of the term *captions* (Barthes 1977, 16).

2. For more on apartheid in Brazil and South Africa, see Marx (1998).

3. It is important to note here that voting is legally required in Brazil. And while it may seem that the example of voting draws away from my argument, I would in fact argue that voting is not a right so much as it is a requirement employed by the state in order to validate state sovereignty and rule.

4. In drawing on Foucault's notion of docile bodies here, I want to acknowledge that my emphasis on death rather than the management of life goes against Foucault's theorization. However, as I mentioned in the introduction to this book, one of my goals is to grapple with this space between the management of life and the management of death (necropolitics) (Mbembe 2003).

5. *Disjunctive democracy* is a "simultaneous expansion and disrespect for citizenship rights" and "although social rights are reasonably legitimated, the civil aspects of citizenship are continuously violated" (Caldeira 2000, 339; Holston and Caldeira 1998; Holston 2008).

6. Alysia Mann Carey argues that domestic violence is a uniquely gendered racialized aspect of antiblack genocide in Brazil. State violence against black women in Brazil is one manifestation of this violence—reading the state as patriarch and racial democracy as an ideology that requires the rape/violation of black women both by the state and individual actors (Mann Carey 2014).

7. Deputy Luiz Alberto was a key organizer in the Movimento Negro Unificado (MNU) before his election to congress.

8. Liisa Malkki (1995) discusses how anthropological witnessing can be a lot like police interrogation.

9. Part of the neighborhood sits on a large hill and the other portion is at ground level near the main access avenue, Avenida San Martins.

10. See, for example, Johannes Fabian (1983).

11. See Benedict Anderson (1991).

12. Sue et al. (2007) define *racial microaggressions* as "brief and commonplace daily verbal, behavioral, or environmental indignities, whether intentional or unintentional, that communicate hostile, derogatory, or negative racial slights and insults toward people of color" (271).

13. Like the piece "Driving While Black Becomes Flying While Brown" by Visible Collective/Naeem Mohaiemen and Aimara Lin (Puar 2007).

14. A notable exception would be Michael Hanchard's (1999a) essay "Black Cinderella."

15. There is interesting literature in the United States that explores black police officers' attitudes toward their work. This research particularly addresses the tensions between being black and doing police work; see Wilkins and Williams (2008).

16. For a more detailed conversation about the nuances between the definitions of performativity and the theatrical, see, for example, Taylor (2003) and Carlson (1996).

17. Black Brazilian feminist scholars have extensively explored the connections between racial democracy, racism, classism, and sexism. Much of this research has focused on perceptions about black women's "proper" place in Brazilian society (e.g., Carneiro 2003; Gonzalez 1983).

18. A recent study by Edward Telles and Tianna Paschel finds that "Brazil's polarization into black and white categories by high status . . . seems to combine a traditional pattern of money whitening . . . with a more recent (and larger) effect of education darkening, leading overall to racial identification by status that moves away from the white and mixed-raced category (*pardo*)" (2014, 897). Telles and Paschel attribute this hybrid phenomenon to multicultural policies.

19. Patricia Hill Collins (2004) presents an interesting critique of gendered, sexualized racism and its relationship to the perceived hypermasculinity of black men in the United States that is also applicable and relevant to Brazil.

20. It is interesting to note that Mattoso argues that the enslaved were situated slightly above the homeless and vagabonds in this pyramid.

21. Crioulos were Brazilian-born people of African descent in the epoch of colonialism and slavery.

22. The theory of internal colonialism has its roots in the earlier work of Martin Delany ([1852] 2004) and W. E. B. DuBois (1948), who likened the condition of black people in the United States to a colonial status. Robert Allen (2005) recalls the long list of black-activist scholars who articulate the black condition in the Americas as one of colonialism from 1852 through the 1960s: Martin Delany, W. E. B. DuBois, Harold Cruse, Malcolm X and Kenneth Clark, and Stokely Carmichael and Charles Hamilton.

23. Although Mignolo articulates this idea of internal colonialism with respect to historic processes, his framework is different from the notion of the transtemporal that I wish to invoke here.

24. Although the theory of internal colonialism emerged out of the U.S. black experience, Latin American scholars (including black Brazilian scholars) have also applied it to the Latin American modern nation-state, even if they have not used the exact term. One of the first Latin American scholars to use the term *internal colonialism* in print was Pablo Gonzalez Casanova (1965).

25. An important aspect of the black radical discourse of internal colonialism is also the topic of war. This association comes out most strongly in Fanon (1967), but also emerges in DuBois's (1948) observations.

26. It is important to note that within Latin American studies, the work of Gonzalez, Moura, and Nascimento predates that of Anibal Quijano (2000) and Walter Mignolo (2005), who apply the theory of internal colonialism to Latin America, particularly engaging with the internal conditions of black and indigenous people.

27. Lélia Gonzalez's work is also helpful for thinking of the center as a symbolic space of the urban city and the periphery the symbolic place of blackness.

28. Moura bases his criticism in a denunciation of Brazilian anthropology and its neocolonialism (to use his terminology).

29. For Nascimento, the symbolic violence of Brazil's racial democracy is, in effect, genocide against people of African descent in Brazil. Nascimento played an active role in the pan-Africanist movement of the 1960s and 1970s. He makes his claims about genocide in conversation with pan-Africanist thought, specifically the work of Julius Nyerere (1968), Maulana Karenga (1975), and Amílcar Cabral (1974).

30. The terms *synchrony* and *diachrony* originate from the linguistic work of Ferdinand de Saussure ([1916] 1983). The term *synchronic* was used to refer to the contemporaneous moment and *diachronic* to describe a sequence of states ([1916] 1983, 98). Within anthropology, temporality has been used to distinguish the West from the colonial Other, associating savagery with a lack of time (an existence outside of linear Time), and consequently a lack of history (Fabian 1983). Diachrony then becomes a classification associated with the possession of history and therefore the possession of agency, a mastery of time, and a mastery of destiny.

31. The affirmation of a synchronic concept of blackness, as it is employed by the state, constructs blackness as temporally removed from linear history and situated in frozen time, an artifact (Anderson 1991; Fabian 1983).

Interlude III: "Terrorism"

1. The word *merenda* in Portuguese literally means "snack" but refers to the lunch provided to students in the middle of the day at school in this context.

Chapter 3: The White Hand

1. For a detailed social and cultural history of hip-hop, see Rose (1994).

2. People inside and outside of the movement use varied spellings of his alias. These include Negro Blul and Nego Blue (although there may be other variations I have not seen).

3. Some estimates put the total of killings by the White Hand at 160; *O Dia* only corroborates ninety-one assassinations (Rose 2005, 257).

4. The period toward the end of the military dictatorship when the regime had agreed to gradually give up power and transition to a civilian government.

5. Phelan seeks to "find a theory of value for that which is not really there . . . that which cannot be surveyed within the boundaries of the putative real" (1993, 1).

6. John Charles de Menezes was assassinated at the hands of the London police in 2005. He was shot because they misidentified him as a terrorism suspect. For a discussion of his death, see Amar (2010).

7. This video is at http://www.theguardian.com/world/video/2013/mar/06/james-steele-america-iraq-video.

8. The most famous of these training programs was the School of the Americas (e.g., Gill 2004).

9. *Marginal*, in addition to being a referent for criminality, carries a geographic connotation and is conceptually linked to the geographic concept of *periphery*. This has interesting implications for understanding how the periphery (*a periferia*) gets scripted as a space of criminality.

10. For more on the classification of police operations in Brazil, see Ramos and Musumeci (2005).

11. All states in Brazil have some version of the shock police, although these special forces go by many different names.

12. For years there has been a push among militantes to demilitarize the police forces in Brazil. The militarization of state police forces is required by the Brazilian constitution. Consequently, demilitarization would require a constitutional amendment. There have been several proposals presented to Brazil's Parliament to end police militarization, however, as of the writing of this book, none of those proposals has passed through legislation. For more on the politics of de-militarizing the Brazilian police see Kawaguti (2013).

13. Similar to SWAT teams in places like Los Angeles, the state uses these shock battalions for special, militaristic assignments in the city, like neighborhood raids. In thinking about Culture Shock's commentaries on transnationalism, it is important to historicize the emergence of SWAT teams not only in terms of Brazil but also in terms of global cold war politics and racialized paranoias. See, for example, Davis (1990); Bayley (2010); and Huggins (2005).

14. For a more in-depth analysis of the spatial-social connotation of the Contorno, see Perry (2013).

15. It is also important to note that the Brazilian police have a long history of actually killing street children as well (Hecht 1998).

16. See particularly Das's chapters "The Event and the Everyday" and "In the Region of Rumor" (2007).

17. The distinction here is made between the everyday foot soldiers of the military police and the Choque police squad, even though they are both part of the military police.

18. After fleeing Napoleon's impending invasion of Portugal, Emperor Dom Pedro I declared Brazil the seat of the Portuguese Empire in 1808 (Fausto 1999).

19. The Portuguese police force of that time was modeled after the French police.

20. In São Paulo, Boris Fausto notes that the disproportionate representation of black people in prisons in the nineteenth century was due to the "stigma of color." As much as thirty years after slavery, courts continued to use derogatory language to classify black people and associate them with slave status (1984, 54).

21. Historian João Reis (2003) explains that the wars occurring across the western coast of Africa throughout the slavery period defined the forced migration of enslaved Africans throughout the colonial and imperial periods, up through the legal ban of trafficking in 1850 through the Lei Eusébio de Queiróz.

22. Rose also argues that the *culture* of death squads should be traced back to slavery. We might define raids on quilombos, batuques, and capoeira meetings that involved the

torture and/or killing of black "enemies of the state" as proto-death-squad activity (2005, 234).

23. For more on the specific legacy of the Death Squadron, see Bicudo (2002).

24. There is a need to take patriarchy and heterosexism into account when analyzing violence of all kinds in Brazil. As researchers note, although women are not nearly as likely to be the victims of homicide as men, most women who are killed are killed as the result of domestic disputes with their partners (Soares and Borges 2004). Moreover, the discrepancies in homicide rates according to gender reinforce hegemonic social scripts of patriarchy. *Travestis*—transgendered men who often take hormones to enlarge their breasts and buttocks and acquire "feminine" body types but do not identify themselves as women—are frequently the victims of harsh police abuse as well (Kulick 1998).

25. The split between the civil and military police formalized the unwritten rivalry that had been practiced during the military regime.

26. One of Nancy Scheper-Hughes's (1992; 2006) primary theses is that "the every-day experience of violence leads poor people to accept their own deaths and those of their children as predictable, natural, *cruel but usual* events. The history of authoritarian rule—whether by local landowners, political bosses, or military police—*extinguished any incipient culture of protest*" (2006, 152; my emphasis).

27. Traditionally, researchers have read death squads as vigilante groups who kill petty criminals for hire when contracted by local merchants, and police raids as excessive, un-sanctioned uses of force by the police in a necessary, justifiable fight against crime (e.g., Chevigny 1995; Espinheira 2004; Huggins 1998; Pinheiro 1991).

28. During its active years, GERCE imprisoned twenty-five people and denounced thirty death squads, many of which were directly associated with the police (Cirino 2007).

29. *Grupo de Atuação Especial de Combate às Organizações Criminosas e de Investigações Criminais.*

30. *Comissão Parlamentar de Inquerito do Exterminio no Nordeste.*

31. In 2015, React or Die! representatives testified in front of CPI on police death squads in Bahia. I briefly discuss this in chapter 2.

32. While Scheper-Hughes does not engage in a racial analysis of death squads, she observes, "Poor black youth are freely referred to as 'bandits' because crime is 'in their blood,' because they are *bichos da Africa,* 'wild African beasts'" (2006, 153).

33. On February 9, 2007, React or Die! held a march to protest the racism of Bahia's public security system, police brutality, and death squads. Blue participated in this.

34. In 1997, Congressman Luiz Alberto became the first black congressman elected from Bahia.

35. The journal *Irohin,* founded by Edison Cardoso in Brasilia, is no longer in operation.

36. Although Brazil has guaranteed universal health care through SUS (*Sistema Único de Saude*) (Unified Health System), access to the system is structured like a pyramid, where most Brazilians have access to basic services, but specialized services are more difficult to obtain. Those who have access to the more specialized services tend to be people who have more social, economic, and cultural capital.

37. The phrase *survival pending revolution* was coined by the Black Panther Party in the 1970s and refers to the measures that black revolutionaries take to ensure survival

when complete revolution is not in the realistic future. This concept is particularly tied with the work of Huey P. Newton.

38. Although Mbembe rejects using the term *war* to define entanglement in his discussion of contemporary Africa (2001, 8), I believe war is an appropriate concept that is applicable to Bahia precisely because of the violent nature of the colonial, racial antagonisms that we find between the state and black residents.

39. Luís Mir in *Guerra Civil: Estado e Trauma* (2004) also defines the crisis of Brazilian urban violence in terms of war, paying close attention to structural inequality and its connections to the history of slavery.

Chapter 4: Palimpsestic Embodiment

1. Prêmio Esso de Fotografia, 1983, http://www.premioesso.com.br/site/premio_principal/index.aspx?year=1983.

2. The reporters who wrote the article about this incident also classified the young men as black (Rodrigues, Lindsay, and Oliveira 2001).

3. Sérgio Pinheiro (1991) reminds us that there are explicit connections between death squads and the civil police.

4. I want to thank one of my anonymous readers for this important point.

5. Mbembe also cautions us that the poststructuralist tendency to overemphasize the hybrid, fluid, negotiated, and constructed nature of identity (and, by extension, social relationships) "reduce[s] the complex phenomena of the state and power to 'discourses' and 'representations,' forgetting that discourses and representations have materiality" (2001, 5).

6. Teresa Caldeira (2000) addresses how policing protects the rich and violates the rights of the poor. She does not address the question of race as it directly relates to this topic.

7. I build this argument in conversation with the work of Robyn Wiegman (1995) and William Pinar (2007), who argue that there is a sexual-racial configuration of lynching in the United States as a torture practice. For a longer discussion of the relationship between the history of lynching in the United States and police violence in Brazil, see Smith (2013b).

8. Fernando Conceição (1998) similarly makes the association between Debret's painting and Morier's photograph.

9. See Ramos (2007).

10. Mbembe suggests that "there is a close relationship between subjectivity and temporality . . . in some way, one can envisage subjectivity itself as temporality" (2001, 14–15). Violent encounters between the police and black people in Brazil are sited at the juncture of time, space, and the body.

11. The bodies of the black men pictured being stepped on have been "disciplined" (both altered and bounded by violence) as a way of abstracting their materiality. The result, as Foucault suggests, is the production of knowledge that comes from this exercising of power (Foucault [1978] 1995). The production of knowledge in this case is the production of knowledge about blackness. However, as Joy James reminds us, Foucault's theorization of the "disappearance of torture as a public spectacle" completely ignores

the use of torture and public spectacle on the Other body, particularly the black body, as a cultural, social, and political practice from the colonial/conquest/slavery period onward (1996, 24–25). Jared Sexton (2007) argues that the spectacular use of torture and punishment against the black body and the minute, biopolitical mechanisms of control that Foucault outlines are not mutually exclusive, and the two in many ways are mutually constitutive. On the one hand, these scenarios are spectacular displays of state authority executed through the torture of the black body. On the other hand, they are also sites of disciplining.

Chapter 5: In and Out of the Ineffable

1. Robin Sheriff (2001) also theorizes silence as the result of trauma in Brazil. However, she focuses on silences around the topics of race and racism. By contrast, I suggest that, in fact, the conditions that produce cultural silence are not just racism but also war.

2. Witnessing in this sense is part of the human-rights narrative and the theater of human-rights restorative justice; see Feldman (2004).

3. They included Manfred Nowak, UN special rapporteur on torture, and Doudou Diène, UN special rapporteur on contemporary forms of racism, racial discrimination, xenophobia, and related intolerance.

4. For a rich discussion on women and the gendered politics of violence in Bahia, see Hautzinger (2007).

5. In one of the play's vignettes not discussed in this book (April 22 vignette), Culture Shock discusses the mediatization of black suffering.

6. *The political power of the dead* refers to Katherine Verdery's (1999) research on how the dead become political symbols.

7. Ruth Wilson Gilmore defines *social mothers* as black women who practice "techniques developed over generations on behalf of black children and families within terror-demarcated racially defined enclaves" (1999, 26). By employing this phrase, I want to resist the temptation to define black mothers only as those who are the biological parents of children, but to think of black women in a broader caretaking role of black children, families, and communities.

8. Historically indigenous people have often been targets of state violence in Brazil (e.g., Garfield 2001).

9. The PCC is an organization/resistance movement for some and a criminal faction for others, founded by people involved in or accused of criminal activity in São Paulo after the Carandiru prison massacre of 1994. That year the PCC coordinated an attack from the state penitentiary on São Paulo that shut down the city for days.

10. See also Smith (2015).

11. *Le cirque*; they had been traveling around the country.

12. I explore the complexity of this emotional experience in Smith (2013a).

13. In using the term *humanity* here, I once again invoke the work of Sylvia Wynter (1994).

14. Ricardo's story reminds us of the diasporic echoes of antiblack state violence once again. The image of Ricardo running away from the police is like the image of Walter

Scott, a black man who was shot to death while running away from a police officer in North Charleston, South Carolina, in April 2015.

15. Kimbundu is a Bantu language from the Congo-Angola region of Africa.

16. The word *quilombismo* was coined by Abdias do Nascimento in 1980 to describe the black cultural practice of creating quilombos (maroon societies) in Brazilian society.

17. Palmares was actually a cluster of ten quilombos; see Gomes (2005). For a more detailed discussion of the quilombo tradition in Brazil, see Reis and Gomes (1996). Richard Price (1973) has done extensive comparative work on maroons and the tradition of marooning throughout the Americas.

18. Founded in the state of Pernambuco, it lasted from the 1500s until 1695.

19. A representative of the Portuguese Crown sent to govern Bahia, a capacity similar to governor; also called vice king.

20. I think that the impact of the politics of affirmative action—which cannot and should not be dissociated from the black movement efforts that led to affirmative action policies—and the correspondent recent social phenomenon of "blackening" in Brazil are also interesting entry points for this conversation (Telles and Paschel 2014).

21. João Reis (2003) and Eduardo de Caldas Britto (1903) both cite the Conde da Ponte's use of the term *war against whites* in his correspondence. I chose to change this terminology to a war against white supremacy because of the racial messiness of the conflict. For example, the anger and violence that rebels directed toward whites were also often articulated against mulattos and black traitors as well. I read these choices in conversation with their direct, purposeful targeting of symbols of white oppression, like the church and the Customs House (where enslaved Africans arrived in ships from the Middle Passage). Their anger was directed at the total system of white supremacy, not just the elite white people who held positions of power in society.

22. For a rich discussion of the history of women in leadership roles in candomblé in Bahia, see Ruth Landes's *The City of Women* (1947).

23. Most large plantations were located in Recôncovo region. João Reis particularly cites the Conceição de Itapagipe Mill as one of the primary centers of slave insurrection in Paripe (2003, 88).

24. Fred Moten's (2003) exegesis of utterance, the break, and the genealogy of black suffering is also an interesting point to reference here.

25. Local communities engaged in social-protest performance use similar techniques to make connections between the theater and local and national social processes and events (Burvill 1998).

26. D. Soyini Madison defines *tactic* as "creating a means and a space from whatever elements or resources are available in order to resist or subvert the strategies of more powerful institutions, ideologies or processes" (2010, 2).

27. Madison (2010) uses the concept of emergence to reflect on the affective energy that is produced during the moment of performance. It is this affective energy that she suggests constitutes the social significance of theater activism.

Appendix: Methodology and Timing

1. I have observed a profound distrust for foreign researchers since I began doing research in Brazil. Despite observations, like those of Teresa Caldeira (1988; 2000), that it

is much easier to gain access to working-class/lower-class communities than it is to gain access to the upper class, I have found that subaltern communities exercise a considerable amount of agency about whom they allow access to their communities and whom they do not. This is of course always mediated by class, race, and gender, but there is a great deal of critique from the community about researchers' sense of entitlement when attempting to do research on the economic and racial Other.

2. This is a big set of elevators that takes residents and tourists from the lower city (Cidade Baixa) to the upper city (Cidade Alta) in downtown Salvador. The elevators are located on the lip of the historic city center Pelourinho and in front of the open-air artisanal market Mercado Modelo.

3. My methodological approach to this project is firmly grounded in politically engaged anthropology (Hale 2008). Following the Austin School Manifesto, my goal has been to "form clearer conceptualizations of our collective condition and, more pointedly, to contribute to the liberation of African-descended peoples, and all others, from socially constructed limitations and diminished life chances" (Gordon 2007, 93). I do not make gestures toward false objectivities. My motivation has been, and continues to be, my firm belief that we must speak out against global patterns of antiblack violence in order to redress injustice, exact liberation, and stay alive.

Bibliography

A Tarde. 2001. "Grupo de extermínio mata jovem." *A Tarde,* July 7, sec. 1, 1, 20.

Ackerman, Spencer. 2015a. "The Disappeared: Chicago Police Detain Americans at Abuse-Laden 'Black Site.'" *Guardian,* February 24, http://www.theguardian.com/us-news/2015/feb/24/chicago-police-detain-americans-black-site.

———. 2015b. "Guantánamo Torturer Led Brutal Chicago Regime of Shackling and Confession." *Guardian,* February 18, http://www.theguardian.com/us-news/2015/feb/18/guantanamo-torture-chicago-police-brutality.

Agamben, Giorgio. 1995. *Homo Sacer.* 3 vols. Vol. 1, *Potere sovrano e la nuda vita: Einaudi contemporanea.* Torino: G. Einaudi.

———. 2005. *State of Exception.* Chicago: University of Chicago Press.

Agier, Michel. 2000. *Anthropologie du Carnaval: La Ville/La Fête et l'Afrique à Bahia.* Marseilles, Paris: Parenthèses/IRD.

Alexander, Elizabeth. 1994. "Can You Be Black and Look at This: Reading the Rodney King Video(s)." In *Black Male: Representations of Masculinity in Contemporary American Art,* edited by Thelma Golden, 91–110. New York: Whitney Museum of American Art.

Alexander, M. Jacqui. 2006. *Pedagogies of Crossing: Meditations on Feminism, Sexual Politics, Memory, and the Sacred.* Durham, NC: Duke University Press.

Allen, James. 2000. *Without Sanctuary: Lynching Photography in America.* Santa Fe, NM: Twin Palms.

Allen, Robert. 2005. "Reassessing the Internal (Neo)Colonialism Theory." *Black Scholar* 35 (1): 2–12.

Alston, Phillip. 2007. *Promotion and Protection of All Human Rights, Civil, Political, Economical, Social and Cultural Rights Including the Right to Development, Addendum: Mission to Brazil.* Geneva: United Nations Human Rights Council.

Alvarez, Sonia E. 2009. "Beyond NGO-ization? Reflections from Latin America." *Development* 52 (2): 175–84.

Amado, Jorge. 1945. *Bahia de Todos os Santos.* São Paulo: Marins.

Amar, Paul. 2010. "New Racial Missions of Policing: Comparitive Studies of State Authority, Urban Governance, and Security Technology in the Twenty-First Century." *Ethnic and Racial Studies* 33 (4): 575–92.

Amnesty International. 2005. "Brazil: 'They Come in Shooting': Policing Socially Excluded Communities." Amnesty International. https://www.amnesty.org/en/documents/ AMR19/025/2005/en/.

Anderson, Benedict. 1991. *Imagined Communities: Reflections on the Origin and Spread of Nationalism.* London: Verso.

Andrews, George Reid. 1991. *Blacks and Whites in São Paulo 1888–1988.* Madison: University of Wisconsin Press.

Angel-Ajani, Asale. 2008. "Expert Witness: Notes toward Revisiting the Politics of Listening." *Anthropology of Humanism* 29 (2): 133–44.

Araujo, Ana Lucia. 2012. *Politics of Memory: Making Slavery Visible in Public Space.* Hoboken, NJ: Taylor and Francis.

Araujo, Major Oseas Moreira de. 1997. *Noticias sobre a Polícia Militar no século XIX.* Salvador, Brazil: Claudiomar Gonçalves.

Asad, Talal. 2004. "Where Are the Margins of the State." In *Anthropology in the Margins of the State,* edited by Veena Das and Deborah Poole, 279–88. Santa Fe: School of American Research Press.

Austin, J. L. 1962. *How to Do Things with Words.* Cambridge, MA: Harvard University Press.

Azevedo, Lena. 2013a. "Crueldade e impunidade marcam crimes de policiais." *Pública: Agência de Reportagem e Jornalismo Investigativo,* July 11, http://apublica.org/2013/07/ crueldade-impunidade-marcam-crimes-de-policiais/, 1–6. São Paulo: Pública.

———. 2013b. "Jovens negros na mira de grupos de extermínio na Bahia." *Pública: Agência de Reportagem e Jornalismo Investigativo,* July 11, http://apublica.org/2013/07/jovens -negros-na-mira-de-grupos-de-exterminio-na-bahia/. São Paulo: Pública.

———. 2015. "CPI da Câmara dos Deputados apura o extermínio de jovens negros: Reaja!" *Geledes,* May 15, http://www.geledes.org.br/cpi-da-camara-dos-deputados-apura -o-exterminio-de-jovens-negros-reaja/#gs.f5a24b008b4c421bbdcf9a76d2d9b543.

Baierle, Sérgio Gregório. 1998. "The Explosion of Experience: The Emergence of a New Ethical-Political Principle in Popular Movements in Porto Alegre, Brazil." In *Cultures of Politics, Politics of Cultures: Re-Visioning Latin American Social Movements,* edited by Sonia E. Alvarez, Evelina Dagnino, and Arturo Escobar, 118–40. Boulder, CO: Westview Press.

Bailey, John, and Lucía Dammert. 2006. *Public Security and Police Reform in the Americas.* Pittsburgh: University of Pittsburgh Press.

Bailey, Stanley R. 2009. *Legacies of Race: Identities, Attitudes, and Politics in Brazil.* Stanford, CA: Stanford University Press.

Bailey, Stanley R., and Edward E. Telles. 2006. "Multiracial versus Collective Black Categories: Examining Census Classification Debates in Brazil." *Ethnicities* 6 (1): 74–101.

Bakhtin, Mikhail. 1981. *The Dialogic Imagination: Four Essays.* Edited by Michael Holquist. Translated by Caryl Emerson and Michael Holquist. Austin: University of Texas Press.

———. 1984. *Rebelais and His World.* Translated by Hélène Iswolsky. Bloomington: Indiana University Press.

Bandeira, Julio, and Pedro Corrêa do Lago. 2007. *Debret e o Brasil*. Rio de Janeiro: Capivara Editora.

Barros, Ricardo, et al. 2010. *Determinantes de Queda na Desigualdade de Renda no Brasil*. Instituto de Pesquisa Econômica Aplicada (IPEA).

Barthes, Roland. 1977. *Image, Music, Text*. Translated by Stephen Heath. London: Fontana.

Basch, Linda G., Nina Glick Schiller, and Cristina Szanton Blanc. 1994. *Nations Unbound: Transnational Projects, Postcolonial Predicaments, and Deterritorialized Nation-States*. N.p.: Gordon and Breach.

Bauman, Richard, and Charles Briggs. 1990. "Poetics and Performance as Critical Perspectives on Language and Social Life." *Annual Review of Anthropology* 19:59–88.

Bayley, David H. 2010. "Foreword." In *Police Use of Force: A Global Perspective*, edited by Joseph B. Kuhns and Johannes Knutsson, xiii–xvi. Santa Barbara, CA: Praeger.

Belchior, Douglas. 2013. "Shopping Vitória: Corpos negros no lugar errado." December 2, http://negrobelchior.cartacapital.com.br/2013/12/02/shopping-vitoria-corpos-negros-no-lugar-errado/.

Bicudo, Hélio Pereira. 2002. *Meu Depoimento Sobre o Esquadrão da Morte*. São Paulo: Martins Fontes.

Biehl, João Guilherme. 2001. "Vita: Life in a Zone of Social Abandonment." *Social Text* 19 (3): 131–49.

———. 2005. *Vita: Life in a Zone of Social Abandonment*. Berkeley: University of California Press.

Boal, Augusto. 1979. *Theater of the Oppressed*. New York: Urizen Books.

Bonilla-Silva, Eduardo. 1997. "Rethinking Racism: Toward a Structural Interpretation." *American Sociological Review* 62 (3): 465–80.

"Brazil's Rolezinhos: The Kids Are Alright." 2014. *Economist*, January 25, http://www.economist.com/news/americas/21595011-youngsters-gathering-shopping-malls-want-attention-not-political-change-kids-are-all.

Brisolla, Fabio. 2007. "Diários de Guerra: Quem São os Policiais do Bope, a Tropa de Elite da PM que Enfrenta Uma Guerra Sem Fim Contra o Tráfico nas Favelas Cariocas." *Veja*, June 6.

Britto, Eduardo de Caldas. 1903. "Levantes de pretos na Bahia." *Revista do Instituto Geographico Histórico da Bahia* 10 (29): 69–119.

Brittos, Valério Cruz, and César Ricardo Siqueira Bolaño. 2005. *Rede Globo: 40 anos de poder e hegemonia*. São Paulo: Paulus.

Brogden, Michael, and Preeti Nijhar. 2005. *Community Policing: National and International Models and Approaches*. Cullompton, UK: Willan.

Brown, Kimberly Juanita. 2014. "Regarding the Pain of the Other: Photograph, Famine, and the Transference of Affect." In *Feeling Photography*, edited by Elspeth H. Brown and Thy Phu, 181–203. Durham, NC: Duke University Press.

Brown, Vincent. 2003. "Spiritual Terror in Jamaican Slave Society." *Slavery and Abolition* 24 (1): 24–53.

Burdick, John. 2013. *The Color of Sound: Race, Religion, and Music in Brazil*. New York: New York University Press.

Burvill, Tom. 1998. "Playing the Faultlines." In *Staging Resistance: Essays on Political The-ater*, edited by Jeanne M. Colleran, 229–46. Ann Arbor: University of Michigan Press.

Butler, Judith P. 1990. *Gender Trouble: Feminism and the Subversion of Identity*. New York: Routledge.

———. 1993. *Bodies That Matter: On the Discursive Limits of "Sex."* New York: Routledge.

———. 1997. *Excitable Speech: A Politics of the Performative*. New York: Routledge.

———. 2004. *Precarious Life: The Powers of Mourning and Violence*. New York: Verso.

———. 2009. *Frames of War: When Is Life Grievable?* New York: Verso.

Butler, Kim D. 1998. *Freedoms Given, Freedoms Won: Afro-Brazilians in Post-Abolition São Paulo and Salvador*. New Brunswick, NJ: Rutgers University Press.

Cabral, Amílcar. 1974. *Textos políticos*. Porto, Portugal: Afrontamento.

Caldeira, Teresa P. R. 1988. "The Art of Being Indirect: Talking about Politics in Brazil." *Cultural Anthropology* 3 (4): 444–54.

———. 2000. *City of Walls*. Berkeley: University of California Press.

Caldwell, Kia Lilly. 2007. *Negras in Brazil: Re-Envisioning Black Women, Citizenship, and the Politics of Identity*. New Brunswick, NJ: Rutgers University Press.

Cano, Ignacio. 2010. "Racial Bias in Police Use of Lethal Force in Brazil." *Police Practice and Research* 11 (1): 31–43.

Capoeira, Nestor. 2002. *Capoeira: Roots of the Dance-Fight-Game*. Berkeley, CA: North Atlantic Books.

Carby, Hazel. 2004. "A Strange and Bitter Crop: The Spectacle of Torture." *Open Democracy: Free Thinking for the World*, October 11, https://www.opendemocracy.net/media-abughraib/article_2149.jsp.

Carlson, Marvin A. 1996. *Performance: A Critical Introduction*. London: Routledge.

Carmichael, Stokely. 1967. *Black Power: The Politics of Liberation in America*. New York: Random House.

Carneiro, Sueli. 2003. "Mulheres em movimento." *Estudos Avanlçados* 17 (49): 117–32.

Casanova, Pablo Gonzalez. 1965. "Internal Colonialism and National Development." *Studies in Comparative International Development* 1 (4): 27–37.

Cascudo, Luis da Câmara. 1950. *O Simbolo Jurídico do Pelourinho*. Natal, Brazil: A Revista do Instituto Histórico.

CBS News. 2014. "Brazilian Police Kill 6 People a Day, Study Finds." November 12, http://www.cbsnews.com/news/brazilian-police-kill-6-people-a-day-study-finds/.

Chalhoub, Sidney. 2006. "The Politics of Silence: Race and Citizenship in Nineteenth-Century Brazil." *Slavery and Abolition* 27 (1): 73–87.

Chevigny, Paul G. 1990. "Police Deadly Force as Social Control: Jamaica, Argentina, and Brazil." *Criminal Law Forum* 1 (3): 389–425.

———. 1995. *Edge of the Knife: Police Violence in the Americas*. New York: New Press/ Norton.

Chevigny, Paul, et al. 1987. *Police Abuse in Brazil: Summary Executions and Torture in Sao Paulo and Rio de Janeiro*. New York: Americas Watch Committee.

Chow, Rey. 2006. *The Age of the World Target: Self-Referentiality in War, Theory, and Comparative Work*. Durham, NC: Duke University Press.

Cirino, Helga. 2007. "Cinco Homens Chacinahdos em Terreno no Bairro da Paz." *A Tarde*, September 19, 1, 4–5.

Clarke, Kimari. 2013. "Notes on Cultural Citizenship in the Black Atlantic World." *Cultural Anthropology* 28 (3): 464–74.

Collins, John. 2011. "Melted Gold and National Bodies: The Hermeneutics of Depth and the Value of History in Brazilian Racial Politics." *American Ethnologist* 38 (4): 683–700.

———. 2014. "Policing's Productive Folds: Secretism and Authenticity in Brazilian Cultural Heritage." *Journal of Latin American and Caribbean Anthropology* 19 (3): 473–501.

Comaroff, Jean, and John L. Comaroff. 2006. *Law and Disorder in the Postcolony*. Chicago: University of Chicago Press.

Conceição, Fernando Costa da. 1998. "Qual a Cor da Imprensa." In *A Cor do Medo*, edited by Dijaci David de Oliveira, Elen Cristina Geraldes, Ricardo Barbosa de Lima, and Augusto Sales Santos, 153–61. Brasilia: Universidade de Brasília.

Conrad, Robert Edgar. 1983. *Children of God's Fire: A Documentary History of Black Slavery in Brazil*. Princeton, NJ: Princeton University Press.

Correio24horas. 2013. "Policiais militares impedem exibição do filme 'Menino Joel' no Nordeste de Amaralina." *Correio24horas*, June 8, http://www.correio24horas.com .br/detalhe/noticia/policiais-militares-impedem-exibicao-do-filme-menino-joel-no -nordeste-de-amaralina/, accessed February 18, 2015.

Costa, Ana Cláudia, et al. 2007. "Para polícia, operação no Alemão vai enfraquecer tráfico em outras favelas." *O Globo*, Extra online ed., June 28, http://extra.globo.com/ noticias/rio/para-policia-operacao-no-alemao-vai-enfraquecer-trafico-em-outras -favelas-680548.html.

Covin, David. 2006. *The Unified Black Movement in Brazil, 1978–2002*. Jefferson, NC: McFarland.

CPI, Comissão Parlamentar de Inquerito do Exterminio no Nordeste. 2005. *Relatório Final da Comissão Parlamentar de Inquérito do Extermínio no Nordeste*, edited by Câmara d. Deputados, 596. Brasilia: Câmara dos Deputados.

Crenshaw, Kimberle. 1991. "Mapping the Margins: Intersectionality, Identity Politics, and Violence against Women of Color." *Stanford Law Review* 43 (6): 1241–99.

Crook, Larry, and Randal Johnson, eds. 1999. *Black Brazil: Culture, Identity, and Social Mobilization*. Los Angeles: UCLA Latin American Center Publications, University of California.

Curtin, Philip D. 1968. *Two Jamaicas: The Role of Ideas in a Tropical Colony, 1830–1865*. New York: Greenwood Press.

D'Eça, Aline. 2008. "MP Cria Núcleo de Combate aos Grupos de Extermínio." *Ministério Público do Estado da Bahia*, April 11, http://www.mpba.mp.br/noticias/2008/abr_11 _exterminio.asp#, accessed June 8, 2015.

Dagnino, Evelina, ed. 1994a. *Os Anos 90: Política e sociedade no Brasil*. São Paulo: Editora Brasiliense.

———. 1994b. "Os movimentos sociais e a emergência de uma nova noção de cidadania." In *Os Anos 90: Política e sociedade no Brasil*, edited by Evelina Dagnino, 103–15. São Paulo: Editora Brasilense.

Das, Veena. 2007. *Life and Words: Violence and the Descent into the Ordinary*. Berkeley: University of California Press.

Davies, Carole Boyce, and Babacar M'Bow. 2007. "Towards African Diaspora Citizenship: Politicizing an Existing Global Geography." In *Black Geographies and the Politics of Place*, edited by Katherine McKittrick and Clyde Woods, 14–45. Boston: South End Press.

Davis, Mike. 1990. *City of Quartz: Excavating the Future in Los Angeles.* New York: Verso.

de Certeau, Michel. 1984. *The Practice of Everyday Life.* Berkeley: University of California Press.

DeFrantz, Thomas, and Anita Gonzalez, eds. 2014. *Black Performance Theory.* Durham, NC: Duke University Press.

Debord, Guy. (1970) 1994. *The Society of the Spectacle.* New York: Zone Books.

Degler, Carl N. 1971. *Neither Black nor White: Slavery and Race Relations in Brazil and the United States.* New York: Macmillan.

Delany, Martin. (1852) 2004. *The Condition, Elevation, Emigration, and Destiny of the Colored People of the United States and Official Report of the Niger Valley Exploring Party.* Amherst, NY: Humanity Books.

Deleuze, Gilles, and Félix Guattari. 1987. *A Thousand Plateaus: Capitalism and Schizophrenia.* Minneapolis: University of Minnesota Press.

Diamond, Elin. 1996. *Performance and Cultural Politics.* London: Routledge.

DuBois, W. E. B. 1948. "Race Relations in the United States 1917–1947." *Phylon* 9 (3): 237–47.

Dunn, Christopher. 1992. "Afro-Bahian Carnival: A Stage for Protest." *Afro-Hispanic Review* 11 (1–3): 11–20.

———. 2007. "Black Rome and the Chocolate City." *Callaloo* 30 (3): 847–61.

Dyson, Michael Eric. 1996. *Between God and Gangsta Rap: Bearing Witness to Black Culture.* New York: Oxford University Press.

———. 2007. *Know What I Mean? Reflections on Hip-Hop.* New York: Basic Civitas Books.

Dzidzienyo, Anani. 1971. *The Position of Blacks in Brazilian Society.* London: Minority Rights Group.

———. 1985. "The African Connection and the Afro-Brazilian Condition." In *Race, Class and Power in Brazil*, edited by Pierre-Michel Fontaine, 135–53. Los Angeles: Center for Afro-American Studies, University of California.

Elam, Harry Justin. 1997. *Taking It to the Streets: The Social Protest Theater of Luis Valdez and Amiri Baraka.* Ann Arbor: University of Michigan Press.

Espinheira, Gey, ed. 2004. *Sociabilidade e violência: Criminalidade no cotidiano de vida dos moradores do Subúrbio Ferroviário de Salvador.* Salvador, Bahia: Ministério Publico da Bahia.

Estanislau, Lídia Avelar. 2000. "Feminino Plural: Negras do Brasil." In *Brasil, Afro Brasileiro*, edited by M. N. S. Fonseca, 211–28. Belo Horizonte, Brazil: Autêntica.

Evaristo, Conceição. 2003. *Ponciá Vicêncio.* Belo Horizonte, Brazil: Mazza Edições.

Fabian, Johannes. 1983. *Time and the Other: How Anthropology Makes Its Object.* New York: Columbia University Press.

———. 1990. *Power and Performance: Ethnographic Explorations through Proverbial Wisdom and Theater in Shaba, Zaire.* Madison: University of Wisconsin Press.

Fanon, Frantz. 1965a. *A Dying Colonialism.* New York: Grove Press.

———. 1965b. *The Wretched of the Earth.* New York: Grove Press.

———. 1967. *Black Skin, White Masks.* New York: Grove Press.

FASEC, Fundação de Assistência Sócio Educativa e Cultural. 2007. *Carnaval: Violência contra a mulher, racismo e homofobia, na opinião de quem faz a festa.* Salvador, Bahia: Fundação de Assistência Sócio Educativa e Cultural—FASEC.

Fausto, Boris. 1984. *Crime e cotidiano: A criminalidade em São Paulo, 1880–1924.* São Paulo: Brasiliense.

———. 1999. *A Concise History of Brazil.* Cambridge: Cambridge University Press.

Federico, Vicente. 1999. *Um Caso de Polícia: Reorganização, Capacitação Profissional e Polícia Comunitária na PM da Bahia.* Salvador, Bahia: Escola de Administração da UFBA.

Feldman, Allen. 1991. *Formations of Violence: The Narrative of the Body and Political Terror in Northern Ireland.* Chicago: University of Chicago Press.

———. 2004. "Memory Theaters, Virtual Witnessing, and the Trauma-Aesthetic." *Biography* 27 (1): 163–202.

Félix, Anísio. 1995. *Pelo Pelourinho.* Salvador: EGBA.

Ferreira, Carla. 2005. "ONU visita Salvador de contrastes." *A Tarde,* October 19, 2005, 7.

Fonsêca, Adilson. 2003. "Subúrbio de Salvador é o reverso do progresso." *A Tarde,* October 2, 3, local.

Fonseca, Carolina Ferreira da. 2008. "Baianas do Acarajé: Patrimônio Urbano Imaterial?" In *IV ENECULT: Enconro de Estudos Multidisciplinares em Cultura.* Fourth ENECULT conference, Salvador, Bahia, Brazil.

Fontaine, Pierre-Michel. 1985. *Race, Class, and Power in Brazil.* Los Angeles: Center for Afro-American Studies, University of California.

Fórum Brasileiro de Segurança Pública (FBSP). 2013. *Anuário Brasileiro de Segurança Pública.* São Paulo: Fórum Brasileiro de Segurança Pública.

Foucault, Michel. (1977) 2003. *Discipline and Punish: The Birth of the Prison.* New York: Pantheon Books.

———. 1978. *The History of Sexuality.* 3 vols. New York: Pantheon Books.

Frazier, E. Franklin. 1942. "The Negro Family in Bahia, Brazil." *American Sociological Review* 7 (4): 465–78.

Freyre, Gilberto. 1933 (1973). *Casa-Grande e Senzala: Formação da Família Brasileira sob o Regime de Economia Patriarcal.* Rio de Janeiro: Livraria Jose Oympio Editora.

Fry, Peter. 2007. *Divisões perigosas: Políticas raciais no Brasil contemporâneo.* Rio de Janeiro: Civilização Brasileira.

Fry, Peter, and Yvonne Maggie. 2004. "Cotas Raciais: Construindo um pais dividido?" *Econômica* 6 (1): 153–61.

Gaggino, Max, dir. 2013. *Menino Joel.* 71 min. Salvador, Bahia: Max Filmes e Ecletique.

Garfield, Seth. 2001. *Indigenous Struggle at the Heart of Brazil: State Policy, Frontier Expansion, and the Xavante Indians, 1937–1988.* Durham, NC: Duke University Press.

Gates, Henry Louis, and Sunday Ogbonna Anozie, eds. 1984. *Black Literature and Literary Theory.* New York: Methuen.

Gill, Lesley. 2004. *The School of the Americas: Military Training and Political Violence in the Americas.* Durham, NC: Duke University Press.

Gilmore, Ruth Wilson. 1999. "'You Have Dislodged a Boulder': Mothers and Prisoners in the Post-Keynesian California Landscape." *Transforming Anthropology* 8 (1–2): 12–38.

Gilroy, Paul. 1987. *"There Ain't No Black in the Union Jack": The Cultural Politics of Race and Nation.* London: Hutchinson.

———. 1993. *The Black Atlantic: Modernity and Double Consciousness.* Cambridge, MA: Harvard University Press.

Glycerio, Carolina. 2007. "68% africano, ativista queria mais detalhes." BBC Brasil.com, May 31, http://www.bbc.co.uk/portuguese/reporterbbc/story/2007/05/070507_dna _freidavid_cg.shtml.

Glycerio, Carolina, and Silvia Salek. 2007. "Especial traça perfil genético de nove negros famosos." BBC Brasil.com, May 28, http://www.bbc.co.uk/portuguese/reporterbbc/ story/2007/05/070521_dna_apresentacao_projetocg.shtml.

Glymph, Thavolia. 2008. *Out of the House of Bondage: The Tranformation of the Plantation Household.* Cambridge: Cambridge University Press.

Goffman, Erving. 1959. *The Presentation of Self in Everyday Life.* Garden City, NY: Doubleday.

Goldberg, David Theo. 2002. *The Racial State.* Malden, MA: Blackwell Publishers.

Goldsby, Jacqueline Denise. 2006. *A Spectacular Secret: Lynching in American Life and Literature.* Chicago: University of Chicago Press.

Gomes, Flávio dos Santos. 2005. *Palmares: Escravidão e liberdade no Atlântico Sul.* São Paulo: Contexto.

Gonzalez, Lélia. 1983. "Racismo e Sexismo na Cultural Brasileira." In *Movimentos Sociais Urbanos, Minorias Étnicas e Outros Estudos,* edited by P. F. Carlos Benedito da Silva, Carlos Vogt, Maurizio Gnerre, Bernardo Sorj, and Anthony Seeger, 223–44. Brasilia: ANPOCS.

———. 1985. "The Unified Black Movement: A New Stage in Black Political Mobilization." In *Race, Class, and Power in Brazil,* edited by Pierre-Michel Fontaine, 120–34. Los Angeles: Center for Afro-American Studies, University of California.

Gonzalez, Lélia, and Carlos Alfredo Hasenbalg. 1982. *O Lugar de Negro.* Rio de Janeiro: Editora Marco Zero.

Gordon, Edmund T. 1991. "Anthropology and Liberation." In *Decolonizing Anthropology: Moving Further toward an Anthropology for Liberation,* edited by Faye V. Harrison, 149–67. Washington, DC: Association of Black Anthropologists, American Anthropological Association.

———. 2007. "The Austin School Manifesto: An Approach to the Black or African Diaspora." *Cultural Dynamics* 19 (1): 93–97.

Goulart, José Alipio. 1971. *Da palmatória ao patíbulo: Castigos de escravos no Brasil, Temas brasileiros.* Rio de Janeiro: Conquista.

Gramsci, Antonio. 1992. *Prison Notebooks.* 3 vols. Translated by Joseph A. Buttigieg. New York: Columbia University Press.

Guimarães, Antonio Sérgio Alfredo. 2003. "Racial Insult in Brazil." *Discourse and Society* 14 (2): 133–51.

Habermas, Jürgen. 1989. *The Structural Transformation of the Public Sphere: An Inquiry into a Category of Bourgeois Society.* Cambridge, MA: MIT Press.

Haddad, Mônica. 2008. "Bolsa Família and the Needy: Is Allocation Contributing to Equity in Brazil?" *Journal of International Development* 20:654–69.

Hale, Charles. 2004. "Rethinking Indigenous Politics in the Era of the 'Indio Permitido.'" *NACLA Report on the Americas* 38 (2): 16–20.

———. 2006. "Activist Research v. Cultural Critique: Indigenous Land Rights and the Contradictions of Politically Engaged Anthropology." *Cultural Anthropology* 21 (1): 96–120.

———, ed. 2008. *Engaging Contradictions: Theory, Politics, and Methods and Activist Scholarship*. Berkeley: University of California Press.

Hall, Stuart, ed. 1997. *Representation: Cultural Representations and Signifying Practices*. Thousand Oaks, CA/London: Sage/Open University.

Hanchard, Michael. 1994. *Orpheus and Power: The Movimento Negro of Rio de Janeiro and São Paulo, Brazil, 1945–1988*. Princeton, NJ: Princeton University Press.

———. 1999a. "Black Cinderella? Race and the Public Sphere in Brazil." In *Racial Politics in Contemporary Brazil*, edited by Michael Hanchard, 59–81. Durham, NC: Duke University Press

———, ed. 1999b. *Racial Politics in Contemporary Brazil*. Durham, NC: Duke University Press.

Harrison, Faye Venetia. 1991. *Decolonizing Anthropology: Moving Further toward an Anthropology for Liberation*. Washington, DC: Association of Black Anthropologists, American Anthropological Association.

———. 2008. *Outsider Within: Reworking Anthropology in the Global Age*. Urbana: University of Illinois Press.

———. 2012. "Building Black Diaspora Networks and Meshworks for Knowledge, Justice, Peace, and Human Rights." In *Afro-Descendants, Identity, and the Struggle for Development in the Americas*, edited by Bernd Reiter and Kimberly Eison Simmons, 3–18. East Lansing: Michigan State University Press.

Hartman, Saidiya V. 1997. *Scenes of Subjection: Terror, Slavery, and Self-Making in Nineteenth-Century America*. New York: Oxford University Press.

Hasenbalg, Carlos Alfredo. 1984. *Race Relations in Modern Brazil*. Alburquerque, NM: Latin American Institute, University of New Mexico.

Hasenbalg, Carlos Alfredo, and Nelson do Valle Silva. 1988. *Estrutura social, mobilidade e raça*. Rio de Janeiro/São Paulo: Instituto Universitário de Pesquisas do Rio de Janeiro/Vértice.

Hautzinger, Sarah J. 2007. *Violence in the City of Women: Police and Batterers in Bahia, Brazil*. Berkeley: University of California Press.

Hecht, Tobias. 1998. *At Home in the Street: Street Children of Northeast Brazil*. New York/Cambridge: Press Syndicate of the University of Cambridge/Cambridge University Press.

Herman, Edward S. 1982. *The Real Terror Network*. Boston: South End Press.

Hill Collins, Patricia. 1990. *Black Feminist Thought: Knowledge, Consciousness, and the Politics of Empowerment*. Boston: Unwin Hyman.

———. 2004. *Black Sexual Politics: African Americans, Gender, and the New Racism*. New York: Routledge.

Hinton, Alexander Laban, ed. 2002. *Annihilating Difference: The Anthropology of Genocide*. Berkeley: University of California Press.

Hoffman-French, Jan. 2013. "Rethinking Police Violence in Brazil: Unmasking the Public Secret of Race." *Latin American Politics and Society* 55 (4): 161–83.

Holley, Emmajean. 2014. "Wole Soyinka: 'I Have Not Merely Reflected but Anticipated.'" *Brown Daily Herald*, October 1, http://www.browndailyherald.com/2014/10/01/wole-soyinka-merely-reflected-anticipated/.

Holloway, Thomas H. 1993. *Policing Rio de Janeiro: Repression and Resistance in a Nineteenth-Century City.* Stanford, CA: Stanford University Press.

Holston, James. 2008. *Insurgent Citizenship: Disjunctions of Democracy and Modernity in Brazil.* Princeton, NJ: Princeton University Press.

———. 2009. "Insurgent Citizenship in an Era of Global Urban Peripheries." *City and Society* 21 (2): 245–67.

Holston, James, and Teresa P. R. Caldeira. 1998. "Democracy, Law, and Violence: Disjunctions of Brazilian Citizenship." In *Fault Lines of Democracy in Post-Transition Latin America,* edited by F. a. J. S. Aguero, 263–96. Miami: University of Miami North-South Center Press.

HoSang, Daniel, Oneka LaBennett, and Laura Pulido. 2012. *Racial Formation in the Twenty-First Century.* Berkeley: University of California Press.

Huggins, Martha Knisely. 1998. *Political Policing: The United States and Latin America.* Durham, NC: Duke University Press.

———. 2005. "Torture 101: Lessons from the Brazilian Case." *Journal of Third World Studies* 22 (2): 161–73.

Ickes, Scott. 2005. "'Adorned with the Mix of Faith and Profanity That Intoxicate the People': The Festival of the Senhor do Bonfim in Salvador, Bahia, Brazil, 1930–1954." *Bulletin of Latin American Research* 24 (2): 181–200.

Incite! Women of Color Against Violence. 2006. *Color of Violence: The Incite! Anthology.* Cambridge, MA: South End Press.

James, Joy. 1996. *Resisting State Violence.* Minneapolis: University of Minnesota Press.

———. 2007. *Warfare in the American Homeland: Policing and Prison in a Penal Democracy.* Durham, NC: Duke University Press.

Jung, Moon-Kie, João H. Costa Vargas, and Eduardo Bonilla-Silva. 2011. *State of White Supremacy: Racism, Governance, and the United States.* Stanford, CA: Stanford University Press.

Justiça Global. 2013. "Declarações do governador do Rio e de sua cúpula de segurança deixam clara a necessidade do fim da PM," July 19, http://global.org.br/arquivo/noticias/declaracoes-do-governador-do-rio-e-de-sua-cupula-de-seguranca-deixam-clara-a-necessidade-do-fim-da-pm/. Rio de Janeiro: Justiça Global.

———. 2015. "Brasil reconhece extermínio da juventude negra em audiência na OEA." March 20, http://global.org.br/programas/brasil-reconhece-exterminio-da-juventude-negra-em-audiencia-na-oea/. Rio de Janeiro: Justiça Global.

Kahan, Dan M., and Tracey L. Meares. 1998. "The Coming Crisis of Criminal Procedure." *Georgetown Law Journal* 86:1153–84.

Karenga, Maulana. 1975. "Ideology and Struggle: Some Preliminary Notes." *Black Scholar* 4 (5): 23–30.

———. 1982. *Introduction to Black Studies.* Inglewood, CA: Kawaida.

Kawaguti, Luis. 2013. "Como desmilitarizar a polícia no Brasil?" *BBC Brasil,* August 22, http://www.bbc.co.uk/portuguese/noticias/, accessed June 8, 2015.

Kellerman, Dana. 1981. *New Webster's Dictionary of the English Language,* edited by Henry E. Clarke and Lucinda R. Summers et al. n.d.: Delair.

Kershaw, Baz. 1992. *The Politics of Performance: Radical Theatre as Cultural Intervention.* London: Routledge.

Knight, Franklin. 2000. "The Haitian Revolution." *American History Review* 105 (1): 103–15.

Kondo, Dorinne K. 1997. *About Face: Performing Race in Fashion and Theater*. New York: Routledge.

Kulick, Don. 1998. *Travesti: Sex, Gender, and Culture among Brazilian Transgendered Prostitutes*. Chicago: University of Chicago Press.

Lacerda, Fernanda Calasans Costa, and Henrique Dantas Neder. 2010. "Pobreza multi-dimensional na bahia: Uma análise fundamentada no indicador multidimensional de pobreza." *Revista Desenbahia* 13:33–70.

Landes, Ruth. 1947. *The City of Women*. New York: Macmillan.

Lara, Sylvia Hunold. 1988. *Campos da Violência, Oficinas da História*. Rio de Janeiro: Paz e Terra.

Lefebvre, Henri. 1991. *The Production of Space*. Translated by Donald Nicholson-Smith. Oxford: Blackwell.

Lemgruber, Julita, et al. 2003. *Quem vigia os vigias? Um estudo sobre controle externo da polícia no Brasil*. Rio de Janeiro: Record.

Lewis, J. Lowell. 1999. "Sex and Violence in Brazil: *Carnaval, Capoeira,* and the Problem of Everyday Life." *American Ethnologist* 26 (3): 539–57.

Lima, Samuel. 2007. "PMs Acusados de Invasão e Tortura." *A Tarde*, May 22, 11.

Lin, Justin, dir. 2011. *Fast Five* (a.k.a. *Fast and Furious 5*). 130 min. Hollywood, CA: Universal Pictures.

Lipsitz, George. 2006. *The Possessive Investment in Whiteness: How White People Profit from Identity Politics*. Philadelphia: Temple University Press.

Lopes, Nei. 1995. *Diccionario Bantu do Brasil*. Rio de Janeiro: Centro Cultural José Bonifácio.

Lorde, Audre. (1984) 2012. *Sister Outsider*. New York: Random House Press.

Loveman, Mara, Jeronimo Muniz, and Stanley R. Bailey. 2012. "Brazil in Black and White? Race Categories, the Census, and the Study of Inequality." *Ethnic and Racial Studies* 38 (8): 1466–83.

Madison, D. Soyini. 2007. "Co-Performative Witnessing." *Cultural Studies* 21 (6): 826–31.

———. 2010. *Acts of Activism: Human Rights as Radical Performance*. Cambridge: Cambridge University Press.

Malkki, Liisa H. 1995. *Purity and Exile: Violence, Memory, and National Cosmology among Hutu Refugees in Tanzania*. Chicago: University of Chicago Press.

Mann Carey, Alysia. 2014. "Racialized Gendered Violence: 'Domestic' Violence, Black Women and Genocide in Brazil." Master's thesis, University of Texas–Austin.

Marenin, Otwin. 1998. "The Goal of Democracy in International Police Assistance." *Policing: An International Journal of Police Strategies and Management* 21 (1): 159–77.

Marx, Anthony W. 1998. *Making Race and Nation: A Comparison of South Africa, the United States, and Brazil*. Cambridge: Cambridge University Press.

Matta, Roberto da. 1979. *Carnavais, malandros e heróis: Para uma sociologia do dilema brasileiro*. Rio de Janeiro: Zahar Editores.

———. 1991. *Carnivals, Rogues, and Heroes: An Interpretation of the Brazilian Dilemma*. Notre Dame, IN: University of Notre Dame Press.

Mattos, Waldemar. 1978. *Evolução histórica e cultural do Pelourinho*. Rio de Janeiro and Salvador, Bahia: Editado pelo Serviço Nacional de Aprendizagem Comercial, Departamento Regional da Bahia.

Mattoso, Kátia M. de Queirós. 1978. *Bahia, a Cidade do Salvador e seu mercado no século XIX.* São Paulo, Salvador: Editora Hucitec; Departamento de Assuntos Culturais, Secretaria Municipal de Educação e Cultura, Prefeitura Municipal de Salvador.

———. 1986. *To Be a Slave in Brazil, 1550–1888.* New Brunswick, NJ: Rutgers University Press.

Mbembe, Achille. 2001. *On the Postcolony.* Berkeley: University of California Press.

———. 2003. "Necropolitics." *Public Culture* 15 (1): 11–40.

———. 2012. "Metamorphic Thought: The Works of Frantz Fanon." *African Studies Review* 71 (1): 19–28.

McDuffie, Erik S. 2011. *Sojourning for Freedom: Black Women, American Communism, and the Making of Black Left Feminism.* Durham, NC: Duke University Press.

McKittrick, Katherine, and Clyde Adrian Woods. 2007. *Black Geographies and the Politics of Place.* Toronto/Cambridge, MA: Between the Lines/South End Press.

McSherry, J. Patrice. 2005. *Predatory States: Operation Condor and Covert War in Latin America.* Lanham, MD: Rowman and Littlefield.

Meirelles, Marcio, and Bando de Teatro Olodum. 1995. *Trilogia do Pelô.* Salvador, Bahia: Edições Olodum.

Mendes, Miriam Garcia. 1993. *O negro e o teatro brasileiro.* São Paulo/Rio de Janeiro/ Brasília: Editora Hucitec/Instituto Brasileiro de Arte e Cultura/Fundação Cultural Palmares.

Menjívar, Cecilia, and Néstor Rodriguez. 2005. *When States Kill: Latin America, the U.S., and Technologies of Terror.* Austin: University of Texas Press.

Mesquita Neto, Paulo de. 2011. *Ensaios sobre segurança cidadã.* São Paulo: Quartier Latin/ FAPESP.

Mesquita Neto, Paulo de, and Adriana Loche. 2003. "Police-Community Partnerships in Brazil." In *Crime and Violence in Latin America: Citizen Security, Democracy, and the State,* edited by Hugo Frühling, Joseph S. Tulchin, and Heather A. Golding, 179–204. Washington, DC: Woodrow Wilson Center Press.

Mignolo, Walter D. 2005. *The Idea of Latin America.* Malden, MA: Blackwell.

Mills, Charles W. 1997. *The Racial Contract.* Ithaca, NY: Cornell University Press.

Mir, Luís. 2004. *Guerra Civil: Estado e Trauma.* São Paulo: Geração Editorial.

Mitchell, Michael, and Charles Wood. 1999. "Ironies of Citizenship: Skin Color, Police Brutality, and the Challenge to Democracy in Brazil." *Social Forces* 77:1001–20.

Morrison, Toni. 1987. *Beloved: A Novel.* New York: Knopf/Random House.

Moten, Fred. 2003. *In the Break: The Aesthetics of the Black Radical Tradition.* Minneapolis: University of Minnesota Press.

Moura, Clóvis. 1987. *Os quilombos e a rebelião negra.* São Paulo: Brasiliense.

———. 1988. *Sociologia do Negro Brasileiro.* São Paulo: Editora Ática S.A.

Movimento Negro Unificado. 1988. *1978–1988, 10 anos de luta contra o racismo: Movimento Negro Unificado.* Salvador: Movimento Negro Unificado.

Mullings, Leith. 2005. "Interrogating Racism: Toward an Antiracist Anthropology." *Annual Review of Anthropology* 34:667–93.

Munoz, José. 2006. "Feeling Brown, Feeling Down: Latina Affect, the Performativity of Race, and the Depressive Position." *Signs* 31 (3): 675–88.

Nascimento, Abdias do. 1961. *Dramas para Negros e Prólogo para Brancos.* Rio de Janeiro: Teatro Experimental do Negro.

————, ed. 1966. *Teatro Experimental do Negro: Testemunhos.* Rio de Janeiro: Edicões GRD.

————. 1979. "Genocide: The Social Lynching of Africans and Their Descendants in Brazil." In *Brazil, Mixture or Massacre? Essays in the Genocide of Black People.* Dover, MA: Majority Press.

————. 1980. "Quilombismo: An African-Brazilian Political Alternative." *Journal of Black Studies* 11 (2): 141–78.

————. 2004. "Teatro Experimental do Negro: Trajetória e reflexões." *Estudos Avançados* 18 (50): 209–24.

Nascimento, Maria Beatriz. 1982. "Kilombo e memória comunitária: Um estudo de caso." *Estudos Afro-Asiáticos* 6 (7): 259–65.

Nelson, Diane M. 2009. *Reckoning: The Ends of War in Guatemala.* Durham, NC: Duke University Press.

Newton, Huey P., and J. Herman Blake. 1973 (2009). *Revolutionary Suicide.* Deluxe ed. New York: Penguin Books.

Nyerere, Julius K. 1968. *Ujamaa.* Dar es Salaam: Oxford University Press.

O Globo. 2007. "OAB: Apenas oito dos 19 mortos no Alemão seriam traficantes." *O Globo,* Extra online ed., June 28, http://extra.globo.com/noticias/rio/oab-apenas-oito-dos-19 -mortos-no-alemao-seriam-traficantes-680863.html.

————. 2012. "PMs são suspeitos de '25 a 30' homicídios durante greve na Bahia." *O Globo, February 13,* http://oglobo.globo.com/brasil/pms-sao-suspeitos-de-25–30-homicidios -durante-greve-na-bahia-3966205, accessed June 9, 2015.

Oliveira, Dijaci David de, Elen Cristina Geraldes, Ricardo Barbosa de Lima, and Augusto Sales Santos. 1998. *A Cor do Medo: Homicídios e Relações Raciais no Brasil, Série Violência em manchete.* Brasília-DF/Goiânia-GO/Brasília, Brazil: Editora UnB/Editora UFG/MNDH.

Omi, Michael, and Howard Winant. 1986. *Racial Formation in the United States: From the 1960s to the 1980s.* New York: Routledge/Kegan Paul.

————. 1994. *Racial Formation in the United States: From the 1960s to the 1990s.* 2nd ed. New York: Routledge.

Ong, Aihwa. 1996. "Cultural Citizenship as Subject-Making: Immigrants Negotiate Racial and Cultural Boundaries in the United States." *Current Anthropology* 37 (5): 732–62.

————. 1999. *Flexible Citizenship: The Cultural Logics of Transnationality.* Durham, NC: Duke University Press.

Paes-Machado, Eduardo, and Ceci Vilar Noronha. 2002. "Policing the Brazilian Poor: Resistance to and Acceptance of Police Brutality in Urban Popular Classes (Salvador, Brazil)." *International Criminal Justice Review* 12:53–76.

Paim, Jarnilson Silva, Maria da Conceição Nascimento Costa, Joane Carla S. Mascarenhas, and Lígia Maria Vieira da Silva. 1999. "Distribuição espacial da violência: Mortalidade por causas externas em Salvador (Bahia), Brasil." *Pan American Journal of Public Health* 6 (5): 321–32.

Pardue, Derek. 2008. *Ideologies of Marginality in Brazilian Hip Hop.* New York: Palgrave Macmillan.

Pateman, Carole. 1988. *The Sexual Contract.* Stanford, CA: Stanford University Press.

Patterson, Orlando. 1982. *Slavery and Social Death: A Comparative Study.* Cambridge, MA: Harvard University Press.

Patterson, William L. 1951 (2007). *We Charge Genocide: The Historic Petition to the United Nations.* New York: International.

Perrone, Charles A. 1992. "*Axé, Ijexá, Olodum*: The Rise of Afro- and African Currents in Brazilian Popular Music." *Afro-Hispanic Review* 11 (1/3): 42–50.

Perrone, Charles A., and Christopher Dunn, eds. 2001. *Brazilian Popular Music and Globalization*. Gainesville: University Press of Florida.

Perry, Imani. 2004. *Prophets of the Hood: Politics and Poetics in Hip Hop*. Durham, NC: Duke University Press.

Perry, Keisha-Khan Y. 2005. "Social Memory and Black Resistance: Black Women and Neighborhood Struggles in Salvador, Bahia, Brazil." *Latin Americanist* 49 (1): 7–38.

———. 2011. "State Violence and the Ethnographic Encounter: Feminist Research and Racial Embodiment." *African and Black Diaspora: An International Journal* 5 (1): 135–54.

———. 2013. *Black Women against the Land Grab: The Fight for Racial Justice in Brazil*. Minneapolis: University of Minnesota Press.

Phelan, Peggy. 1993. *Unmarked: The Politics of Performance*. London: Routledge.

Pierson, Donald. 1947. *Negroes in Brazil: A Study of Race Contact at Bahia*. Chicago: University of Chicago Press.

Pinar, William F. 2007. "Cultures of Torture." In *Warfare in the American Homeland: Policing and Prison in a Penal Democracy*, edited by Joy James, 290–304. Durham, NC: Duke University Press.

Pinheiro, Paulo Sérgio. 1991. "Police and Political Crisis: The Case of the Military Police." In *Vigilantism and the State in Modern Latin America: Essays on Extralegal Violence*, edited by Martha K. Huggins, 167–88. New York: Praeger.

Pinho, Patricia de Santana. 2010. *Mama Africa: Reinventing Blackness in Bahia*. Durham, NC: Duke University Press.

Polícia Militar da Bahia. 2015. "Batalhão de Choque" [informational website]. Estado da Bahia. http://www.pm.ba.gov.br/index.php?option=com_content&view=cate, accessed June 8, 2015.

Poole, Deborah. 1997. *Vision, Race, and Modernity: A Visual Economy of the Andean Image World*. Princeton, NJ: Princeton University Press.

Pratt, Mary Louise. 1992. *Imperial Eyes: Travel Writing and Transculturation*. London: Routledge.

Price, Richard. 1973. *Maroon Societies: Rebel Slave Communities in the Americas*. Garden City, NJ: Anchor Press.

Puar, Jasbir K. 2007. *Terrorist Assemblages: Homonationalism in Queer Times*. Durham, NC: Duke University Press.

———. 2013. "Rethinking Homonationalism." *International Journal of Middle East Studies* 45:336–39.

Queiroz, Maria Isaura Pereira de. 1992. *Carnaval brasileiro: O vívido e o mito*. São Paulo: Editora Brasiliense.

Quijano, Anibal. 2000. "Coloniality of Power, Eurocentrism, and Latin America." *Nepantla* 1 (3): 533–81.

Rahier, Jean Muteba. 2014. *Blackness in the Andes: Ethnographic Vignettes of Cultural Politics in the Time of Multiculturalism*. New York: Palgrave Macmillan.

Ramos, Aguinaldo. 2007. "Luiz Morier: Todos Negros." *A História bem na Foto* [blog]. http://ahistoriabemnafoto05.blogspot.com/2007/09/depoimento-5.html.

Ramos, Cleidiana. 2005. "Maioria das vítimas é formada por negros." *A Tarde*, July 20, 3.

Ramos, Sílvia, and Leonarda Musumeci. 2005. *Elemento Suspeito: Abordagem policial e discriminação na cidade do Rio de Janeiro*. Rio de Janeiro: Civilização Brasileira/CESEC, Centro de Estudos de Segurança e Cidadania.

Rawls, John. 2005. *A Theory of Justice*. Cambridge, MA: Belknap Press.

Rebouças, Danile, and Samuel Lima. 2009. "MP Investiga Mortes em Canabrava." *Grupo A Tarde*, June 18, http://atarde.uol.com.br/materias/imprimir/1267436, accessed June 9, 2015.

Reinelt, Janelle. 1998. "Notes for a Radical Democratic Theater: Productive Crises and the Challenge of Indeterminacy." In *Staging Resistance: Essays on Political Theater*, edited by Jeanne M. Colleran and Jenny S. Spencer, 283–300. Ann Arbor: University of Michigan Press.

Reis, João José. 2003. *Rebelião escrava no Brasil*. São Paulo: Editora Schwarcz.

Reis, João José, and Flávio dos Santos Gomes. 1996. *Liberdade por um fio: História dos quilombos no Brasil*. São Paulo: Companhia das Letras.

Reis, Pablo. 2008. "Jovens negros são vítimas preferenciais de grupos de extermínio." *Correio da Bahia*, March 2.

Reis, Vilma. 2005. "Atoiçaoados pelo estado: As políticas de segurança pública implementadas nos bairros populares de Salvador e suas representações 1991–2001." Master's thesis. Federal Unviersity of Bahia, Salvador.

Reiter, Bernd. 2009. *Negotiating Democracy in Brazil: The Politics of Exclusion*. Boulder, CO: First Forum Press.

Reiter, Bernd, and Gladys L. Mitchell. 2010. *Brazil's New Racial Politics*. Boulder, CO: Lynne Rienner.

Rios, Flavia. 2012. "O protesto negro no Brasil contemporâneo." *Lua Nova* 85:41–79.

Risério, Antonio. 1981. *Carnaval Ijexá*. Salvador: Corrupio.

Roach, Joseph R. 1996. *Cities of the Dead: Circum-Atlantic Performance*. New York: Columbia University Press.

Roberts, Dorothy. 1999. "Foreword: Race, Vagueness, and the Social Meaning of Order-Maintenance Policing." *Journal of Criminal Law and Criminology* 89 (3): 775–836.

Rocha, Janaina, Mirella Domenich, and Patricia Casseano. 2001. *Hip Hop: A Periferia Grita*. São Paulo: Editora Fundação Perseu Abramo.

Rocha, Luciane de Oliveira. 2012. "Black Mothers' Experiences of Violence in Rio de Janeiro." *Cultural Dynamics* 24 (1): 59–73.

———. 2014. "Outraged Mothering: Black Women, Racial Violence, and the Power of Emotions in Rio de Janeiro's African Diaspora." PhD diss., University of Texas–Austin.

Rodrigues, Cristovaldo, Jorge Lindsay, and Flávio Oliveira. 2001. "Três rapazes executados a tiros." *A Tarde*, July 17, 16.

Rodrigues, João Jorge Santos. 1999. "Olodum and the Black Struggle in Brazil." In *Black Brazil: Culture, Identity, and Social Mobilization*, edited by Larry Crook and Randal Johnson, 43–52. Los Angeles: UCLA Latin American Center Publications, University of California.

Romero, Simon. 2013. "Boom Town of 'Eternal Beauty' Faces Dark Side." *New York Times*, November 11, A4.

Romo, Anadelia A. 2010. *Brazil's Living Museum*. Chapel Hill: University of North Carolina Press.

Rose, R. S. 2005. *The Unpast: Elite Violence and Social Control in Brazil, 1954–2000.* Athens: Ohio University Press.

Rose, Tricia. 1994. *Black Noise: Rap Music and Black Culture in Contemporary America.* Hanover, NH: University Press of New England.

Roso, Jayme Vita. 2005. "Tribunal empossa hoje novos desembargadores." *Diário do Poder Judiciário* 15 (3.801): 1–3.

Rubin, Joel, and Sarah Ardalani. 2012. "Killings by Local Police Jump Sharply," *Los Angeles Times,* June 10, 2012, http://articles.latimes.com/print/2012/jun/10/local/la-me-cop -shootings-20120610.

Sansone, Livio. 2001. "The Localization of Global Funk in Bahia and in Rio." In *Brazilian Popular Music and Globalization,* edited by Charles A. Perrone and Christopher Dunn, 136–60. Gainesville: University Press of Florida.

———. 2002. "Fugindo para a Força: Cultura Corporativista e 'Cor' na Polícia Militar do Estado do Rio de Janeiro." *Estudos Afro-Asiáticos* 24 (3): 513–32.

———. 2003. *Blackness without Ethnicity: Constructing Race in Brazil.* New York: Palgrave.

Santos, Augusto Sales. 2006. "Who Is Black in Brazil? A Timely or False Question in Brazilian Race Relations in the Era of Affirmative Action." *Latin American Perspectives* 33 (30): 30–50.

Santos, Dyane Brito Reis. 2002. "O Racismo na Determinação da Suspeição Policial." Master's thesis, Universidade Federal da Bahia, Salvador.

———. 2003. "Fear as the Commodity Blacks Own the Most: An Essay on Police Violence against Black People and the Poor in Salvador, Bahia, Brazil." In *Race and Democracy in the Americas,* edited by Georgia A. Persons, 96–104. New Brunswick, NJ: Transaction.

Santos, Milton. 1995. "Salvador: Centro e Cenralidade na Cidade Contemporânea." In *Pelo Pelô,* edited by A. A. d. F. Gomes, 13. Salvador: Editora da Universidade Federal da Bahia.

Santos, Milton, and María Laura Silveira. 2001. *O Brasil: Território e sociedade no início do século XXI.* Rio de Janeiro: Editora Record.

Saussure, Ferdinand de, et al. (1916) 1983. *Course in General Linguistics.* London: Duckworth.

Scarry, Elaine. 1985. *The Body in Pain: The Making and Unmaking of the World.* New York: Oxford University Press.

Schechner, Richard. 1985. *Between Theater and Anthropology.* Philadelphia: University of Pennsylvania Press.

———. 1988. *Performance Theory.* New York: Routledge.

Scheper-Hughes, Nancy. 1992. *Death without Weeping: The Violence of Everyday Life in Brazil.* Berkeley: University of California Press.

———. 2006. "Death Squads and Democracy in Northeast Brazil." In *Law and Disorder in the Postcolony,* edited by Jean Comaroff and John L. Comaroff, 150–87. Chicago: University of Chicago Press.

Schiller, Nina Glick, Linda G. Basch, and Cristina Szanton Blanc. 1992. *Towards a Transnational Perspective on Migration: Race, Class, Ethnicity, and Nationalism Reconsidered.* New York: New York Academy of Sciences.

Schuller, Mark, and Deborah A. Thomas. 2013. "Archiving Violence: A Conversation on the Making of *Poto Mitan* and *Bad Friday.*" *Transition* 112:153–68.

Schwartzman, Luisa Farah. 2007. "Does Money Whiten? Intergenerational Changes in Racial Classification in Brazil." *American Sociological Review* 72 (6): 940–63.

Scott, David. 2000. "The Re-Enchantment of Humanism: An Interview with Sylvia Wynter." *Small Axe* 8:119–207.

Secretaria da Segurança Pública (Governo do Estado de São Paulo). 2015. "Organograma: CPChq—Comando de Policiamento de Choque." http://www.ssp.sp.gov.br/institucional/organograma/pm_cpchq.aspx, accessed June 8, 2015.

SEPPIR, Secretaria de Políticas de Promoção da Igualdade Racial. 2013. "Presidenta diz que combate à violência contra jovens negros é prioritário." http://www.seppir.gov.br/noticias/ultimas_noticias/2013/08/presidenta-diz-que-combate-a-violencia-contra-jovens-negros-e-prioritario, accessed June 8, 2015.

Seremetakis, C. Nadia. 1991. *The Last Word: Women, Death, and Divination in Inner Mani.* Chicago: University of Chicago Press.

Sexton, Jared. 2007. "Racial Profiling and the Societies of Control." In *Warfare in the American Homeland,* edited by Joy James. Durham, NC: Duke University Press.

Sharpe, Christina. 2010. *Monstrous Intimacies: Making Post-Slavery Subjects.* Durham, NC: Duke University Press.

Sheriff, Robin E. 1999. "The Theft of Carnaval: National Spectacle and Racial Politics in Rio de Janeiro." *Cultural Anthropology* 14 (1): 3–28.

———. 2001. *Dreaming Equality: Color, Race, and Racism in Urban Brazil.* New Brunswick, NJ: Rutgers University Press.

Shohat, Ella, and Robert Stam. 1994. *Unthinking Eurocentrism: Multiculturalism and the Media.* London: Routledge.

Silva, Denise Ferreira da. 2007. *Toward a Global Idea of Race.* Minneapolis: University of Minnesota Press.

———. 2009. "No-Bodies: Law, Raciality and Violence." *Griffith Law Review* 18 (2): 212–38.

Silva, José Raimundo dos Santos. 2007. "Uma Nação Africana chamada Bahia?" Afropress, February 8, http://www.afropress.com/post.asp?id=12936, accessed June 9, 2015.

Silva, Maria Auxiliadora, and Délio José Ferraz Pinheiro. 1977. "De Picota a Ágora: La transformaciones del Pelourinho (Salvador, Bahía, Brasil)." *Anales de Geografía de la Universidad Computense* 7:69–97.

Skidmore, Thomas E. 1974. *Black into White: Race and Nationality in Brazilian Thought.* New York: Oxford University Press.

———. 1985. "Race and Class in Brazil: Historical Perspectives." In *Race, Class, and Power in Brazil,* edited by Pierre-Michel Fontaine, 11–24. Los Angeles: Center for Afro-American Studies, University of California.

Skogan, Wesley G., and Susan M. Hartnett. 1997. *Community Policing, Chicago Style.* New York: Oxford University Press.

Sluka, Jeffrey A. Sluka, ed. 2000. *Death Squad: The Anthropology of State Terror.* Philadelphia: University of Philadelphia Press.

Smith, Christen A. 2008. "Scenarios of Racial Contact: Police Violence and the Politics of Performance and Racial Formation in Brazil." *e-misférica* 5 (2), available at http://hemisphericinstitute.org/hemi/en/e-misferica-52/smith.

———. 2009. "Strategies of Confinement: Environmental Injustice and Police Violence in Brazil." In *Environmental Justice in the New Millennium: Global Perspectives on Race, Ethnicity, and Human Rights,* edited by Filomina Chioma Steady, 93–114. New York: Palgrave MacMillan.

———. 2013a. "An Open Love Note to My Son: On Mourning, Love, and Black Mother-hood." *The Feminist Wire,* July 14, http://thefeministwire.com/2013/07/an-open-love -note-to-my-son-on-mourning-love-and-black-motherhood/.

———. 2013b. "Strange Fruit: Brazil, Necropolitics, and the Transnational Resonance of Torture and Death." *Souls* 15 (3): 177–98.

———. 2014. "Putting Prostitutes in Their Place." *Latin American Perspectives* 41 (1): 107–23.

———. 2015. "Between Soapboxes and Shadows: Activism, Theory, and the Politics of Life and Death in Salvador, Bahia, Brazil." In *Bridging Scholarship and Activism: Reflections from the Frontlines of Collaborative Research,* edited by Bernd Reiter and Ulrich Oslender, 135–50. East Lansing: Michigan State University Press.

Soares, Fábio, Rafael Perez Ribas, and Rafael Guerreiro Osório. 2010. "Evaluating the Impact of Brazil's Bolsa Família." *Latin American Research Review* 45 (2): 173–90.

Soares, Gláucio Ary Dillon, and Doriam Borges. 2004. "A Cor da Morte." *Ciência Hoje* 35 (209): 26–31.

Soares, Luiz Eduardo, MV Bill, and Celso Athayde. 2005. *Cabeça de Porco.* Rio de Janeiro: Objetiva.

Soja, Edward. 1980. "The Socio-Spatial Dialectic." *Annals of the Association of American Geographers* 70 (2): 207–25.

Sontag, Susan. 2002. "Looking at War: Photography's View of Devastation and Death." *New Yorker,* December 9, 82–98.

———. 2004. "Regarding the Torture of Others." *New York Times,* May 23, 25.

Souza, Itamar. 2001. *Nova história de Natal.* Natal, Brazil: Diário de Natal.

Soyinka, Wole. 1976. *Myth, Literature, and the African World.* Cambridge: Cambridge University Press.

Spencer, Jenny S., ed. 2012. *Political and Protest Theatre after 9/11: Patriotic Dissent.* New York: Routledge.

Sterling, Cheryl. 2012. *African Roots, Brazilian Rites: Cultural and National Identity in Brazil.* New York: Palgrave Macmillan.

Staub, Ervin. 1989. *The Roots of Evil: The Origins of Genocide and Other Group Violence.* Cambridge: Cambridge University Press.

Straubhaar, Joseph. 1989. "Television and Video in the Transition from Military to Civilian Rule in Brazil." *Latin American Research Review* 24 (1): 140–54.

Styron, William. 2002. *The Confessions of Nat Turner.* New York: Random House.

Sue, Derald Wing, et al. 2007. "Racial Microaggressions in Everyday Life: Implications for Clinical Practice." *American Psychologist* 62 (4): 271–86.

Taylor, Diana. 2003. *The Archive and the Repertoire: Performing Cultural Memory in the Americas.* Durham, NC: Duke University Press.

Telles, Edward. 2004. *Race in Another America: The Significance of Skin Color in Brazil.* Princeton, NJ: Princeton University Press.

Telles, Edward, and Tianna Paschel. 2014. "Who Is Black, White, or Mixed Race? How Skin Color, Status, and Nation Shape Racial Classification in Latin America." *American Journal of Sociology* 120 (3): 864–907.

Thomas, Deborah A. 2004. *Modern Blackness: Nationalism, Globalization, and the Politics of Culture in Jamaica.* Durham, NC: Duke University Press.

————. 2011. *Exceptional Violence: Embodied Citizenship in Transnational Jamaica*. Durham, NC: Duke University Press.

Turner, Victor. 1974. *Dramas, Fields and Metaphors: Symbolic Action in Human Society*. Ithaca, NY: Cornell University Press.

Turra, Cleusa, Gustavo Venturi, and Datafolha. 1995. *Racismo Cordial: A Mais Completa Análise Sobre o Preconceito de Cor no Brasil*. São Paulo: Editora Atica.

Twine, France Winddance. 1998. *Racism in a Racial Democracy: The Maintenance of White Supremacy in Brazil*. New Brunswick, NJ: Rutgers University Press.

UNESCO World Heritage Centre. 1992–2013. "Historic Centre of Salvador de Bahia." http://whc.unesco.org/en/list/309/, accessed October 3, 2013.

United States General Accounting Office. 1996. *School of the Americas U.S. Military Training for Latin American Countries: Report to the Ranking Minority Member, Committee on National Security, House of Representatives*. Washington, DC: U.S. General Accounting Office.

Uzel, Marcos. 2003. *O Teatro do Bando: Negro, Baiano e Popular*. Salvador, Bahia: Teatro Vila Velha, P555 Edições, Ministério da Cultura Fundação Palmares.

Vargas, João H. Costa. 2004. "Hyperconsciousness of Race and Its Negation: The Dialectic of White Supremacy in Brazil." *Identities: Global Studies in Culture and Power* 11:443–70.

————. 2005. "Genocide in the African Diaspora: United States, Brazil, and the Need for a Holistic Research and Political Method." *Cultural Dynamics* 17:267–92.

————. 2008. *Never Meant to Survive: Genocide and Utopias in Black Diaspora Communities*. Lanham, MD: Rowman and Littlefield.

Vartabedian, Ralph. 2014. "Ferguson Unrest Reflects Decades of Racial Tension in St. Louis Area." *Los Angeles Times*, August 15, http://www.latimes.com/nation/nationnow/la-na-nn-ferguson-racial-history-20140815-story.html.

Verdery, Katherine. 1999. *The Political Lives of Dead Bodies: Reburial and Postsocialist Change*. New York: Columbia University Press.

Viana, Itana. 2004. "Sociabilidade e Violência: Programa de Reduão de Danos Sociais." In *Sociabilidade e Violência: Criminalidade no cotidiano de vida dos moradores do Subúrbio Ferroviário de Salvador*, edited by G. Espinheira, 300–800. Salvador, Bahia: Ministério Publico.

Waiselfisz, Julio Jacobo. 2012. *Mapa da Violência: A Cor dos Homicídios no Brasil*. Brasilia: Centro Brasileiro de Estudos Latino-Americanos (CEBELA), FLACSO Brasil, Secretaria de Políticas de Promoção da Igualdade Racial, Governo Federal do Brasil.

————. 2013. *Mapa da Violência 2013: Mortes matadas por armas de fogo*. Brasilia: Centro Brasileiro de Estudos Latino-Americanos (CEBELA), FLACSO Brasil, Secretaria de Políticas de Promoção da Igualdade Racial, Governo Federal do Brasil.

Walker, Sheila S. 1973. *Ceremonial Spirit Possession in Africa and Afro-America: Forms, Meanings, and Functional Significance for Individuals and Social Groups*. Leiden, Netherlands: Brill.

Whitehead, Neil L. 2004a. "On the Poetics of Violence." In *Violence*, edited by Neil L. Whitehead, 55–77. Santa Fe, NM: School of American Research Press.

————. 2004b. "Rethinking the Anthropology of Violence." *Anthropology Today* 20 (5): 1–2.

Wiegman, Robyn. 1995. *American Anatomies: Theorizing Race and Gender*. Durham, NC: Duke University Press.

Wikipedia. 2013. "Salvador, Bahia." http://en.wikipedia.org/wiki/Salvador,_Bahia.

Wilderson, Frank B. 2008. "Biko and the Problematic of Presence." In *Biko Lives! Contesting the Legacies of Steve Biko*, edited by Andile Mngxitama, Amanda Alexander, and Nigel C. Gibson, 95–114. New York: Palgrave MacMillan.

———. 2010. *Red, White, and Black: Cinema and the Structure of U.S. Antagonisms*. Durham, NC: Duke University Press.

Wilkins, Vicky M., and Brian N. Williams. 2008. "Black or Blue: Racial Profiling and Representative Bureaucracy." *Public Administration Review* 68 (4): 654–64.

Willett, John, trans and ed. 1964. *Brecht on Theatre: The Development of an Aesthetic*. New York: Hill and Wang.

Williams, Erica Lorraine. 2013. *Sex Tourism in Bahia: Ambiguous Entanglements*. Urbana: University of Illinois Press.

Winant, Howard. 2001. *The World Is a Ghetto*. New York: Basic Books/Perseus Books.

Wood, Marcus. 2013. *Black Milk: Imagining Slavery in the Visual Cultures of Brazil and America*. New York: Oxford University Press.

Wynter, Sylvia. 1994. "'No Humans Involved': An Open Letter to My Colleagues." *Forum N.H.I.: Knowledge for the 21st Century* 1 (1): 42–73.

———. 1995. "1492: A New World View." In *Race, Discourse, and the Origin of the Americas: A New World View*, edited by Vera L. Hyatt and Rex Nettleford, 5–57. Washington, DC: Smithsonian Institution Press.

———. 2003. "Unsettling the Coloniality of Being/Power/Truth/Freedom: Towards the Human, After Man, Its Overrepresentation—An Argument." *New Centennial Review* 3 (3): 257–337.

Zaluar, Alba. 1994. *Condomínio do Diabo*. Rio de Janeiro: Editora Revan/UFRJ Editora.

———. 2004. *Integração Perversa: Pobreza e Tráfico de Drogas*. Rio de Janeiro: Editora FGV.

———. 2010. *Violência e Juventude*. São Paulo: Editora HUCITEC.

Zaluar, Alba, and Marcos Alvito. 1998. *Um Século de Favela*. Rio de Janeiro: Fundação Getulio Vargas Editora.

Index

91; resistance to slavery, 197–98; *sequelae* of violence and, 149, 184–85, 188–93; sexual assaults during carnival, 43; state-sponsored domestic violence, 83. *See also* mothers (black mothers, mothering)

Wood, Marcus, 57

Wretched of the Earth, The (Fanon), 77

Wynter, Sylvia, 14, 20, 105–6, 107, 109–10

Xhosa, 201

Yoruba/Nagô, 194

Youth Statute (Brazil), 9

Zuley, Richard, 128

Zumbi, 84–85, 193–94

CHRISTEN A. SMITH is Assistant Professor of African and African Diaspora Studies and Anthropology at The University of Texas at Austin.

The University of Illinois Press
is a founding member of the
Association of American University Presses.

University of Illinois Press
1325 South Oak Street
Champaign, IL 61820-6903
www.press.uillinois.edu